W9-BEE-507

GAME OF MY LIFE

TEXAS

LONGHORNS

MEMORABLE STORIES OF LONGHORNS FOOTBALL

MICHAEL PEARLE
AND BILL FRISBIE

FOREWORD BY LEE CORSO

Sports Publishing books may be purchased in bulk at special discounts for sales promotion, corporate gifts, fund-raising, or educational purposes. Special editions can also be created to specifications. For details, contact the Special Sales Department, Sports Publishing, 307 West 36th Street, 11th Floor, New York, NY 10018 or sportspubbooks@skyhorsepublishing.com.

Sports Publishing® is a registered trademark of Skyhorse Publishing, Inc.®, a Delaware corporation.

Visit our website at www.sportspubbooks.com

10 9 8 7 6 5 4 3 2 1

Library of Congress Cataloging-in-Publication Data is available on file.
ISBN: 978-1-61321-073-4

Printed in the United States of America

Michael Pearle:

For
Mikey and Nicole.

Bill Frisbie:

To my daughters,
Chandler and Darby.

Contents

Foreword

I began my coaching career in 1958 as an assistant at my alma mater Florida State, so *Game of My Life Texas Longhorns* covers a period of college football history that I know and love.

Beginning with beloved Texas coach Darrell Royal, who describes his first win against Oklahoma in 1958, up through receiver Jordan Shipley, Class of '09, who tells of how the Longhorns upset No. 1 Oklahoma during the controversial 2008 campaign, the people who tell their stories in *Game of My Life* cover the last fifty years of UT football.

And what great college football games there were during those years! The "Great Shootout" game between Texas and Arkansas in 1969 is described in these pages by Steve Worster, the Longhorns' powerful wishbone fullback. The Horns' wins over Bear Bryant's Crimson Tide in the 1982 Cotton Bowl and the third-ranked Houston Cougars on a wild night in Austin in 1990, a game shown nationally on ESPN, are also covered. Texas's upset defeat of Nebraska in the 1996 Big 12 championship game and—of course, the granddaddy of them all—the win over Southern Cal in the 2006 Rose Bowl, one of the greatest games ever in college football (and a game I picked Texas to win, incidentally!) are all retold in this book.

And there are many more. Earl Campbell, Roosevelt Leaks, Jerry Gray, Major Applewhite, and Ricky Williams are just some of the players that tell the stories of the games they remember most from their days as a Longhorn. These mostly were games Texas won that fans will love reading about, but there's also a loss or two. For example, Johnny Lam Jones, who entered Texas after winning a gold medal in the 1976 Montreal Olympics, talks about losing big to the Houston Cougars his freshman year, and what that taught Jones and his teammates about the effort it would take to win in big-time college football.

As for the writers of this book, I've known Michael Pearle since the days he and my son David became friends back in the 1980s while they were at UT Law School together. Michael has interviewed me a couple of times for his magazine *Inside Texas*, and I know he is a guy who bleeds Texas orange. Ditto for his co-author, Bill Frisbie, who started writing about Texas football during his days as senior sportswriter with the UT student newspaper, the *Daily Texan*, as well as when he was former editor of a Texas ex-students association publication, *The Longhorn Letter*. Frisbie is currently lead writer for *Inside Texas*. Between them, Michael and Bill either watched as a fan or covered professionally almost every game they write about in this book.

If you love Texas Longhorn football, or are just somebody who loves college football like I do, then this is a book you will thoroughly enjoy. Hook 'em!

—Lee Corso
Co-host, ESPN College Game Day

Chapter One

DARRELL K ROYAL

Texas Coach (1957-76)

A few days before the second Saturday in October, 1958, evangelist Billy Graham announced that there had been discernable signs of the Second Coming.

For University of Texas football faithful, the thing that mattered most was whether the longed-for revival of the Longhorn program had found its savior in a young, relatively unknown coach named Darrell K Royal. College football would find out soon enough. October's second Saturday, traditionally the date of Texas's annual showdown with archnemesis Oklahoma, loomed ominously. For nearly one decade, the beatings that the once-proud Longhorn program suffered at the hands of the Sooners bordered on apocalyptic.

Oklahoma coach Bud Wilkinson had created a monster program. The Sooners reeled off 47 straight wins from early 1953 to late 1957, Royal's first-year on the Longhorn sideline. OU had won eight of nine against Texas heading into the 1958 season, dominating the three previous mismatches by a combined score of 86-7.

In short, the 1950s were not Happy Days for Horns fans.

The Texas program hit rock bottom with a 1-9 finish in 1956, coach Ed Price's sixth and final year. In early December, the five-member Texas Athletics Council was looking not for just a quick fix, but rather a hire for the ages. Ironically, Texas turned to a former Sooner All-American quarterback to restore its fortunes. Incredibly, Royal was just thirty-two years old when he agreed to work for $15,000 annually.

Few had heard of him. Royal's rise through the ranks was so meteoric—he was on the payroll of five different programs during a seven-year stretch—that he and his wife Edith barely had time to unpack their boxes. But a pair of legendary coaches, Georgia Tech's Bobby Dodd and Michigan State's Duffy Daugherty, spoke so highly of Royal that Texas officials granted him an interview.

Royal's job description was basically to rebuild the program and beat Oklahoma, though not necessarily in that order. During Royal's interview, a council member asked, "Now what's the *first game* you're going to win?" Royal replied, "I think we open with Georgia."

Indeed, Royal's Texas tenure began with a 26-7 decision over the Bulldogs in Athens on September 21, 1957. But Royal clearly understood the question's intent.

"I knew what they were talking about," Royal said, "but I wasn't going to take the job and promise we'd beat Oklahoma my first year."

By the opener, Royal had helped launch significant upgrades to athletic facilities that had begun to reflect the downtrodden spiral of the football program. In fact, the practice field was in such sorry shape that Longhorn officials had to import grass from Texas A&M. That same year, Texas became the country's first public university to require entrance exams. Royal responded by creating what became the forerunner of modern day academic advisers when he hired a science teacher from nearby Lockhart High to work with his student-athletes. It was such an innovative move that players dubbed the latest addition as the "brain coach," but Royal commented, "You go to college, first and foremost, to learn and to have a chance to better yourself."

It helped that players were also bettering themselves on the field.

When Royal's Horns opened at home against Tulane one week later, the Texas program had entered the weekly *Associated Press* poll for the first time since losing to Oklahoma in 1954. Royal's inaugural campaign resulted in a respectable 6-4-1 finish, including a 9-7 win against No. 4 Texas A&M and a berth in the Sugar Bowl. But the Horns fell to Oklahoma for the seventh time that decade. Now, three games into the 1958 season, Texas would face a loaded Sooner squad ranked No. 2 nationally in both major polls.

Royal was no longer an unknown, but he remained relatively unproven. He was still searching for a signature win against a traditional power to validate his program.

Coach Darrell Royal at the Cotton Bowl, 1963

"The Oklahoma game became a personal crusade for coach Royal," said former All-Southwest Conference linebacker Pat Culpepper. "He knew that was why they had hired him."

On October 11, 1958, the "crusade" reached the Cotton Bowl in Dallas. It was Texas versus Oklahoma for the 53rd time, but Texas entered the tilt undefeated for the first time in seven seasons.

The Second Coming of Texas football had begun.

No. 16 TEXAS vs. No. 2 OKLAHOMA

October 11, 1958
Cotton Bowl—Dallas, Texas

Texas was listed as a 2-touchdown underdog against the Sooners, so there was little reason to expect that a recent rule change in college football would factor so prominently in the outcome. The 1958 season marked the first time the NCAA allowed the 2-point conversion following a touchdown. The measure succeeded, in no small part, because the highly influential Wilkinson served on a committee that lobbied heavily for its passage.

Not all coaches, however, were pleased with the new-fangled concept. Royal made no secret of his opposition to the 2-point play; he likened it to playing with someone else's money and hardly worth the risk. Yet a six-game losing streak to Oklahoma called for some moxie.

Late in the first quarter, Royal called for a pass on fourth-and-goal from the three rather than the chip-shot field goal. Sooner David Baker broke up QB Vince Matthews's attempt on the first play of the second quarter to turn Texas away. Royal would face another fourth-down decision inside the red zone on Texas's next series. This time, halfback Rene Ramirez rolled left and hooked up with George Blanch for the 10-yard score.

For the second-straight year, Texas scored first against its interstate rival but, to nearly everyone's surprise, Texas went for two. It was a simple handoff with RB Don Allen charging over left guard, but it gave the Horns an 8-0 lead. The Sooners responded with a 61-yard drive in seven plays, but missed a 30-yard field goal by inches.

Texas took its surprising 8-point advantage into the locker room, but the Sooners owned the third quarter. Texas could not muster a first down during the entire frame on an afternoon when it rushed for all of 57 yards. Royal's defense put the clamps on a thirteen-play drive, turning away the Sooners on downs at the Longhorn five. Oklahoma would finally hit pay dirt on its next possession, marching 38 yards on eight plays to score on a five-yard run. The Horns nursed an 8-6 lead with 3:56 left in the quarter after the 2-point attempt failed. Oklahoma drove 59 yards in twelve plays to the Longhorn 34, but the defense held on fourth-and-2.

Texas desperately needed to establish some semblance of a running game. Instead, the very next play resulted in one of the flukiest turn-of-events in series history: Oklahoma's Jim Davis grabbed a Longhorn fumble—the ball never touched the ground because a botched handoff landed on FB Mike Dowdle's rump—and returned it 24 yards for the defensive touchdown. This time, Oklahoma completed the 2-point try and led for the first time, 14-8.

Both squads exchanged punts, but Oklahoma kept Texas's defense on the field for most of the fourth quarter with a nine-play drive. Texas took over on its own 28 with 6:50 remaining. The Sooners had stuffed Texas's ground game all day, but now the Horns took to the air with Matthews behind center. He completed a critical third-and-18 at midfield with an 11-yard screen pass to Blanch. He followed with a seven-yard toss to Bob Bryant before connecting with Ramirez for 11 to set up shop at the Sooner 19. From there, Royal caught Oklahoma off guard with a fullback draw play as Dowdle rumbled for 14 yards. Now, all that separated Texas from its biggest win of the decade was five yards of prime real estate.

It came down to a third-and-goal from the seven with little more than 3 minutes remaining. Another Royal surprise: After twelve plays, the second-year Texas coach replaced Matthews at quarterback with Bobby Lackey. The taller signal caller rolled right, faked a handoff, and then threw a jump pass over the middle. He hit Bryant, who was at least three steps from the nearest defender, in stride. Bryant crossed the goal line untouched before Lackey kicked the PAT.

Texas 15, Oklahoma 14.

The Longhorns still needed one more big play from Lackey. After the Sooners drove to the Longhorn 44, Lackey's one-handed interception sealed the improbable upset. It was just the second Texas win against Oklahoma in ten years. Texas fans stormed the field at the final whistle and tore down the goal posts. Later that night, the team's aircraft had to circle an Austin landing strip for 20 minutes until airport officials could clear more than 2,000 jubilant fans from the runway. Royal knew then that his fledgling program had taken flight.

The Game of My Life

By Darrell K Royal

I guess you could say the [1958] Oklahoma game was the one that started it all for us. There had been a six-year streak of Oklahoma wins against Texas. That win probably helped more than anything else to getting me established at Texas. All I was thinking at the time was about trying to be around for a while. I was just trying to win enough games to keep from being chased off. I was a young coach trying to earn the confidence of players, alumni, fans, and sportswriters. We were trying to get back the winning tradition that Texas had under Coach [Dana X.] Bible.

It was one of those situations where the pupil was playing the teacher. Coach Wilkinson had more influence on me as a coach than any other coach. I played for him, but now I was coaching against him at Texas. I elected to be a coach, and I was lucky that The University of Texas selected me to come here.

That was the year the NCAA brought in the 2-point play. I was very much opposed to the 2-point conversion. I always thought it was too much of a gamble. The odds are three-to-one against you. It put a lot of strain on coaches. You'd probably wind up wearing a straw hat to a Christmas party if you went for two every time. But we had to take some gambles that day. We felt like we had to swing from the floor and be as aggressive as we could possibly be. So, after we scored first, we decided to jump up quick from the huddle and go for two. Fortunately for us, it was successful. It was the difference in the ball game.

Of course, we had to score again. They [OU] had a fumble return for a touchdown and we had to collect ourselves in a hurry. I'm sure it seems strange that after Vince Matthews had passed us all the way down to the goal line, I would put [QB Bobby] Lackey in for the [winning] pass. But Lackey was taller (6-foot-3) and had more experience with that play. He had run that play more in practice than Vince had and I wanted to send in that play, anyway. I substituted Lackey back in; he faked the handoff and threw a jump pass to [end] Bobby Bryant.

I remember we had a hard time running the ball that day. Most teams don't run on Oklahoma. I didn't mind the reputation I had that we didn't throw the ball but, if you look at all the big games that we won, we did a lot of throwing in them. The 1969 Arkansas game, the [1963] A&M game, the [1964] Cotton Bowl game where we played Navy, we did a lot of throwing to win those games. We ended up throwing to beat Oklahoma that day.

As a young coach, beating Oklahoma that day meant a lot. It meant a lot to me, it meant a lot to our team, and it meant a lot to our future because now the players learned that it's possible.

Upon Further Review

Oklahoma was the better team that year, but Texas was the better team that day. The Sooners would finish No. 5 in both polls while leading the nation in scoring defense (4.9 ppg). Meanwhile, Texas would drop three conference games and was shut out of the postseason. Six Sooners went on to First-Team All-Big Eight status while Texas did not field a single All-Southwest Conference athlete for the only time in Royal's tenure. But the 1-point Longhorn win signaled a dramatic reversal of fortune in the series. Including the 1958 game, Texas would take 12 of 13 from Oklahoma.

The rest, of course, is Burnt Orange history. When Royal called it a career after twenty seasons, his resume included eleven Top Ten finishes, eleven conference titles, sixteen bowl games and three national championships. ABC-TV named him the Coach of the Decade for the 1960s. He never had a losing season.

There will always be those who insist Royal was gradually shown the door, at age fifty-two, after stumbling to a 0-5-1 mark against the Sooners to end his tenure. Royal is generally content to allow those folks to think that.

"I wanted to quit while I was still having fun," Royal said. "I didn't want to coach until I didn't like it. I wanted to get out before people wanted me out."

Others continue to point to the fact that Texas, like so many other southern programs, was slow to recruit African-American players. For the record, Royal had coached black players while at Edmonton [1953] and Washington [1956]. Texas will always bear the dubious distinction of being the last all-white team to win the national championship in 1969, but the program was integrated the year before when the freshman team included three African-American players (two walk-ons and a scholarship player who would transfer).

At the end of the day, Royal would go out the way he came in: as a winner. Including the 1957 season-opening win against Georgia and his career-ending 29-12 nationally televised win against Arkansas in 1976, Royal's record at Texas stood at 167-47-5. It was the best mark in college football during that two-decade span. In 1996, the University honored its all-time winningest head coach by naming its football stadium Darrell K Royal-Texas Memorial Stadium.

Perhaps the only thing more impressive than Royal's final tally is an enduring legacy that cannot be quantified. Case in point: current Texas coach Mack Brown chuckled a few years ago when asked what type of legacy he wanted to leave at the Forty Acres. "There will only be one legacy at The University of Texas," Brown said, "and that's coach Royal."

Chapter Two

DUKE CARLISLE

Safety, Quarterback (1961-63)

It was the first day of 1962 and, to some extent, the first day of Texas football as we know it.

Yet, for Longhorn coach Darrell Royal—no less than for his staff with Magnolia State roots running deeper than the Mississippi River bottom—all that mattered on this New Year's Day was that Texas beat the hell out of Ole Miss. A 1-point Cotton Bowl nail-biter would have been just as satisfying, given all that had gone on before. But to fully appreciate the moment, one must consider the immediate history preceding it.

Royal's rapid ascendancy through the coaching ranks included an assistant coaching stint at Mississippi State before returning to Starkville a few years later as the Bulldogs' head coach. Assistants Charley Shira and Jim Pittman lettered at Mississippi State and were among Royal's staff when he coached the Bulldogs from 1954-55. Mike Campbell had suited up for Ole Miss and was then a high school football coach in Kenton, Mississippi. But Royal was quickly convinced that Campbell would make for an outstanding defensive coordinator.

"I noticed that every time we were around any kind of coaching convention, or where a bunch of coaches were, they were always hovering around Mike," Royal recalled. "It really impressed me how much respect he had from other high school coaches. When I went to the University of Washington, I asked him to join my staff."

One year later, Royal brought his Mississippi-flavored assistants to Austin. By the end of Royal's inaugural 1957 campaign, the Horns capped their first winning season in four years with a 9-7 upset at No. 4 Texas A&M. It put Texas in the Sugar Bowl against Ole Miss, the program that had begun to supplant Oklahoma in the late 1950s as college football's most dominant program. The Rebels had their way with Royal's teams during his time with the Bulldogs, and the 1958 Sugar Bowl continued that trend. Final score: Ole Miss 39, Texas 7.

"The years that coach Royal was at Mississippi State, Ole Miss was at its height and he couldn't beat them," former All-Southwest Conference Longhorn linebacker Pat Culpepper said. "Every experience he had against Ole Miss was a bad one. It stuck in his craw like getting beat by Oklahoma."

A Texas-Mississippi matchup on New Year's Day, 1962, would be just as personal to safety Duke Carlisle, albeit in a more affable fashion. Carlisle's family moved from Athens, Texas, to McComb, Mississippi, shortly after he graduated from high school in 1959. His father went to work with his uncle in the oil business, and Carlisle worked in the oil fields during the summer. There, he befriended Ole Miss standouts Louis Guy and Billy Ray Adams. When the trio wasn't working in the oil fields, they worked out on football fields as part of a self-paced strength and conditioning regimen.

"We parted ways at the end of the summer and wished each other luck," Carlisle said. "I would naturally follow what Ole Miss did each season, because of them, and they kept up with Texas."

By December 1961, Carlisle completed his sophomore year in what was Royal's fifth season in Austin. Texas's 9-1 mark represented its most successful campaign in years, but Royal was still looking for his first bowl victory. The general perception was that the Sooner program was in decline and that Royal needed a signature bowl win against a national opponent. A national opponent along the lines of, say, Ole Miss.

"As fate would have it," Carlisle said, "we both had outstanding seasons and ended up playing each other in the Cotton Bowl."

The Rebels were not a consensus national champion in 1959 or 1960, but several ratings services listed them as college football's best following 10-1 and 10-0-1 campaigns. Ole Miss coach John Vaught had forged a 29-2-1 record and a South-

Duke Carlisle on the run against Navy in the Cotton Bowl, 1964

eastern Conference Championship in the three seasons prior to the 1962 Cotton Bowl. The Oxford program was coming off consecutive Sugar Bowl wins and was on its way toward another title in 1961. By mid-October, the Rebels were No. 1 in the *Associated Press* poll while Texas was No. 3 following Royal's fourth-straight win over Oklahoma.

It appeared that both squads would run the table and, during the pre-BCS Bowl era, land in separate postseason venues. But Ole Miss suffered a 10-7 setback to LSU. Texas inherited college football's top spot and had only to get past unranked TCU and Texas A&M to finish the 1961 regular season unscathed. In one of the biggest upsets in Southwest Conference history, a 2-4-1 Horned Frog team came to Austin and stunned Texas, 6-0, scoring the game's only touchdown on a flea-flicker.

"They had a touchdown pass that they lateraled back and forth several times," Carlisle recalled. "We couldn't get it in the end zone that day. It was a huge upset."

The unforeseen set of events reshuffled bowl projections. Texas took out its frustration on Texas A&M, 25-0, and earned a spot in the Cotton Bowl as the SWC co-champion. Its New Year's Day opponent, of course, was Ole Miss. No. 3 Texas entered the showdown as the higher-ranked team but also as a 3-point underdog. Many pigskin pundits believed No. 5 Mississippi's 17-pound weight advantage per lineman would be too much for the Horns to overcome.

"There's nothing you can do about that," Royal recalled. "We couldn't put weight on our guys all of a sudden."

Instead, Mike Campbell devised a scheme for slowing the Rebels' outstanding quarterback Glynn Griffin, whose sprint-out passing attack had devoured acres of real estate. Campbell brought linebackers Culpepper and Johnny Treadwell closer to the line of scrimmage so that both could trail Griffin on sprint-outs. Texas went from a wide-tackle six formation and played most of the ball game in a split-six look, with both tackles in a three-technique.

Just before kickoff, Campbell told his players that he wouldn't trade them for anyone else in the country. Still, very few outside of the Texas locker room gave the undersized Horns much of a chance to unseat a national-champion-caliber foe. But it wasn't so much the size of the opposition, but rather Royal's recent history against Ole Miss that had lit a burnt-orange fire among his troops during bowl preparation.

"Our coaches were so tight that day," Culpepper said, "that you couldn't drive a nail up their asses."

No. 3 TEXAS vs. No. 5 MISSISSIPPI

January 1, 1962
Cotton Bowl—Dallas, Texas

Texas did not record a first down until the second quarter, but its defense would notch five interceptions on the day. Treadwell picked off the first one in front of the Rebels' bench, while defensive back Jerry Cook was responsible for three of the thefts, including on a tipped ball from Treadwell near the Longhorn goal line.

"We didn't really have nickel backs during that era," Royal said. "Everybody just backpedaled and broke on the ball."

One of Royal's favorite plays was the speed option out of a two-tight end, wing set. It was a blind pitch from quarterback Mike Cotten, who never took his eyes off of the defensive end and, in effect, gradually wore down the larger Ole Miss defense. The play set up Texas's first score, courtesy of halfback James Saxton, who would finish the year as a consensus All-American and No. 3 in the Heisman balloting. Texas missed the extra point but would drive for another touchdown just before halftime. One of the most widely recruited Longhorns of that era would cap his senior season with a play that all but sealed the deal in Dallas.

Jack Collins was a 1959 All-SWC halfback after leading his team in rushing, receiving and total offense. During his senior year, Collins moved to wingback in Royal's new Wing-T formation. Technically, he was a receiver. Essentially, he was the lead blocker for Saxton on sweeps. In 1961, it was Saxton who led the league with 846 rushing yards and 7.9 yards per carry. But it was Collins who collected 'otton's screen pass and, behind Charlie Talbert's clearing block, scampered in from 24 yards out. Texas took a 12-0 lead into the locker room at halftime.

It was a precarious lead, given Ole Miss's vaunted passing attack. Yet Texas held the Rebels in check most of the afternoon before surrendering a second-half touchdown. Now, it was anybody's contest at 12-7, and the Rebels were on the move again. Ultimately, it came down to a fourth-and-2 defensive stand. Defensive end Bobby Moses slipped inside the offensive tackle and stopped Griffin just short of the first-down marker. Shortly after the final seconds ticked from the game clock, jubilant Longhorns hoisted Royal on their shoulders following his first postseason victory.

The Game of My Life

By Duke Carlisle

The game was probably the best bowl game that year because of the matchup. Both teams had been ranked No. 1 at some point in the season and had a shot at the national championship. Ole Miss actually went into the game as a slight favorite. In the late 1950s and early 60s, Ole Miss was one of the strongest teams in the country. They consistently had good teams. In those (pre-scholarship limit) days, they had enough good players that they could redshirt every guy moving from freshmen to sophomores. They would bring a couple guys up, but they could redshirt almost the entire freshman class. It's almost unbelievable. It basically meant that when you played them that you were playing guys that were a year older than you.

Both teams, with the bitter disappointment of being one loss away from winning the national championship, had extra incentive to do well. We were both fired up and excited. It was obviously a hard-fought and close game. It was a great season for both teams, but it was disappointing to not quite make it. Beating a strong team in the bowl game would be some consolation.

My parents, living in McComb, were surrounded by people who were for the other team. They took a lot of heat because everybody in town was hoping Ole Miss was going to win the game. The other interesting twist on the game was that coach Royal had picked up much of his staff when he was coaching at Mississippi State. Coach Campbell, Shira, and Pittman all had Mississippi connections. They still had family and friends in Mississippi. Of course, I still had the friends that I had made from working in Mississippi during the summer. [Fullback] Billy Ray Adams was involved in a serious automobile accident that December and would have to miss that game. He made most of the All-America teams that year. It was a severe enough injury it kept him from having a shot at the pros, which I'm sure he would have had.

Ole Miss was a big team. It surprised me how large they were, consistently across the board. They outweighed us quite a bit at each position. After we had the pregame warm-up, we got back in the dressing room and somebody made the comment that it was interesting Ole Miss did their pregame without their shoulder pads. I remember thinking that it couldn't possibly have been the case because I had never seen a team larger than that. They looked like the New York Giants warming up. It was really discouraging to find out they weren't even wearing their shoulder pads. An interesting sidenote to that: The next season, early in the year when it's still hot in September, one of my teammates asked coach Royal if we could not wear our shoulder pads during the pregame. Without missing a beat, coach Royal said, "That's fine. Anybody who is willing to play without their shoulder pads is certainly free to warm-up without them." He didn't get any takers.

Just before kickoff, Pat Culpepper's eyes would roll back in his head. He was a wild man. I didn't get into this, but a lot of the defensive guys would bang each other's shoulder pads just before kickoff. I was, unfortunately, standing near Pat when we came out on the field. He automatically did that to me, but he hit me so hard it knocked the right strap on my shoulder pad loose. It almost hit me in the face. I figured that was the hardest I was going to get hit all day. Pat was so excited that he looked over at Ole Miss and was shaking his fist to show we were ready to play. I thought, "Man, those big guys are probably fired up enough as it is without Pat throwing gasoline on it."

Johnny Treadwell was also a very intense guy. He thought if you smiled any time during the season then you weren't ready to play. He didn't have as much natural athletic ability as Pat, but he worked hard and had great determination and made himself into an All-American his senior year.

The base defense we ran that year had six down-linemen with two linebackers, two [defensive halfbacks], and a safety. I think we went to a 4-4 look for that game: four guys who were more like linebackers instead of two. I think we took our defensive ends, stood them up, and moved them back. Ole Miss had great speed and a terrific passing attack. Coach Campbell tried to adjust for that. You had time to do that in the bowl season, but that would have been hard in the season when it's week to week. There were some Southwest Conference teams that threw it more than others, but none that spread it out like Ole Miss was doing. Ole Miss probably threw it more than most and still had a good running attack. They also had a good defense. I mean, they were a good team.

I played safety, and that ended up being a particular challenge against Ole Miss. They had an extremely effective passing attack. They had been one of the leaders in the country for passing offense. They had a couple of quarterbacks who were very good and they had a lot of good receivers. I didn't have an interception in the game, but our team intercepted five. That was obviously an important part of the victory. Jerry Cook had three that day.

Their two ends would come at me and cross in front of me. It was nerve-racking trying to figure out how I was going to manage both of these guys. I tried to stay deep of both of them and still stay close enough to them. The good thing was we rushed the passer effectively. I don't think they hit any big passes that day, but they made some yardage. Later on, I told coach Royal in practice that we ought to put that in our game plan. I said we ought to criss-cross our receivers, especially if they had just one safety back there.

Ole Miss was down on the goal line, at one point, and they were throwing to a receiver in the end zone. Johnny Treadwell got a hand on it, tipped it, and Cook intercepted it in the end zone. Those five interceptions on the day were critical to slowing them down. They moved the ball on us but only had one touchdown.

Upon Further Review

Texas's 10-1 finish was its best in fourteen years. Yet the program's best days were still on the horizon and Carlisle was largely responsible for Texas's first national championship two seasons later. Carlisle played both safety and quarterback when Royal decided he would put the option back in the Split-T just in time for the 1963 season. (Carlisle struggled just enough with the added wrinkle that he jokes, "At the end of spring football, coach Royal said that either I had to change or he would have to change the offense.")

The Carlisle-led Longhorns were involved in a pair of matchups that season pitting the nation's top two teams. No. 2 Texas thumped No. 1 Oklahoma, 28-7, on a day where Carlisle ran the option as if he invented it. Arguably, Carlisle's biggest play of 1963 was on defense. Texas nursed a 7-0 lead against pass-happy Baylor but, with 29 seconds left, the Bears were within striking distance at the 19-yard line. For a moment, receiver Lawrence Elkins was wide open as he approached the end zone. Carlisle covered nearly 15 yards as he closed in on Elkins. His over-the-shoulder interception ranks as one of the top defensive plays in program history, preserving Texas's national championship hopes and clinching Royal's third-straight conference title.

It took another near-miracle for Texas to get past Texas A&M. Kyle Field was a rain-soaked quagmire and the country was still reeling from President John F. Kennedy's assassination just six days earlier in Dallas. Texas trailed very late in the game when an Aggie linebacker intercepted Carlisle. Had he taken a knee, A&M would have knocked Texas out of the national title hunt. Instead, he lateraled the ball to . . . no one. Fullback Tom Stockton, the closest to the ball, recovered not only the fumble but Texas's title hopes. (Stockton said: "I later read in the paper that the linebacker was asked why he did what he did. He said, 'My teammate was behind me and I was going to lateral to him.' But if you look at the film, there was no one else in the picture but me.") Royal inserted passing quarterback Tommy Wade, who deftly moved his team down the field. Texas was just shy of the end zone and, with seconds remaining, Royal replaced Wade with Carlisle. He crossed the goal line on a quarterback sneak, and Texas snuck away with a sloppy 15-13 comeback.

Eastern sportswriter Myron Cope, however, was so unimpressed with the ugly win that he wrote, "Texas is the biggest fraud ever perpetuated on the football public" prior to the Horns' Cotton Bowl showdown against No. 2 Navy. Carlisle was the quarterback of the nation's No. 1 team, but the Midshipmen boasted Heisman Trophy signal caller Roger Staubach. But it was Carlisle who came out throwing after Texas coaches discovered Navy's defense remained in a 5-2 and did not shift to the strong side of the offensive set. It meant the cornerback responsible for containing the option was left on an island against receiver Phil Harris. Carlisle would throw for 213 yards in his final collegiate game, leading Texas to a 28-6 win and putting the finishing touches on Royal's first national championship.

Carlisle was Green Bay's fifth-round pick of the 1964 NFL Draft in an era when franchises would select players virtually sight unseen.

"Professional teams would draft you based on what they heard about you or from what little film they'd seen of you," Carlisle said. "They sent me a questionnaire, and asked me to list my ideal playing weight. I had never weighed more than 173, but I'd always thought my ideal playing weight was about 193. So, I put that on there. I ended up getting a no-cut contract with Green Bay. I'd never seen a guy's face fall like [Packers coach] Vince Lombardi's did when he saw me naked for the first time. I was on the scale, and I hit about 172. I'm sure he was thinking, 'Good grief, what are we doing with this shrimp?'"

It wasn't long before Carlisle was traded to the Dallas Cowboys. Coach Tom Landry desperately needed a quarterback and knew that former SMU star John Roach, just one year removed from pro football, was in the Dallas area as a realtor. It's just that Green Bay still had the rights to him.

"Tom Landry called Lombardi and said he needed to make a deal for Roach," Carlisle said. "The way I tell it is Lombardi said, 'You can have Roach if you take Carlisle.'"

Carlisle spent one season in Dallas before hanging up his cleats. He then worked in hospital administration in Landstuhl, Germany, during the Vietnam War. Five years in the investment banking business shuttled him between Dallas and New York. Then, in 1973, Carlisle returned to where the mystique of a Texas-Mississippi matchup essentially began. He returned to McComb to work with his father-in-law in the oil business. He remains there to this day.

Chapter Three

PAT CULPEPPER

Linebacker (1960-62)

It was 1959 when Darrell Royal and Mike Campbell pulled up to the house in Cleburne to recruit Pat Culpepper to play football for Texas. In January of that year, Fidel Castro had taken control in Cuba after driving Fulgencio Batista from the presidency. Senator Joseph McCarthy had died, but America was still feeling the aftershocks of the Red Scare. No wonder, then, that Mrs. Culpepper had a few pointed questions for the coaches that needed answering.

"My mother was a schoolteacher so she was interested in the academic part of it," said Culpepper. "But she was scared Texas had communists as professors. She didn't like that, but coach Royal did a good job of explaining himself. He said, 'Well, if some professor is going to change Pat, then we haven't done a very good job in this house.' And she liked that, and said, 'They're not going to change him, but I just don't like that influence.'"

Texas football faced a red scare of a different kind during that era—under Bud Wilkinson, Oklahoma had beaten Texas six straight times before Royal's Longhorns ended that streak in 1958. But during his playing days from 1960-62, Culpepper's Horns never lost to the Sooners. And that was especially sweet for Pat. "The only ones that recruited me hard were Rice, Texas, and Texas A&M," Culpepper recounted. "Oklahoma turned me down. They sent me a 'Dear John' letter, which I kept on my wall, you better believe it. They were the power then.

With coach Wilkinson, that was the team of the 1950s. They said I could walk on up there, that they'd run out of scholarships. Well, you couldn't run out of scholarships in those days. It was impossible."

Culpepper loved A&M under Bear Bryant, because Bryant's toughness reminded him of his high school coach at Cleburne, and he admired John David Crow, the Aggies' 1957 Heisman Trophy winner. But Bryant left College Station for Alabama in 1958, opening the door for Darrell Royal and Texas. "When Bryant left, the atmosphere changed at A&M. I got to see Texas work out during spring practice, and I was impressed with the way they were organized, how they did things. You could just tell these guys were winners."

Indeed, "winning" and "Texas" were becoming synonymous under Royal. Texas went 26-5-2 during Pat Culpepper's Longhorn career. But while they never lost to the Sooners, the Horns had to deal with another red menace to the north—Arkansas.

The Horns and Razorbacks had been slugging it out in down-to-the-wire contests for years. In 1959, Culpepper's freshman year on campus, Texas escaped Little Rock with a 13-12 squeaker, a game Pat sweated out in his dorm room listening on the radio. In 1960, the Hogs returned the favor, breaking Horn hearts with a 24-23 win in Austin on a field goal with 16 seconds left. In 1961, Texas registered a rare blowout in the series utilizing its brand new "Flip-flop Wing-T" offense, which featured the explosive running talents of James "the Rabbit" Saxton. Although Texas and Arkansas would share the conference crown that year, on that day Texas dominated, winning 33-7 in Fayetteville.

"That's how intense those games were," recalled Culpepper. "You had two coaches that were among the elite of college football in coach Royal and Frank Broyles. In 1961, we really had a great football team with all of that offensive firepower. We took the ball and marched right down the field using that Flip-flop Wing-T. When they got the ball, Lance Alworth would split to my side and I would run out there and run with him and jam him, but they couldn't match us. But those previous Texas and Arkansas teams were building up to it."

"It" was the 1962 game between the Horns and Hogs. After Texas finished the '61 season at 10-1, including a Cotton Bowl victory over Ole Miss, the team lost a ton of offensive talent, including Saxton. But the defense in 1962 was suffocating. Featuring Culpepper, All-American Johnny Treadwell at linebacker, and Scott Appleton at defensive tackle, the Horns allowed only 59 points in 10 regular season games, including three shutouts. But the season almost began with a loss.

Longhorns Pat Culpepper (31) and Johnny Treadwell (60) stop the Hogs' Danny Brabham (Photo courtesy of the University of Texas)

"We played Oregon the first game with Mel Renfro, who later played with the Dallas Cowboys and was a great player," Culpepper said. "That bunch had the NCAA sprint relay champions in that backfield. They could fly, and they came *that* close to beating us. Knox Nunnally barely made a tackle on Renfro on the second half kickoff. He dove and got his shoe or Renfro'd have gone all the way. But we just wore them down." After that 25-13 victory, Texas blew out Texas Tech and Tulane before outlasting Oklahoma 9-6. That set up the classic showdown in Austin with Arkansas and its high-octane offense.

"All of our games starting with the Oregon game were such close games," said Culpepper. "We beat Texas Tech pretty good, but then the OU game we won just 9-6. The year before, we were scoring points by the bucketfuls."

In 1962, it was the Razorbacks scoring points in buckets, and then some. The undefeated Hogs brought a No. 7 national ranking to Austin to face undefeated Texas, the nation's No. 1-ranked team. The Hogs had scored an average of over 36 points in their first four games, while Texas had allowed an average of just under seven. Irresistible force, meet immoveable object.

No. 1 TEXAS vs. No. 7 ARKANSAS

October 20, 1962
Austin, Texas

"Coach Broyles had Billy Moore at quarterback and a good football team behind him," said Culpepper. "They had a great staff at Arkansas; they were great coaches. They had Jerry Jones, the current owner of the Dallas Cowboys, on the offensive line. They had a real fine football team. They were explosive and scoring a lot of points. We were number one but thinking, 'Are we really that good?' We were winning the way we had to win. We had Ernie Koy at punter who could put the other teams in bad field position, because he was a punter who could flip the field. We had a defense that had played together in '61 with all those young players like Scott Appleton; we had a good secondary with Joe Dixon and Tommy Ford and Duke Carlisle at safety, and good defensive ends. Our defensive ends were good athletes who could do anything."

The first half saw Texas struggle offensively, netting only one first down. The Hogs fared only slightly better, notching a 41-yard field goal to take a 3-0 lead into halftime. As the third quarter wore on, Arkansas mounted a drive that took it to the Texas five-yard line. There, it's back to the goal line, the Texas defense dug in, and turned in one of the most famous defensive stands in school history.

On third down, Arkansas called on its giant fullback, 6-foot-4, 218-pound Danny Brabham, to thrust into the Texas line. As Brabham dove for the goal line, he met a meat grinder in the form of linebackers Culpepper and Treadwell and lineman Marvin Kubin. Culpepper speared the ball with his head, ejecting it from Brabham's grasp. The Horns' Joe Dixon fell on it in the end zone, and the Hogs were denied. A photographer snapped a shot at the precise moment Culpepper jarred the ball loose, and that photo to this day is among the most famous in Longhorn football history.

But the defense's day was not over. After the Horns took over on the 20, they fumbled the ball back to Arkansas, which a few plays later faced a fourth-and-one at the Texas 12. Electing to go for it, Broyles called a quarterback sneak, but Treadwell stopped Billy Moore cold, giving Texas the ball on its own 12-yard line. The ensuing Texas series would forever be known as "The Drive." After quarterback Duke Carlisle suffered a 2-yard loss, the Longhorns drove 90 yards in twenty plays, scoring on a 3-yard Tommy Ford run with only 36 seconds to play. Texas would hang on to claim the 7-3 victory.

The Game of My Life

By Pat Culpepper

In Austin that week we had Dan Jenkins of the Fort Worth *Press,* Bill Van Fleet of the Fort Worth *Star-Telegram,* Blackie Sherrod of the Dallas *Times Herald,* Jimmy Banks of the Austin *Statesman*—those were the sportswriters of that generation. That was your ESPN *Gameday* at that time. When they came in and started interviewing players in the lunch hall and watching practice, you knew it was a big ball game.

The campus at Texas had gone through such an exciting time in 1961 when we were No. 1 during the season, with parades down Congress Avenue. We had pep rallies every night on campus, marching up from Clark Field. They'd march up to Moore-Hill Hall after supper and there would be 300 students following the band. Well, it started up again that week against Arkansas in '62. We would hear the band practicing at Clark Field while we were practicing. It was just a great time because there was a closeness about the university. We had school dances on the steps right in front of the UT Tower. There were about 24,000 students, and Austin wasn't that big of a town. You could get around the whole town easy in a car. It was a little different that way.

Arkansas would come down to Texas and beat everybody. They would come down to Baylor and SMU and TCU and beat all of these people, and then they would get Texas so it was a big game. So they would come down with all of their army. It was one of those games where everybody knew they were going to have to play their best. You didn't need to hear any pep talk. So you had two great staffs with teams that had winners on them, and they were both nationally ranked teams. The Southwest Conference was no pushover then.

It was the first sellout that coach Royal had. They put bleachers up in the end zone and that stadium was already filled to capacity when we went out to warm up. The Arkansas fans were on the east side. They had their confederate flags and Razorback flags, and they would start that, "Woo, Pig! Sooie!" and I'll never forget, our fans would answer woo pig with, "We're No. 1!" from both sides of the stands. So it was like a pep rally before the game. Man, we were wired up.

Some of the Arkansas fans had cut the back fence at Memorial Stadium with wire cutters and they were all standing on the track, walking all along the south end zone. I bet there were 2,500 of them. At the end of the game, when the referee Curly Hayes held up the ball he got hit in the stomach by an Arkansas fan. They were mad because we hadn't had any penalties in the game, but coach Royal coached that way. We were not going to have holding penalties. He detested late hits. He knew how to win big football games, from the kicking game on down, and he was not going to let us lose the football game because we were stupid or selfish.

So into the third quarter we were still down 3-0. Arkansas ran a sweep down near our goal line. The wire fence was three yards behind the goal line, in the south end zone. There were four thousand people back there and man they were raising hell, yelling, "Stop 'em, stop 'em!" They got a first down on our five-yard line, and that's when we could really hear those people screaming. And that's when Al Panzera of the Fort Worth *Star Telegram* ran down there to the end zone and got right behind the goal post with his camera. And all these people were yelling and waiving their coats, and we couldn't hear anything. The humidity was over 80 percent that night, and everyone had sweated through their jerseys. Both teams were fighting hard.

What coach Campbell would do was target actions by different players that he thought would help the linebackers get to the play. And we targeted on Billy Moore. Jesse Branch was the tailback, who took off to the right. Moore pivoted and gave it to the big fullback, Danny Brabham. We are in a goal line defense, and all of our lineman have their butts up in the air and are getting underneath their lineman to take them out. Johnny Treadwell and I are standing on the goal line, and everybody is yelling, including our linemen. One of our linemen, Marvin Kubin, was yelling, "No! No! No!" I could hear him yelling. But the people behind us along the fence were yelling so loud, you couldn't hear Billy Moore call the signals.

Moore takes the snap and starts to my left, his right, and pivots and hands the ball to Brabham hitting right up the middle, and I've got a clear shot at him. Treadwell and Kubin and I hit him, and when I hit him, I knew something happened because I felt something go over my shoulder. It was a square hit, I caught him just right. He didn't fumble, I knocked it out. Johnny and Kubin came in and the ball rolled over, and then Jerry Lamb, their good receiver, fell on the ball as it was rolling, but Joe Dixon outfought him for it in the end zone. Joe picked up that ball and threw it in the air, higher than the goal post. Tommy Lucas was pointing the other way, and some guy threw his coat over the fence, and that's when the photographer got that great picture.

We got the ball back, but on our 21-yard line, Ray Poage got knocked loose from the ball, so they got it back. As we went back on the field, old Treadwell said, "Dammit, we're gonna do it again!" just like on the goal line. This time they had a fourth-and-a-half-a-yard at our 12-yard line. We go back in a goal line defense. Coach Campbell takes the safety out and brings a lineman in to gut it again. This time Moore tried a quarterback sneak. Our linemen knocked theirs back into him, so Moore had to squirm to his right, and Treadwell hit him right there in the chin and buckled his head back, and we took the ball over. So we had to do it twice.

We worked hard on goal-line defense. That was always our last big hitting period before the season started. We would stop the heavy hitting, and have a goal-line period, good against good. We'd go down on that goal line against that Wing-T and boy, it was getting after it. Coach always felt that he could gauge his defense that way, and his offensive players, the way they'd get after each other.

So now, we get the ball back and we have to go 90 yards. We get it down to a fourth-and-a-half-yard and run our pitch sweep out of the Wing-T, and Jerry Cook made it by the length of a pencil. So now we're on the Arkansas 42 with about 4:30 left. We ran a trap to the 37. Johnny Genung came in at quarterback because Carlisle had run a sprint out and had been knocked out. Genung had been quarterback for the last great Wichita Falls Rider single-wing state championship teams. Johnny was a good thrower, but the first pass he threw, Stan Sparks from Arkansas intercepted it in front of our bench. But he stepped out of bounds! When he came down on that line, Sparks was so mad he took that ball and threw it so far it hit the wall past the track.

So on a third-and-four, about the sixteenth play of our drive, Genung sprints right and throws back to Tommy Ford in the flat, but Mike Parker, who later was defensive line coach at Texas under Fred Akers, stopped him with a tremendous hit. He hit Tommy Ford a lick and leveled him. But that gave us a first-and-10 with 1:48 left. Nobody in the stands sat down. Smokey the Cannon was being fired after every first down.

We got it to a second-and-3 with less than a minute left. That's when Royal started calling for the field goal kicker to be ready. Scott Appleton, our great defensive tackle, thought coach Royal was going to go for the tie and he was yelling, "No, coach, no!"

We got our wing set to the right, and we ran our favorite play, "18 sweep." Tommy Ford made it in to that end zone because he could turn that baby inside. He was not a sideways runner. When you hit Ford, he was going toward your goal line. And he got that ball in there, and we were going nuts. That was the twentieth play of that drive.

After the game, the fans stormed the field. We got in the dressing room and coach Royal was so shaken up, he was crying. And old Staley Faulkner picked him up and coach said, "I can't say anything. What can I say? That was the greatest win we could have. We just outfought 'em." It was really emotional. The fans just stayed in the stadium, and nobody went to bed that night. The horns were going off all night, they were going crazy on the mall in front of the Tower. Since that day, I've met more people who say they were at that game. They never forgot it.

The photograph of the goal line stand did not come out in the Sunday paper; it came out the next week. Coach Royal held it up and said, "This is our Mount Suribachi." Ever since then, that picture captures all of it. We were just lucky that that guy was sitting back there. Frank Broyles thought for a long time that Brabham had crossed the goal line, but his body never crossed that line, much less the ball. After that play was over, we got up and I hit Brabham on the shoulder pads and he touched me back and ran off the field. It wasn't his fault. It was just one of those plays that the defense makes because the linemen executed their charge and the linebackers did what they were supposed to.

Upon Further Review

Given the intensity of the emotions after the Arkansas game, the Horns may have been suffering from an understandable letdown as they stumbled to a 14-14 tie against Rice the next week. But they reeled off four straight victories to finish the regular season, giving them a 9-0-1 record and an outright Southwest Conference championship. Although Texas lost 13-0 to LSU in the Cotton Bowl, it finished the season ranked fourth by both the AP and the UPI, setting the stage for the program's first-ever national championship in 1963.

Following that 1962 season, Pat Culpepper graduated and became an assistant coach under Darrell Royal at Texas. He coached college football for twelve years, including his stint at Texas, and made coaching stops at Colorado, Tulane, Baylor, and Memphis State. He was named head coach at Northern Illinois in 1976 and held that post through 1979. Culpepper also coached in the high school ranks in Texas, holding head coaching positions at some of the state's high school football hotbeds, including Midland, Lufkin, Galveston Ball, Westfield, and Cleburne, his hometown. Culpepper was inducted into the Texas High School Football Hall of Fame in 2011.

In addition to being remembered for his ferocity on the field, Culpepper is also known for his academic accomplishments while at Texas. He earned an Earl Blaik academic fellowship, named for the former coach and athletic director at West Point who mentored Doc Blanchard and Glenn Davis. The Blaik award was given to players found to be leaders in academics as well as football, and who were found to "exert a fine influence on their campuses." Culpepper also earned a Swede Nelson Sportsmanship award, given by the Boston Gridiron Club, and was named an Academic All-American his senior year.

For Pat Culpepper, who would graduate with a history degree from Texas with honors, academics were a vital part of the experience. "Academics were changing at the University of Texas during coach Royal's time," said Culpepper. "By the time I got to be a junior or senior, half of my professors were from Harvard and thought we were all a bunch of hicks, which we probably were. But I had a great experience. Ira Iscoe was head of the psychology department. I didn't even know he knew me, but the week of the Oklahoma game my senior year, I'm walking by the Tower and he's got his head down and he comes up to me and says, 'You've got to hate those bastards, Culpepper!' I didn't even know he cared about football! But I loved all of my professors at Texas. All of them were wonderful teachers."

A fact which no doubt would have made his mother smile.

Chapter Four

TOMMY NOBIS

Linebacker, Guard (1963-65)

Tommy Nobis had his doubts. He wasn't sure if he had the stuff to play football at the collegiate level. Yes, that Tommy Nobis.

The same Tommy Nobis to win both the Outland and Maxwell trophies recognizing college football's most outstanding lineman. The same Tommy Nobis named All-American at both linebacker and guard. The same Tommy Nobis whom Darrell Royal said was the best two-way lineman he ever coached. The same Tommy Nobis whose jersey number 60 still represents the gold standard for burnt-orange defensive excellence more than fifty-five years after completing his eligibility.

But before he was that Tommy Nobis, he was a tall redhead with a twenty-inch neck, and one of a half-dozen linebackers Texas inked in the spring of 1962. Two decades before the NCAA imposed scholarship limits, major programs typically overloaded their rosters with upwards of fifty freshmen each year. It meant that hundreds of talented youngsters, who likely would have earned starting jobs at other schools, simply got lost in the shuffle. That's why, when Nobis scanned the field on his first day of college practice, the thought occurred to him that he just might be a perpetual bench-warmer.

After all, he wasn't even a First-Team All-State linebacker when recruited out of San Antonio Jefferson. And, yes, the linebackers who finished ahead of Nobis in the balloting also signed with Texas that year. "I knew I had to do something to get the coaches' attention," Nobis recalled.

That he did, to say the least.

A combination of toughness, tenacity, focus, drive, and rare talent pushed Nobis to the top of his class, regardless of position. Freshmen were still ineligible for varsity sports, so it spoke volumes that Nobis was the only sophomore starter on Texas' 1963 national championship team. Nobis was selected to the All-Southwest Conference team that season, but he had just begun to make a name for himself.

Texas entered the 1964 campaign undefeated in 21 straight regular-season games but needing to replace eight starters. It was also the year the NCAA began allowing any number of substitutions with the clock stopped, but Royal still preferred two-way players. It meant that the likes of Nobis would continue to start on both sides of the ball.

The Longhorns opened at No. 4 in the preseason *Associated Press* rankings and vaulted to the top spot after posting wins against Tulane and Texas Tech by a combined score of 54-0. Then came the season-defining stretch in which Texas played No. 10 Army, Oklahoma, and No. 8 Arkansas in a row.

The Horns had to rally from a 6-3 halftime deficit against the visiting Cadets. Nobis would register 24 tackles in 28 minutes in an eventual 17-6 Texas win. He notched 21 tackles the following week in a 28-7 thumping of the Sooners. However, Arkansas had methodically replaced Oklahoma as the highest-rated team on Texas' schedule. Five times during the 1960s, the Texas-Arkansas rivalry featured two Top 10 teams. The 1964 game in Austin was no exception.

Razorback Ken Hatfield returned a punt 81 yards early in the second quarter to erase a scoreless tie. It would remain a 7-0 ballgame until Phil Harris knotted the affair with a two-yard run early in the fourth. Texas forced a punt, but the Hogs got a fresh set of downs after Texas was guilty of a substitution infraction. Arkansas parlayed the penalty into a 34-yard touchdown pass to regain the lead. The Horns answered with a 70-yard drive and scored on tailback Ernie Koy's two-yard run with 87 seconds left. Texas trailed by a point, and Royal had a decision to make. The head coach who publicly opposed the 2-point conversion when it was implemented just six seasons earlier opted to go for broke, or "for the whole load of watermelon," as he later said. Under a heavy rush, Marvin Kristynik's pass to TB Hix Green fell short. Arkansas left town with a 14-13 upset despite managing just 55 yards rushing.

Both teams would run the table the rest of the season. Undefeated Arkansas was paired with Nebraska in the Cotton Bowl, but No. 5 Texas drew the biggest postseason prize of them all.

Tommy Nobis receives the Maxwell Award, 1966

No. 5 TEXAS vs. No. 1 ALABAMA

January 1, 1965, at the Orange Bowl

The Longhorns would face No.1 Alabama, its legendary coach Paul 'Bear' Bryant and consensus All-American quarterback Joe Namath in the Orange Bowl. The showdown pitted the reigning national champs against a Crimson Tide team that had already been declared the 1964 national champion by most major polls. It would also be college football's first bowl game ever played on prime-time television.

Steve Sloan opened at quarterback for the Tide after Namath earlier injured a knee in practice. Texas's defense set the tone early when it stemmed the Tide at the Longhorn one. The Longhorns took over on downs, setting up Koy's 79-yard touchdown run on a power sweep with 23 seconds left in the first quarter. It set a new Orange Bowl record for the longest TD run from scrimmage in a season where Texas' longest scoring run had covered just 21 yards.

The same kind of substitution penalty that cost Texas dearly six games earlier against Arkansas came back to haunt Alabama. This time, a Tide lineman was offsides as his team substituted liberally prior to a Texas punt. The critical mistake gave Texas a fresh set of downs, and the Horns went for the jugular. Royal subbed strong-armed Jim Hudson at quarterback who connected with George Saur on the next play for a 69-yard touchdown strike.

Crimson Tide coaches determined that a gimpy Namath was better than no Namath. He capped a fourteen-play, 87-yard march with his 7-yard touchdown toss to Wayne Trimble. Texas responded by marching into the Bama red zone, but the Crimson Tide blocked David Conway's 35-yard field goal attempt. The momentum shifted back to the burnt orange just as quickly when Texas recovered an Alabama fumble on the return. Koy capped a six-play, 38-yard drive with a 2-yard TD run.

The Horns held a 21-7 halftime lead, but would be shut out offensively during the final 30 minutes. Namath trimmed the lead with his 20-yard TD toss to Ray Perkins in the third quarter. Alabama added a 26-yard field goal in the fourth quarter to turn this one into a 21-17 nail biter.

Texas abandoned its cover two defense and began tightening up on receivers, but Namath had one last drive in him. He would complete eighteen of thirty-seven passes for 255 yards on the night and orchestrated a march inside the Texas 10-yard line with less than 7 minutes remaining. The rest is the stuff of Longhorn legend.

The Tide had first-and-goal from the Longhorn six. Three Steve Bowman plunges set up fourth-and-goal from the one, as well as one of the most memorable goal-line stands in college football history. It was also one of college football's most disputed. It would come down to Namath versus Nobis.

On fourth down, Namath kept and slid past right tackle. Almost immediately, he was met head-on by Nobis and tackle Frank Bedrick. To this day, Nobis insists he heard the whistle blow the play dead. Meanwhile, Namath fell into the end zone on what he assumed was an apparent touchdown. Officials ruled that Namath was stopped just shy of the end zone, and Texas took over on its one-inch line.

The Tide had a couple of more shots to pull it out, but the night belonged to Nobis and the Longhorn defense. Texas held Alabama to 49 rushing yards while running for 212.

The Game of My Life

By Tommy Nobis

It's a shame that people don't talk as much about the 1964 team. The 1964 team was as good as the 1963 team that won the national championship. We came so close to winning back-to-back national championships. We went for two (against Arkansas in 1964), but a tie would have cost us the national championship. You can't go back and blame it on a player or on a coach, or on whatever. We still had a tremendous year. Arkansas went on to play in the Cotton Bowl for winning the Southwest Conference because of that 1-point conversion. But we played No. 1 Alabama in the Orange Bowl. In those days, the major polls (AP, UPI) awarded the national championship before the bowl season. So, we were playing the national champ in our bowl game. And we, of course, had won it the year before. We thought that by beating Alabama we could make a statement that we were just as good as that year's national champion.

To this day, the Orange Bowl game against Alabama was a bigger game emotionally for me than the Navy (national championship) game. It was larger, on an emotional scale, than any game I ever played in as a pro. It was the first college bowl game to be played on television at night. The Orange Bowl was set up like the Super Bowl is today, with all the pageantry and fireworks and a big halftime show. It was just a spectacle. It had all the elements you could hope for: two major college football schools, the Bear on one sideline, Darrell Royal on the other, and a player like Joe Namath at quarterback. Our team didn't have any All-Americans. It was just a blue-collar, hardworking, give-it-all-you-can kind of team.

Namath had a hurt knee. He didn't start, but he still played and nearly pulled it out. We played outstanding run defense that night. Mike Campbell was my defensive coach. I don't care what you say about him; he could motivate. He could get the most out of young men, and that's what makes you successful. Darrell Royal had the same quality of being able to piss you off to the point where you wanted to show him but still love him. He still had your respect. Some coaches are going to try to push you, and shove you, and cuss you and kick you in the ass. You end up almost hating them. I'm not going to say that we didn't dislike them at times for some of the things they did or said, but we ended up with a lot of respect for our coaches.

We jumped on Alabama early but, very late in the game, we were up by just 4 points. Namath led a drive inside our 10-yard line. They had four shots at us to win the game with a touchdown. It came down to fourth-and-inches. Our coaches knew how to get us in the right position. If you played where they set you up, and you played it right, you had a chance to whip a guy's ass.

We held. We took over on downs and won by a score of 21-17. I'll never forget it.

The scene was one I never got close to copying in the pros because of the emotion of that game. The only thing that would have been bigger was if I had played in the Super Bowl. We (Atlanta Falcons) made it to the Super Bowl after I got here and after I was done playing, but that game didn't come anywhere close to what the Orange Bowl was for me in terms of excitement.

Upon Further Review

Ironically, four Longhorns in this game—Saur, Hudson, Pete Lammons, Josh Elliot—would become NFL teammates with Namath after he signed with the New York Jets for a then-unimaginable $400,000. But one of the biggest NFL recruiting wars was waged for Nobis the following season.

By then, Sports Illustrated had named him the best defender in college football. Nobis was also the only defensive player listed among the 1965 Heisman Trophy finalists. He averaged nearly 20 tackles per game during his collegiate career, despite the effort of opponents to run away from him.

Obviously, the League was salivating at the prospect of signing Nobis. Make that both leagues.

The NFL was still a "mom-and-pop" organization in 1965, according to Nobis, but it also had a distant cousin in the American Football League. Nobis was the first pick in the history of the Atlanta Falcons, but he was also the pick of the

AFL's Houston Oilers. It ignited a tug-of-war between the two organizations. As Nobis pondered his decision, astronaut Frank Borman, commander of the Gemini 7 spacecraft, literally urged from outer space that Nobis sign with Houston.

In the end, Nobis had Georgia on his mind. He became known as Mister Falcon after posting an astonishing 296 tackles his inaugural season, still the team's single-season record. Nobis was named the NFL Rookie of the Year and became the first Falcon voted to the Pro Bowl that same season.

Yet, in many ways, the transition from college to the professional ranks was "a step backward," according to Nobis. NFL teams in the mid-1960s "didn't have traditions. You didn't have loyalties. I went from a very established situation (at Texas) to one that was unproven. The way we operated (on the 1965 Falcons)—and I'm talking about everything from the locker room, the weight rooms, the way we traveled—was a step backward from big-time college football to the NFL. Obviously, the NFL caught up."

To some extent, the NFL also caught up with him. Nobis had never suffered a serious injury but, following his forty-eighth consecutive professional game, he underwent knee surgery in 1969. He had surgery on his other knee two years later. Like every other standout whose life had always been athletics, Nobis wrestled with the ageless questions: Why me? Why now?

"I was laying in a hospital feeling sorry for myself," Nobis said. "I was asking why this happened so early in my career. Your fourth year in the League is when you're finally learning to play."

Then came the event so impactful that Nobis compared it only with the births of his three children. It forever changed his perspective on his injury, his career and, indeed, on life.

Tommy Nobis went to Vietnam.

A member of the U.S. National Guard, Nobis reported to Fort Benning, Georgia, for basic training in March 1967. For four months, his helmet and shoulder pads would be replaced with fatigues and combat boots. When he went to Vietnam two years later, it was part of an NFL-sponsored USO tour to visit American troops. The athletes arrived in Saigon before venturing closer to the actual fighting than Nobis had anticipated.

"We went out to what they called 'fire bases' to visit the troops. You met young men who were going out that very day to put their lives on the line. They didn't know if they were going to come back in one piece, or come back at all. We would be flown in at certain times for our safety. There were some nights when we were out in the field. We weren't directly fired upon, but we were in areas where there were live rounds coming in. We didn't know where the shells would hit."

It amounted to just seventeen days, but those days have since shaped every day of Nobis' existence.

"The Vietnam experience put my life in perspective as to how fortunate I was and to how bad war can be. That was a nasty war in the way it was fought. It was just a brutal, terrible war. I was never so glad to get on an airplane and get out of there, but I felt like I was playing hooky from school in leaving those other guys behind."

It's primarily what Nobis thought about as he lay in a hospital bed, contemplating the arduous recovery from his second knee surgery.

"I knew I was going to get better. I knew I was going to play again. I didn't lose my limbs. Vietnam lent perspective at a time in my life when I was feeling sorry for myself. Rather than dwelling on my injuries, I thought about my blessings."

Nobis returned to earn a fifth Pro Bowl spot in 1972. By then, he had been named to the NFL's All-Decade Team for the 1960s. When Nobis hung up his cleats in 1976, he had led his team in tackles for nine of his eleven seasons. He had so immortalized the number 60 that it became the first jersey the franchise had ever retired.

His responsibility as the Falcons Vice President for Corporate Development meant that his affiliation with the franchise extended for more than forty-five years. It would come as little surprise that Nobis has a framed photograph of nearly every living NFL Hall of Famer in his office. What may come as a complete surprise is that Nobis is not in it. One of the greatest middle linebackers to ever play the game has never been inducted into the Hall, despite grassroots efforts to enshrine him.

The Canton snub was "disappointing, at first," Nobis concedes, but concludes he is in pretty good company. There are many pro players who had outstanding careers but never made it into the Hall, he noted.

"What is the Hall of Fame going to do for me? Is it going to make me a better husband? Is it going to put more food on the table? I don't think it's going to change my life. Now, there are some things that I can do that will make me a better person, and that will have a bigger impact."

No small part of that impact includes his involvement with The Tommy Nobis Center. His namesake has evolved since its inception in 1975 (when it operated out of trailer) into a multimillion-dollar nonprofit organization that trains physically challenged Atlanta citizens, providing them with marketable skills and placing them—many for the first time—in the workplace.

Concludes Nobis: "When you see the look on the face of someone when they show you their first paycheck, well, that is exciting as any touchdown."

Chapter Five

STEVE WORSTER

Running Back (1968-70)

Steve Worster became a legendary figure during his Texas Longhorn career. But truth be told, he'd become a legend before he ever set foot on the 40 Acres.

A tough, physical back from Bridge City in the Golden Triangle area of Southeast Texas, Worster was considered by experts at the time to be the greatest power runner in Texas high school history. No surprise, then, that after his senior season in 1966, in which his team won the state championship, a recruiting war erupted. Virtually every school in the country made its pitch. Coaches like Charley McClendon, Gene Stallings, Paul "Bear" Bryant-and Bum Phillips all took their shot. "The Pursuit of Steve Worster" was chronicled in depth in the 1967 issue of *Dave Campbell's Texas Football* magazine.

"I paid for that article," Worster said with a rueful laugh, recalling the treatment he got from his Texas teammates the next year in Austin. "Every night, *every* night in the cafeteria, I had to get up in front of the team and read from that article. And it really gave me the reds because it sounded like in the article I was just blurting out all of that stuff—not just answering questions, which was all that I did—the magazine made it appear that I was just sitting there talking and all of this stuff is just rolling out of my mouth. And I paid for it every night. They had me up on a table, and every night they would applaud and laugh . . . Finally it got to a point where I quit going down to eat, because hell, I didn't get to eat anyway. What was the purpose of going down there? I was just getting harassed. That went on for weeks . . . "

But Worster survived, and thrived. When he ran with the ball, the chant "Woooo, Woooo" reverberated through Memorial Stadium. But at first, Worster couldn't figure out why the crowd was booing him.

"When it first happened, it was a home game and I had made about a five-yard run," recalled Worster, "and I'm thinking, that was a pretty good run, and I got up and I could have sworn they were booing me, and I went back to the huddle thinking, 'I can't believe they're booing me after that run, why would they be doing that—they don't boo anybody in this stadium,' and I couldn't figure it out. Then I had another pretty good run, a little bit better than the first, and I said, 'What the heck is going on?' and somebody, I think James Street or Ted Koy, said, 'They're not booing you, you dummy, they're saying 'Woo, Woo!' And I said, 'You've got to be kidding me!' And then after that point, it got to where every time we'd have third-and-one, the fans'd get to calling my name, and I'd go 'Shhhhh.' The other team knew I was going to get the ball anyway, but the fans didn't have to remind them—they might have forgotten!"

Whether the defense knew or not, it really didn't matter. The former Bridge City Cardinal spearheaded the Longhorns' famed Wishbone attack from his full-back position. In his career at Texas, from 1967 to 1970, including a five-game stretch as a freshman with the Texas Shorthorns, Worster's UT teams lost only two ball games and tied one, and won two national championships. Worster's Horns reeled off thirty consecutive victories between 1968 and New Year's Day, 1971.

Darrell Royal and the Texas coaches introduced the Wishbone in early 1968. Royal had Chris Gilbert, Ted Koy and Worster vying for two positions in the same backfield, and wanted them all on the field at once. The decision was to move Koy from fullback to halfback along with Gilbert, and to keep Worster at fullback. The result would revolutionize college football.

"After we started beating people, we realized the fact of the uniqueness of the Wishbone," remembered Worster, "that we had a triple option, which we knew was pretty much a nonexistent item before, so we all thought, well hell, this ought to be pretty nifty, but we didn't understand at first the complexities that were involved in trying to defend the thing."

After a sputtering start in 1968 that saw Texas tie Houston and lose to Texas Tech, Royal made a switch at quarterback, from Bill Bradley to James Street. With a 31-3 demolition of Oklahoma State the next game, the Wishbone era had begun.

Steve Worster gallops for yardage against the Irish in the Cotton Bowl, 1970

Nobody could stop it, but opposing coaches pulled out all the stops to try. Much of the formation's success can be attributed to the Texas coaches. They became masters at making game-time adjustments, and always managed to keep a step ahead of their foes.

"The beauty of it was our coaches in the press box," said Worster, "because every team that came out threw a different defense at it. Literally, there was hardly a soul that didn't put together their own creation and way to try and defend the Wishbone. So in the first quarter a lot of the time, we wouldn't necessarily be stumbling and bumbling around, but we sure wouldn't be running over anyone, and what we were doing was figuring out the defense. The coaches would call down adjustments, so for example, the tight end might have been blocking out and kicking out on a defensive end, now he's blocking down and taking on a defensive tackle. The thing was, every film we watched of the opponent, there was no defense for the Wishbone, so we couldn't really prepare. We had no earthly idea because everybody we ran up against had something new, and you never had seen them defense it before. And that was every single solitary game. So you had to be impressed with our coaches up in the press box."

Texas finished that 1968 season with a 36-13 demolition of Tennessee in the Cotton Bowl. Worster led all rushers with 85 yards on only 10 carries. The streak had begun.

The 1969 season was the 100th year of college football. Texas ran the table through its first nine games, leading to an epic showdown between the No. 1-ranked Horns and the No. 2-ranked Arkansas Razorbacks on a cold, drizzly December day in the Ozark Mountains.

No. 1 TEXAS vs. No. 2 ARKANSAS

December 6, 1969
Fayetteville, Arkansas

Billy Graham gave the pregame invocation. President Richard Nixon watched in person, along with future president George H. W. Bush and Arkansas senator William Fulbright, while a national television audience tuned in to the only college football game that day. What they saw was the sharp Razorbacks jump on top of the mistake-prone Longhorns to take a 14-0 lead into the fourth quarter. That's when James Street turned the game around with a 42-yard touchdown slalom to the Arkansas end zone and a sneak for the 2-point conversion.

But Arkansas promptly marched to the Texas seven, only to see Texas's Danny Lester pick off a Bill Montgomery pass intended for Chuck Dicus. Two series later, trailing 14-8 with only 4:47 on the clock, the Horns stared at a fourth-and-3 from their own 43. Instead of relying on his smashmouth Wishbone, coach Royal gambled—and won.

The coach called "53 Veer Pass." Out of the Wishbone, with tight end Randy Peschel lined up beside the left tackle, Street faked to a charging Worster up the middle, rolled left, and flung it deep toward a sprinting Peschel. With two Hogs draped across his back, Peschel hauled it in, finally tumbling down at the Arkansas 13. Two plays later, Jim Bertelsen plunged over from the two. With James "Happy" Feller's kick, the Horns led 15-14. When Tom Campbell picked off Montgomery the next series, Texas clinched the game of the century.

The Game of My Life

By Steve Worster

It was just an amazing time. There were hippies running around, we had women's lib going on, the Vietnam War. Neil Armstrong had walked on the moon that summer. The interesting thing about it is, ABC television were soothsayers when you get right down to it, because during the preseason, they moved the game from October to early December, which was phenomenal. Think about that. They had a feeling each team would be doing exactly what we ended up doing, going undefeated. And then, not only that, but it was the last game of the entire college year, and not only that, but the last game of the 1960s, and the last game of the celebration of the 100th year of NCAA football. That's why we had the "100s" on the sides of our helmets. I mean it was a big deal. We had a pep rally before the game where we had over 25,000 people in the stands. It was fascinating how that all worked out.

I didn't hear anything the night before at our hotel, but we tried desperately to keep our location as much a secret as possible and to not let the information out about where we would be staying. We were not anywhere close to town because I remember it was a good 45-minute drive to town to get to the stadium. But the Hog fans were passionate. Before we left to go out on the field, the last word out of everybody's mouth was "keep your helmets on—when you're sitting on the bench, do not take your helmet off." But the funny part was, I got a kick out of watching them throwing their whisky bottles. All they were doing was wiping out their own people, they couldn't get the throw from up in the stadium to out on the field, so they were just hitting their own people right on the head. But they were radical. In fact, after the game, I heard that they had maybe six or seven heart attacks at the stadium, and lost maybe three people. And obviously that was a real shame, but the way that game ended, I guess it is not that surprising.

But when we were down 14-0 in the fourth quarter, we never panicked, and we never had a negative thought in our minds, never ever. We never thought anything negatively. The group we had were such class acts, and all we were was just a group of country bumpkins from all over the state of Texas. All of us were from little bitty towns all over the state, all coming from blue-collar working families—very few of us even had a parent that had a college education. We just represented Texas, and when we got together, we knew very early that we had something very special.

When James [Street] ran in with the pass play on fourth-and-3, I think all of us were saying, "You've got to be kidding me!" Trust me, James was a heck of an athlete. James was a winner. James just basically knew how to win. But throwing the ball was not a big part of his expertise. But we never questioned anything. I remember when the play was called, I really just kind of took it with a grain of salt, and thought, "Hey, that's the call, coach Royal is the man, and whatever he decides is what we do." In fact, I didn't think about it at the time, but looking back on it, I was kind of glad he didn't call on me. Because we were having a heck of a time gaining even an inch off of those guys, much less four yards. And to be honest with you, I really didn't think that we could make it. So we had to take what they were giving us. And that deep pass was the last thing in the world that they ever expected us to do.

But the amazing thing about it, to show you how good Arkansas was, they defended it perfectly. We normally didn't throw the ball to the tight end, but Randy pulled it in and he did what he had to do.

After we took the lead, I don't remember feeling anything except numbness. In fact, I felt almost numb that whole game. It was almost surreal. It was almost like we weren't even there, it was like somebody else was playing in our bodies and we were watching from the sidelines. It was just a strange, strange deal. I don't remember feeling excitement because it really wasn't excitement to me. When we did it, it was just a relief. When we caught that pass the thought was, "Alright, we did it, that's what we were supposed to do, now we have to go down, and now we have to score. Alright, we scored, OK, now we have to keep those guys from scoring," because hell, they'd been threatening to score every time they got their hands on the ball.

Then after the game, President Nixon was in the locker room with secret service guys just everywhere. But I was over in the corner just stunned. I didn't really participate in all of the celebration at all. In fact, until I later saw a recording of the locker room, I didn't even realize what had happened. It was just like we were in another world. I'm thinking, "We won, but did we really win?" I mean the game wasn't over until almost the last play of the game when we intercepted the ball.

But Arkansas had a hellacious defensive effort going that day. Plus the fact that they were a phenomenal football team. They were excellent. They were as good as anybody we had ever played. In fact, to me, it was almost like playing ourselves. It literally was. It was like our team was out there playing each other. And that was why, in my eyes, it was so difficult that anybody had to lose that day. When we walked off the field after the game, we were thinking that it was just sad that anybody had to lose.

Because, without a doubt, Arkansas was a class team. I felt like our team was just a class act, a total class act, and Arkansas was like our total carbon copy. We just had the ultimate respect for these guys, especially after we got on the field with them. It was just one of these deals where they'd knock you in the dirt, and then they'd help you up out of the pile.

And it all comes down from the coaches. That's who establishes the ideology of the team. And with coach Royal and coach Broyles, what two better gentlemen to be involved than those two guys. So the classiness just exemplified them and their type of football. That was what it was all about. I'm telling you, it was a class act. But I mean, we were killing each other out there, just killing each other. I'm telling you, I've never been hit so hard in my life, and constantly and consistently and time and time again, and there was never, ever a letup, and it was fascinating because that was the way *our* team played.

Upon Further Review

With its 15-14 win over Arkansas, in which Worster ground out 94 yards on 25 carries, Texas won the Southwest Conference championship and the right to play in the Cotton Bowl on New Year's Day, 1970. The Horns' opponent that day would not be Penn State (also undefeated) as coach Joe Paterno elected to send his team to the Orange Bowl to face Missouri. Instead, Notre Dame accepted an invitation to the Cotton Bowl, ending a forty-five-year bowl absence that dated back to the 1925 Rose Bowl, when the Four Horseman shook down the thunder in a win against Stanford.

In a grueling duel that Worster remembers as more alley fight than football game, Texas outlasted Notre Dame 21-17 to clinch the national championship. Worster earned Most Outstanding Player honors that day, as he carried the ball 20 times for 155 yards. In back-to-back Cotton Bowls against Tennessee and Notre Dame, Worster totaled 240 yards on 30 carries for an average of exactly 8 yards a carry.

During the 1970 season, Worster and the Horns continued their dominance, destroying every team in their path en route to their second-straight undefeated season and third-straight Southwest Conference title. The reward was a return trip to Dallas where, on January 1, 1971, they again took on Joe Theismann and the Irish. This time, though, despite racking up over 400 yards of offense, Texas couldn't overcome five lost fumbles and fell 24-11.

Despite the tough finish in the last game of his career, Worster had turned in a season to remember. He earned All-America honors for the second-straight year and was named the team's Most Valuable Player. He finished fourth in the Heisman Trophy balloting behind quarterbacks Theismann, Archie Manning, and winner Jim Plunkett. In its December 14, 1970, issue, *Sports Illustrated* featured Worster on its cover in full gallop under the heading "Texas Slaughters Arkansas" with the subhead, "WooWoo Worster on a Rampage."

In his career at Texas, Worster rampaged, indeed. His 36 rushing touchdowns still ranks him tied for fifth on the all-time list, behind only Ricky Williams, Cedric Benson, Earl Campbell, and Vince Young. For his career, he gained 2,353 yards on 457 carries for a stout 5.1-yard average, thirteenth all-time at Texas.

But after a one-year stint in the Canadian Football League, Worster's rampaging days on the football field came to an end. "I went to Canada and tried it up there," explained Worster, "because I didn't want to be that frustrated jock that says, 'I wish I'd done this or that—I had the opportunity to play pro ball but I didn't,' etc. I just didn't want to second-guess myself. And so I went up there and did it, and didn't like it, so I said I'm going to go back and get my degree, which I did."

After football, Worster returned to his hometown of Bridge City. "My business career mainly centered around sales, outside sales, and sales management," Worster said. "I managed two or three different companies in sales-oriented businesses because I just liked dealing with the people, and that's what I am still doing today." Recently, the Texas Sports Hall of Fame honored Worster by making him one of its Class of 2008 inductees.

Of his memories of his days as a Longhorn, some of his most cherished involve his relationship with coach Royal, who helped Worster deal with the pressures of being a star in the fish-bowl world of college athletics.

"Coach Royal was just a great person," said Worster. "I'll never forget, at the end of my time there at the University of Texas, after I was through playing football altogether, I called him up and said, 'Do you think I may visit with you one day? I need to talk to you,' and he said sure.

"So we meet one morning and he says, 'What's on your mind, Steve?' And I said, 'I'm having a problem, coach. Look, I'm at the point where I don't know who this guy is.' And he said, 'What guy?' And I said, 'This Steve Worster guy.' And he said, 'What do you mean?' And I said, 'Well, every place I go, when I introduce myself, everybody makes such a big deal out of it, you know, they rant and rave, and they won't leave me alone,' and I said, 'I'm miserable, I hate it, that's not me. I'm from Bridge City, that place that has about three thousand people running around.' Then I told him that it got to where I wouldn't tell people my last name, but they'd ask, so I'd tell them, and then they'd think I was just setting it up to put more emphasis on it. So I told him it was just eating me alive, and that I couldn't handle it anymore, and I didn't know what to do.

"He said, 'Man, I went through that same thing and I still do to a certain extent,' but he said, 'Look, everything you've done is well-deserved, and you've earned everything that you've ever gotten.' He said, 'Believe me, I know. I'm your coach and I've been here with you all along. Take that in stride. Be thankful for everything that you have done in your life, and everything that has happened in your life.' And he said, 'Be proud of it. You have a lot to be proud of.'

"From that point on, I just started living my life and it gave me a way to deal with it. And I am happy as a camper that I went to coach Royal and asked him for help because it just made sense to me coming from him, that he believed I had earned all of it, and that I should be proud of it. It just made it all so much easier."

As to that quality about himself and his teammates that made them so beloved to Longhorn fans, Worster believes that the fans simply related to them as hard-working, hard-nosed football players.

"I think a lot of it was that I was just this old country bumpkin from Bridge City that came up to the big city and just played old-fashioned, hard-nosed football," Worster mused. "Kind of like coach Royal played. I was the perfect player for coach Royal because he basically said—and I saw him actually say this a couple of times during my stay there—'Look buddy, if you think you can whip us, fine—you line up your best eleven and I'll line up my best eleven and we'll get after it and see what happens. Your man on my man. I think my guys are better than yours and you think yours are better than mine, so we'll just line 'em up and we'll find out.'

"And that's basically what we did. We played good, honest, clean, hard-nosed football. It was 3 yards and a cloud of dust—what else was the Wishbone? We're not going to try and trick you, we're not going to try to throw the ball over you, we're not going to try to do anything but run right at you. That era of football is long since gone. And I think a lot of people identified with us because they had all come from that type of football growing up in their little hometowns, and I think they identified with me because I was just a hard-nosed guy, nothing fancy about me. And they just liked it because I didn't pull any punches and didn't say the right things, and I didn't tell the sportswriters what they wanted to hear. But the whole team had a personality, a unique personality."

Chapter Six

ROOSEVELT LEAKS

Fullback (1972-74)

It was National Signing Day, and Brenham High head baseball coach Jim Raup thought himself the victim of an early-morning prank. His team had won the 1970 state championship the prior season, but now his senior left fielder greeted him in the school parking lot by flashing the Hook 'Em Horns hand signal. A University of Texas graduate, Raup ordinarily would not have minded the gesture. It's just that he knew his star outfielder, who had made a name for himself as a varsity football fullback, had earlier given a verbal commitment to the University of Houston. During recruiting season, Raup made no secret of the fact that he wished Brenham's top athlete would sign with Texas. Now, he just wished Roosevelt Leaks would stop rubbing it in.

"Don't tease me like that!" Raup implored.

Leaks wasn't kidding. He, too, was a Longhorn—albeit for less than one hour. Texas assistant David McWilliams had been so persistent in courting Leaks that the Brenham standout reconsidered his initial decision.

"I thought about going to the University of Houston," Leaks said, "but they had just signed a lot of running backs. Recruiting back then wasn't done until the end of your senior season. Colleges would contact you, but I didn't go anywhere [for a visit] until after my senior season, in December and in February.

[Laughing] I think I gained 10 or 15 pounds during recruiting season, just like the rest of them."

But Leaks was, by no means, like the rest of them. The 5-foot-10, 200-pounder had the burst of a tailback and was expected to be Texas's first great ball carrier since Steve Worster completed his eligibility. Leaks was also an African-American who had signed on with the last all-white team to win college football's national title [1969]. The 1970 [UPI] national champion Longhorns included tight end Julius Whittier as the program's first African-American letterman, but Leaks's affiliation with Texas was nonetheless groundbreaking.

"Texas probably lagged behind in having a black player on its team," Leaks said. "It was part of the South and there were other teams like that. But it got to a point where coaches at other schools would tell you that Texas was not the place to be because they said it was racist. But, you know, I grew up with that. It wasn't anything new to me. At the same time, Coach Royal, as well as the other coaches, had to contend with alumni who pay the bucks. I understand that was a tough situation for him, but we made tremendous strides."

Many would argue that the strides Leaks made in changing the racial complexion of not only the University of Texas but also the Southwest Conference were even more significant than the strides he made as an All-American fullback. When Whittier completed his eligibility in 1972, there were still no high-profile black players associated with the Longhorn program. However, the perception gradually changed each time Leaks carried the ball. The 1972 Longhorns capped a 10-1 season with a thrilling 17-13 comeback against No. 4 Alabama in the Cotton Bowl. That day, Leaks ran for 120 yards on 25 carries. He finished the regular season with 1,099 rushing yards on the way to consensus All-SWC honors. In short, Leaks is generally regarded as Texas's first black superstar.

"It's probably not as important as folks make it out to be," Leaks said. "I was just playing football and so was everybody else out there. I was doing a job. There are many who want to play college football and I was the same way. Yet, I understood there were some things happening during that time when I was able to make a difference in whatever steps the university wanted to make. I was simply part of those steps."

Yet Leaks would take one giant step toward establishing his legacy while helping Texas clinch its fifth-straight SWC title on a windswept November afternoon in Waco, Texas.

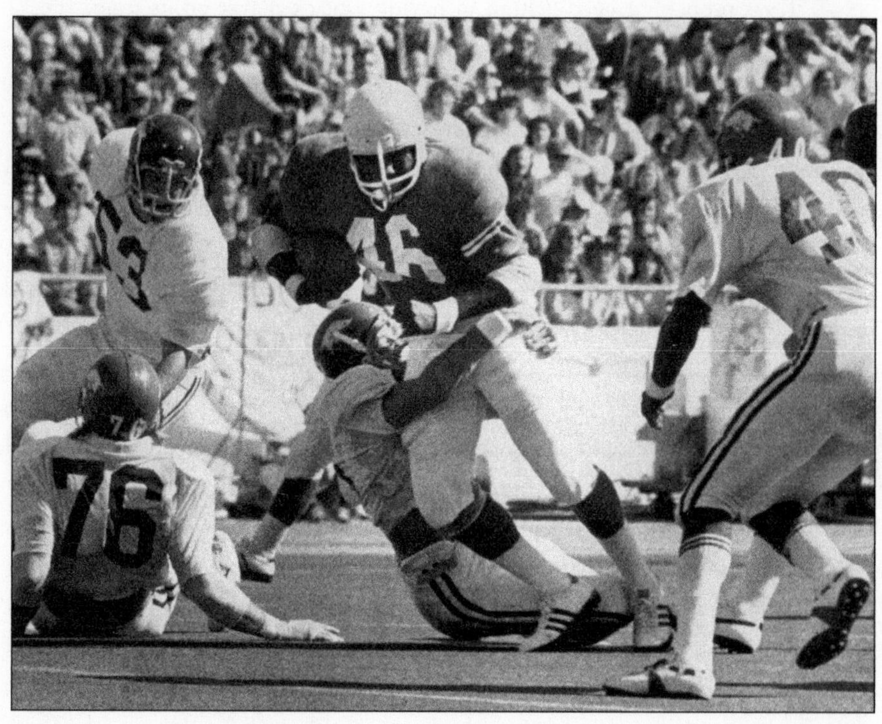

Roosevelt Leaks is surrounded by Razorbacks, 1974

No. 9 Texas vs. Baylor

November 11, 1972
Waco, Texas

Texas had not lost to Baylor since 1956, the year before Darrell Royal was hired to restore the Longhorn program, and the Burnt Orange would travel to Waco as a 14-point favorite and with a No. 9 national ranking. Yet Texas would face not only an improving squad with an outside shot at the league title, but also an ornery group of Bears intent on reversing the fifteen-year nonwinning streak. (Royal would later comment that Baylor came out with "eyes scrunched up like BBs.")

The Bears also entered the game boasting the Southwest Conference's top defense and kept Texas's offense off balance with a steady diet of stunts. The home team forced an early punt, a shank that covered all of 17 yards, and took over at its own 45. The result was a 35-yard field goal and Baylor's first lead against Texas in four years.

Texas's first sustained drive of the afternoon began at its 28 but the Horns fumbled it away at the Baylor 43. The teams exchanged punts, including Alan Lowry's 82-yard quick kick downed at the Baylor two. The Bears moved to midfield but, again, were forced to punt. Then, with 3:20 remaining until halftime, consensus All-American right tackle Jerry Sisemore limped off the field with an ankle injury. Following another Longhorn punt, Texas recovered a fumble deep in Bear territory. A five-yard loss and a five-yard penalty doomed the drive as Texas settled for a game-tying field goal at the break.

Baylor enjoyed a 9-3 advantage in first downs at halftime and outrushed Texas 113-77. Royal tried three different tackles in Sisemore's absence but there was no replacing the two-time All-American. A scoreless third-quarter saw Royal call timeout with 5 seconds remaining to force a Baylor punt into the stiff southerly breeze.

Leaks had just twelve attempts during the first three quarters. Now, his team was 15 minutes from suffering a major upset. Suddenly, Sisemore trotted toward the huddle as Texas began to operate with a two-tight-end set.

Texas's winning drive began on its own 30 when Leaks barreled for four yards. He would add runs of 3, 9, and 13 yards as part of a ten-play march to help move the Horns to the Bear 26. Quarterback Alan Lowry was forced to convert just one third-down conversion on the drive when he carried around left end for 11 yards. Leaks would carry twice on first-and-goal from the two, the second play resulting in the winning touchdown with 10:18 on the game clock.

"That was a hard drive at Baylor," Royal recalled. "We worked Rosey pretty hard on that drive to get in and take the lead. He was running and making tough, tough yardage. He really competed on that drive."

Texas forced a Baylor punt, but it was still anybody's ball game at 10-3. Leaks collected 11 yards on 2 carries up the middle before Texas was guilty of its second fumble of the day. Yet a roused Longhorn defense forced another three-and-out, limiting Baylor to 74 total yards during the second half and just one first down in the final 25 minutes.

The Horns operated from their own 17 and looked to run the clock by running the ball. Leaks and Lowry carried all but one play during Texas's time-chewing seventeen-play march. Leaks blasted over left tackle for the final score with 10 seconds remaining. At the end of the day, Leaks had notched his fifth-straight 100-yard rushing game, churning for 108 yards in the decisive fourth quarter alone. All told, Leaks accounted for 162 yards on 35 carries, a mark that—nearly four decades later—remained among the top 15 rushing days in Texas football history.

The Game of My Life

By Roosevelt Leaks

The early years were my best years, but my senior year, after my knee surgery, that was a little different. But as far as the games went, just getting back on the field was the exciting part for me. People still talk about the [1973] SMU game because of the [342 rushing] yards, but SMU was not that great of a game. Yeah, we ran up and down the field. But we [the starters] shouldn't have been in there midway through the third quarter. The game should have been over with by then. It should have been our game. The second team should have been in. The game shouldn't have even been close, but SMU went up 14-0. We played catch-up by running the ball. I went back into the game for the Southwest Conference record. I broke 342 yards, but that [record] was what that was about. I fumbled two or three times. You can say nobody remembers that, but I do. [Laughing] I have several friends who remember that.

The Arkansas game of my sophomore year was the game where I first proved, or was where I was first considered to be, a back who could run inside and out.

The game that made me a blocker was the Texas Tech game in Austin my junior year. I was the lead blocker when we ran plays to the outside.

The games against Oklahoma were tough games. We ran certain plays and I got tackled the same way every time, year-in and year-out. During that period

[1972-74], we didn't win any games against OU. Of course, my NFL roommate with the Baltimore Colts [former Oklahoma RB] Joe Washington had a lot to say about it.

A difficult game for me was when we played Texas A&M in College Station [1973]. One of their players tackled me and it was the first time I stretched my knee. It was a tough tackle that bent my left knee. He jumped up and down and all around after the play. A lot of folks griped about that, but I didn't think much about it. I said that he was just excited about making the play, and that's all it was. That young man called me the next day and told me it was all about the excitement of the game.

I don't remember as well of those days as some others do. [Laughing] Maybe I've been hit too many times and something is still rattling around up in my head. But if I had to pick one game, I would go with coach Royal's game. I would go with the game coach Royal picked as my top game. He thought my best game was when we played at Baylor during my sophomore year. I carried the ball more than thirty times. I would point to the support that I got from my offensive linemen. Jerry Sisemore was our All-American [offensive tackle] and Julius Whittier was the tight end. Jerry Sisemore got hurt in the first half and didn't come back until the fourth quarter.

We ran one play, the same play, time-in and time-out. It wasn't anything fancy. They kept tackling me, but we kept running the same play. We were running the Wishbone, and Baylor had a good team then. Coach [Grant] Teaff was there. People don't remember that, for a stretch of ten or fifteen years, the home team in that series almost always won that game. Baylor was tough and it just so happened that I carried the ball twelve or thirteen times in a row. Baylor had an outstanding defense that year. That was a tough game that came down to the fourth quarter. We had a long drive where I scored halfway through the fourth quarter and then I scored just before time ran out. But we won, and it meant we were the Southwest Conference champs with two games to go in the season.

Upon Further Review

Leaks's 1972 sophomore campaign was a preview of things to come. His 342 yards on 37 carries against SMU in 1973 established a SWC single-game rushing record and remained the Texas standard until RB Ricky Williams eclipsed the mark by eight yards against Iowa State twenty-five years later. Leaks was named the SWC Most Valuable Player after setting a league single-season rushing record with 1,415 yards. More important, he became the first black student athlete to earn First-Team All-American honors at Texas. He finished third in the 1973 Heisman balloting, trailing only Ohio State's John Hicks and Penn State's Heisman winner John Cappelletti. Both were seniors, and Leaks was considered the Heisman front-runner heading into his senior season.

The 1974 season promised to be glorious for the Burnt Orange. Texas had posted six straight conference titles and its freshmen class, including Tyler running back Earl Campbell, was Royal's finest since landing the Worster Bunch in 1967. But then . . .

"It was a freak accident."

That's how Leaks described his devastating knee injury suffered during spring drills.

"A defensive back hit me. The front of his head hit my leg. Whatever was in there [a knee], it was all torn. There was no pain whatsoever. I felt a 'pop' in my knee, but there was no pain when it actually happened. We weren't even going at full speed. It's just one of those things that happen. It's part of the game."

It obviously wasn't part of Texas's game plan for 1974. And the prognosis was worse than expected.

"The doctors told me that 95 percent of the players who have that kind of surgery never play football again," Leaks continued. "The rare thing was that I never had any swelling in my knee. The doctors said that was extremely rare. That's why, once I got out of my cast, I could start working on it right away. I think the reason I was still able to play football was because I worked at it. I worked out twice a day on my knee. I had the keys to the weight room."

Leaks strongly considered a medical redshirt but opted to try to complete his eligibility with his class. Almost six months from the day of the injury, Leaks played in Texas's 42-19 season opening win against Boston College.

"Coach Royal gave me the opportunity to make the decision about a medical redshirt. I made the decision to go ahead and play. I was the one who made that decision. Folks still ask me about it. I was at the Texas Black Sports Hall of Fame in January [2008], and some of the coaches there were still saying that Coach Royal did me wrong. I had to tell them that I made the decision. And they said, 'OK.' It's a decision I don't look back on. Hindsight is always twenty-twenty. Who knows? I taped my knee the whole time during my senior year, and taping to the skin is not easy. [Laughing] I had to shave my leg."

Leaks was clearly not the same. He slipped off of the national radar as his numbers dipped to 409 yards on 96 carries.

"I was fine when I ran to the left," Leaks explained. "I could hit the whole square. But going right, I would always hit the inside of the hole instead of hitting the hole square. I could never stretch my leg because of the scar tissue."

Texas's string of conference titles came to an end with its stunning 34-24 loss at Baylor. The Horns finished 8-4 following a 27-3 Gator Bowl loss to Auburn. Ohio State's Archie Griffin would win his first Heisman.

"There's no telling what could have happened to me if that injury had not happened," Leaks surmised. "I've got a couple of friends who still remind me of that. Every time Raymond Claiborne sees me, he says, 'Man, you cost us the national championship.' He's kidding, but I don't have any problems with the way I am today. The injury made me think about doing something else besides playing football. I realized that education was a big part of it, too. I really came to Texas to get an education. Of all the talented players I knew in high school, only three of us went to college. You need to have an opportunity to do something else with your life. I had the opportunity to get an education, and I knew I needed to take advantage of it."

Even so, Leaks would emerge as a nine-year NFL veteran. There were plenty of skeptics, however, on 1975's draft day. Concern about the knee injury saw Leaks's stock drop from a likely first-round pick to Baltimore's fifth-round choice.

Then . . . it happened again.

"During my third year at Baltimore, my knee got hit in the same way," Leaks said. "A big lineman fell on me. I was in New York and we were playing the Jets. It tore all the scar tissue through there. For any athlete, there's always going to be the shock of getting hit again like that. You always flinch hard when that happens because you think you tore it again. Nobody likes going through rehabilitation. I knew I had a problem because it swelled up. I came back to Texas the next morning. The doctor looked at my knee and said everything was still intact. Everything had just opened up, that's all. I called Baltimore and told them I was going to be OK, but that it was going to take a couple of weeks for the swelling to go back down. After that, because all the scar tissue had been torn loose, I could hit the whole square."

Leaks spent his final four years at Buffalo and was eventually cut during the 1984 training camp. By then, he had been selling real estate for several years. Leaks and his wife returned to Austin, where he is now the director of appraisals for the Veterans Land Board. His offices are on Congress Avenue, a few blocks from his landmark days at The University of Texas. He has two children and is also committed to the success of an East Austin after-school program that serves more than 800 children and youth from economically disadvantaged and/or single-parent households.

Collectively, it puts football, and the what-might-have-beens, in some perspective.

"Of all the things that have happened, I'm still happy and I'm still healthy, which is the main thing about being an athlete. I played the game long enough that I have no regrets about playing it, but I don't want to play it anymore. I'm through playing. I don't even play sandlot ball with anybody. Sometimes I'll go shoot some basketball with my son and his friends but, other than that, I don't play any ball. The bright side of that is . . . "

Leaks pauses before completing the sentence with a smile.

" . . . is that I made it."

Chapter Seven

JOHNNY "LAM" JONES

Running Back, Wide Receiver (1976-79)

When Johnny "Lam" Jones arrived on the Texas campus as an eighteen-year old freshman in the summer of 1976, the whole country knew who he was.

Jones and teammates Harvey Glance, Millard Hampton, and Steve Riddick had blown past the Soviets and East Germans at the 1976 Olympics in Montreal to claim the gold medal for the United States in the 4x100-meter relay. With Jones running the second leg, the quartet smoked the field with a time of 38.33 seconds. Jones had also competed in the final of the 100-meter dash, having posted qualifying times in three earlier heats to get to the final. Although he finished sixth in the 100, he posted his fastest time of the meet with a time of 10.27 seconds.

So after living in the Olympic Village, racing against and beating the fastest runners on the planet, and taking the stand in Montreal to receive his gold medal to the strains of the Star Spangled Banner, showing up to play football in Austin figured to be no big deal—right?

"Football is the type of sport that, it doesn't matter what the heck you did on the track, it's a whole new ballgame," emphasized Jones, discussing his arrival on the 40 Acres. "So I was just like all of the other incoming freshmen as far as being nervous about school and about football. As far as football goes, I had had the chance to come in and watch practice and see how big and fast the guys were and how hard the hits were, so coming in and seeing all of that, it didn't mean a thing what happened in Montreal. I had enough sense to know that what I did up in Montreal was yesterday, and now when we put those pads on, it was a whole new ballgame."

Jones joined a Longhorn team that had come off a 10-2 season in 1975, including a 38-21 win over tenth-ranked Colorado in the Bluebonnet Bowl. The 1976 Horn offense featured junior Earl Campbell at fullback in the Wishbone, and the defense fielded some of the hardest hitters in Texas football history. Legendary coach Darrell Royal was entering into his twentieth season as head coach of the Horns. Jones knew better than to act like he was someone special.

"I didn't have to tackle Earl," laughed Jones, "but we had guys on defense like Steve McMichael, Brad Shearer, Johnny Johnson, Lionell Johnson, Ricky Churchman, the list goes on and on, and I had to practice against these guys every day. With the type of guys we had on our team, with that many great athletes around, it was real easy to keep a level head. In the company we had, I'd have liked to have seen the guy that could get the big head—they'd have to have been awful good. The other thing was, Coach Royal didn't recruit the type of guys that would have the big egos, no matter how good they were, and that's what made it so special going to Texas and being on that team."

Along with Campbell on the '76 Texas offense, the Longhorns had playmakers like receiver Alfred Jackson, and one of the all-time great placekickers in Russell Erxleben. But the team had lost a spiritual leader, Marty Akins, to graduation in 1975. Akins had led the team at quarterback the three previous seasons, so 1976 saw a transition at the all-important quarterback spot in the Longhorn Wishbone. The Horns started three different quarterbacks in Mike Cordaro, Ted Constanzo, and freshman Mark McBath. The backfield rotated Graylon Wyatt, Johnny "Ham" Jones of Hamlin, Texas, Ivey Suber and Jimmy Walker at halfback, as well as the newcomer from Lampasas, Johnny "Lam" Jones.

Campbell spearheaded the Texas rushing attack, but hurt his hamstring in the opening game of that 1976 season, a 14-13 loss to Boston College. Injuries would plague Campbell throughout the season, as they would other members of the Texas offense, including receiver Jackson, who suffered broken ribs against Oklahoma. The injuries to members of the Texas backfield meant Lam Jones got on the field as a true freshman, earlier than he might have wanted.

But Jones was ready. In the third game of the season, at home against the Rice Owls and their All-American quarterback Tommy Kramer, Jones exploded for 182 yards on only 15 carries as Texas destroyed the Owls 42-15, despite a 397-yard pass-

Johnny Lam Jones turns the corner against Texas Tech (Photo courtesy of the University of Texas)

ing effort from Kramer. Only four Texas freshmen—Cedric Benson, Joe Bergeron, Jamaal Charles, and Charles Hunter—have rushed for more yards in a game during their freshmen seasons. Two games later, Jones romped for 122 yards on only 9 carries against SMU in a 13-12 Texas win. That victory gave the Horns a 3-1-1 record, which included "Spygate," a gut-wrenching 6-6 tie against Oklahoma.

Following the win against the Ponies, the Horns suffered a 31-28 loss to Texas Tech in Lubbock, which dropped Texas another game back in the conference race. The Horns badly needed a victory to keep their title hopes alive. They would try to get it the next week at home in Austin against conference newcomers, the University of Houston.

No. 20 TEXAS vs. No. 19 HOUSTON

November 6, 1976
Austin, Texas

The 1976 season saw the Houston Cougars join the Southwest Conference, and it had been a long wait. The Cougars, under head coach Bill Yeoman, came in to the SWC with a chip on their shoulders and plenty to prove; they were not a team to try and get well against. On November 6, 1976, in front of 77,809 fans (the largest crowd ever at Memorial Stadium at the time), Texas found that out the hard way.

Playing without Earl Campbell, who had again hurt a hamstring against Tech the previous week, the Longhorn offense sputtered to a virtual standstill against the swarming Cougars. The Houston defense, led by defensive tackle Wilson Whitley, the winner of the Lombardi Award that year, completely suffocated the Texas rushing attack, which managed only a paltry 24 yards on the day. Texas never drove the ball beyond the Cougar 28 the entire game.

Jones, playing without the bruising Campbell in front of him to grab the defense's focus, took a beating he remembers to this day. His fumble at the Texas 15 just before halftime, recovered by Cougar linebacker David Hodges, led to a Houston field goal. Behind the passing of quarterback Danny Davis and the rushing of Alois Blackwell, the Cougars routed Texas 30-0, ending the Horns' home winning streak emphatically at forty-two straight games dating back to 1967. Houston would go on to win the Southwest Conference that season, earning its first-ever trip to a New Year's Day bowl game. In the Cotton Bowl, the Cougars would face undefeated and fifth-ranked Maryland. The 30-21 upset of the Terps gave the Cougars a final record of 10-1 and a final national ranking of fourth.

The Game of My Life

By Johnny "Lam" Jones

There's two games that stand out—the Houston game my freshman year and the Notre Dame game in the Cotton Bowl after the 1977 season. And the only difference is that in the Houston game, Earl was hurt. And when I came to Texas as a freshman, I was a running back, so I was running the ball in the Houston game. In the Notre Dame game, Earl wasn't hurt so he was running the ball in that game and they were killing him. In the Houston game, they were killing me because I ran the ball quite a bit!

We were still running the Wishbone and I started four or five games my freshman year, and Earl was hurt along with some other running backs that had gotten injured, so I played a lot more than I would have if not for some injuries. I was playing one halfback in the Wishbone and Ham Jones was playing the other. The nicknames "Ham" and "Lam" just kind of caught on. The other Johnny Jones from Hamlin was playing at the same time and coach Royal came up with the nickname. It was one of those deals that everybody liked and so it made it easy.

But when we went out on the field at Texas, it seemed like everybody played us like it was their bowl game. They didn't play us like they feared us; they didn't lay down. We just knew that other teams respected us. One thing I can relate it to is, I am constantly meeting people and they'll say, 'Man, I wish I had gone to Texas,' or 'I wanted to go to Texas but I couldn't get in.' Or they might say, 'I wanted to play for Texas but they didn't recruit me' or 'they didn't have enough scholarships left.' I also meet people who say, 'I got my degree from so-and-so university but I wish I had gone to Texas.' You never hear anybody from Texas saying, 'I wish I had gone to some other school,' or 'I played for Texas but I wish I had played for somebody else.' You never hear anybody say that. That was one of the good things about playing for Texas.

But as far as the Houston game, playing in a game like that, that early in my career, I think the best thing about it was that it gave me a good taste of how hard I was going to have to work in college football. It wasn't going to be like in high school—not that high school was easy, but in high school, my junior year I averaged 11 yards a carry, and about 9 yards a carry my senior year.

But the Houston game taught me that it was going to be different in college. A game like that lets you know, if you can get beat like that, you are going to have to work a helluva lot harder. And it's not going to be just yourself—everybody on the team is going to have to work harder, too. So those kind of games were just letting you know that it was not going to be a cakewalk.

But Houston whipped up on everybody that year. It was their first year in the Southwest Conference and they had something to prove. They had been trying to get in for a while, and they came in and terrorized the conference. Wilson Whitley won the Lombardi Trophy that year, but it wasn't just him, their whole team was really good. They were tough. I just remember being so frustrated getting shut down like that. It was definitely a wake-up call for what college football was going to be like.

Upon Further Review

Texas went on to beat TCU following the loss to Houston, but would fall to both Baylor and Texas A&M before beating Arkansas in what turned out to the last game of Darrell Royal's legendary career at Texas, a career that saw him win 167 games, three national titles, eleven Southwest Conference championships, and eight bowl wins in twenty seasons. Following the Arkansas game, Royal stepped down, leaving the program in the hands of Fred Akers, an assistant to Royal for nine years who had taken over the program at Wyoming.

"I'm always proud to say that I came through Texas with Coach Royal's last recruiting class," said Jones, "and that I had the chance to play under Coach Royal and Coach Akers. Of course I was just a freshman, and when you play for a great coach like Coach Royal, you don't question anything that he does. I mean I was disappointed just like everybody else that he was leaving, but I'm sure he had sat down and thought about all of the reasons why. We didn't have any idea during the season that he was leaving. While he was there he was 100 percent coaching the team. Every week you are preparing for Saturday, getting ready for that week's game, and I can't remember anything being insinuated or mentioned about it being his last season. Everything was focused on trying to win the games each and every week. But I was really fortunate to play under two great coaches, because Fred Akers was a great coach, too."

Texas finished 5-5-1 in 1976, and did not make the postseason for the first time since 1967. But in 1977, Akers's first year at the helm, the Horns took the lessons learned from the bitter '76 campaign and reeled off an 11-0 regular season behind the devastating running of Campbell, who became the university's first Heisman Trophy winner after galloping over and through opponents for 1,744 yards. Johnny "Lam" Jones moved to receiver and led the team in receptions that year, as he would for the following two seasons. A loss to Notre Dame in the Cotton Bowl kept Texas from winning its fourth national championship.

The 1978 season, for which Jones earned the team's Most Valuable Player award, saw the Horns go 9-3, capped off with a 42-0 blowout of No. 13 Maryland in the Sun Bowl. In 1979, the Horns again finished 9-3, but a disappointing loss to A&M kept the Horns out of a New Year's Day bowl. Instead, they again went to El Paso, where they lost 14-7 to No. 13 Washington. In a 13-0 win over Baylor that year, Jones hauled in eight passes for 198 yards, a school record for nonbowl game receiving yardage that stands to this day. His career total receiving yards of 1,603 are the tenth-most in Texas history. As a kickoff returner, Jones still holds the Texas record for the highest average yards per return for a season when, in 1978, he took back eleven kicks for 356 yards for a 32.3-yard average. His 100-yard return for a touchdown against SMU that season is still tied for the longest kickoff return in Texas history.

After the 1979 season, Johnny "Lam" Jones took his Olympic sprinter's speed to the next level. In the spring of 1980, after trading up with the thirteenth and twentieth picks in the first round, the New York Jets took Jones as the second overall pick in the draft, behind only Billy Sims, who went first to the Detroit Lions, and ahead of Anthony Munoz, who went third to Cincinnati. Jones spent seven injury-plagued seasons in New York, the last two on injured reserve, where he caught 138 passes for 2,322 yards and 13 touchdowns.

"It was quite a transition going from college to the NFL and going from Texas to New York," recalled Jones. "New York is a long way from Lampasas, Texas. Looking back on it, I just wasn't really prepared for going to New York. I probably could have handled that whole situation a lot better. New York's the kind of place where it's great if you are winning, but if not, it can be pretty brutal. My first year up there we had a tough season, and they had traded away two first-round picks to move up to draft me. So combining that with our record, it was a hard place to live. It was a grind, but it was like anything else—when things are going good, it's great, and when it's going bad, it can be difficult. And football wasn't just a sport anymore; now they're paying you money for it. It was just like the business world. If you are not doing your job, it can be brutal. It was just that I got injured a lot. There's so many things involved in sports—timing and just a lot of things other than just talent. The guy with the best talent doesn't always make the team. There's so many more things involved."

Although his NFL career had its frustrations, Jones remains grateful for the opportunity. "Getting drafted is one of those things it's kind of hard to explain,"

Jones said. "You know, you're coming out of school and you're getting ready to go and do something that you would do for free, and now they're going to pay you for it. So it was an exciting time. You were just so happy about getting an opportunity to play, you're not going to get picky about where you're going to play—you don't really care."

Looking back on his days at Texas and in the NFL, Jones remembers it for what it was—a grand ride, despite the ups and downs. "There's so many good memories that I have, it's hard to say that there's any one that stands out," mused Jones. "I've been so fortunate and blessed in my life. I have so many things to be grateful for. By the time I got to Texas, I had already gone to the Olympics, and then after that, I played in the NFL from 1980 to '87. And to reach that level in any of those things, you have so many memories of good things that happened. Like a lot of people ask me, 'What was it like running in the Olympics,' and I tell them, 'It was almost as exciting as running in our state meet in Texas!' And they look at me like I am crazy! But you'd have to grow up in Texas or to have gone to our state meet to understand what I am talking about. At Lampasas, we won our state meet, the 3A state division, but to say that the day we won the meet was the best, I'd be lying, because we had so many happy things happen to get to that point. So I have so many things to be grateful for—it wasn't just the end result that was great, like winning the state meet or getting drafted or going to UT or going to the NFL. There were so many things that happened on the way leading up to those things—it was all good."

After retiring from football for good in 1987, Jones faced his share of personal challenges, but the biggest challenge of his life is the one he is facing now. In 2005, Jones was diagnosed with multiple myeloma, a cancer of the blood and bone. When initially diagnosed, Jones found himself at a time in his life when he was not covered by health insurance. Friends, former teammates, and Texas fans have raised money to help pay for his drugs and treatment, but Jones is also helping himself.

After Texas won the 2005 national championship, Jones, like Orangebloods everywhere, got caught up in the excitement. A photography buff, Jones drove from his home in Leander down to the Texas campus in the middle of the night to shoot photographs of the UT Tower bathed in orange with the number "one" lit up on all four sides. He had to make two different runs after his first batch of shots fell short of his standards, but after the second run, he had what he needed. Framed copies of these photos, signed by Johnny "Lam" Jones, are available from the university co-op for $150, and 100 percent of the proceeds go directly to Jones to help in his fight against cancer.

Though the cancer has weakened his body, it has not diminished his spirit. Through good friendships, a big heart, and an Olympic champion's determination to fight, Jones has made it through. "One thing I have been so blessed with," said Jones, "besides a loving family, is that I have so many people that I feel like I can call friends. I might not talk to them all the time, I might not talk to them for months or even years, but I know that when we do talk again, I can call them a friend."

While at Texas, Jones showed where his heart was by donating his Olympic gold medal to the Special Olympics. Once in New York, pro contract in hand, Jones made the biggest single contribution ever to the Texas Special Olympics, and served as an honorary coach of the New York Special Olympics. But Jones deflects any praise for these acts of generosity.

"If you've ever gone to the Special Olympics, you'd want to give in any way that you could, too," Jones maintains. "Some people have time that they give, some people have money that they give, and at that time, I didn't have much time because I was in school.

"At that time, they used to have the Special Olympics meet at Memorial Stadium when the track was in the stadium, and so even though we were involved in school and sports, the athletes would always volunteer. So when I got the opportunity to go and volunteer and work with them, it was real clear . . . that those kids deserved that gold medal more than myself or any other athlete I'd ever met. And even though I gave that medal, there's a lot of people that gave a lot more than I gave. When you go and see those volunteers that maybe don't have the money, or they don't have a medal to give, and they are giving their genuine time, and the love they show for those kids, they give a lot more than I have ever given.

"After you've been to one of those Special Olympics meets it's real clear—sometimes we athletes complain a lot about stuff, but the truth is, we don't have anything to complain about."

Chapter Eight

EARL CAMPBELL

Running Back (1974-77)

Arguably, no state boasts a richer abundance of high school football talent than Texas. By the mid-1970s, however, the Who's Who among Lone Star State running backs could virtually be divided into two groups: Earl Campbell and everybody else.

Some would insist it's still that way. Most would agree that Campbell's devastating combination of power, size, balance and speed put him in a league of his own. Former Oklahoma coach Barry Switzer once said that Campbell was the only player he had ever seen who could have jumped directly from high school to NFL stardom. Later, one of Switzer's assistants observed, "You don't stop Earl Campbell; you survive him." Darrell Royal remarked that Campbell's patented stiff-arm deserved to be on a box of Arm and Hammer baking soda. And Texas QB Randy McEachern (1977-78) comments that "the hardest I've ever been hit" was when he collided with Campbell on an ill-timed handoff.

By the time Campbell graduated from John Tyler in 1974, he had already traversed through a lifetime's worth of mettle-testing hardships. When Campbell was eleven years old, his father died of a massive coronary. The fifth of eleven children, Campbell assumed more of a financial responsibility for his family. It meant that a fledgling interest in football would be balanced with hours of toil in the blistering heat of local rose fields. He would also enter eighth grade at a recently desegregated middle school. Racial tensions ran higher than the Texas summer sun, but Campbell credits middle school coach Lawrence La Croix for uniting blacks and whites with the common goal of someday winning the football state championship for their future high school. La Croix also served as Campbell's mentor following his father's death. As such, Campbell perceived La Croix's eventual promotion as a John Tyler football assistant and, consequently, his renewed influence in his life, as nothing less than divine intervention.

Campbell was John Tyler's middle linebacker, earning All-American honors his junior campaign. But La Croix could attest to what Campbell, as a middle-school student , was able to do with a football in his hands. Coaches moved Campbell to running back his senior season. All he did was rush for 2,224 yards, lead his team to a 15-0 mark and the Class 4A title (at the time, the state's largest high school classification).

The result only fueled one of the most intense recruiting battles ever waged for a Texas schoolboy. All the usual suspects desperately wanted Campbell to sign with their programs, but Campbell announced he wanted to play college ball close to home. Royal and Switzer made in-home visits, while Campbell took official trips to their respective campuses. Already, Longhorn recruiting coordinator Ken Dabbs spent seventeen straight days at a Tyler hotel. Campbell remained undecided the night before signing day, but his choice would come down to Texas and Oklahoma. Campbell left the decision to his bladder. Before going to bed, Campbell vowed that if he woke in the night to go to the bathroom, he would pick Texas.

Nature called. And Campbell would call Royal that morning with his verdict.

Longhorn fans salivated at the prospect of leading-Heisman Trophy candidate Roosevelt Leaks and Campbell sharing the same backfield, if only for the 1974 season. But Leaks tore three ligaments in his knee earlier that spring. Determined to play, Leaks relentlessly rehabilitated until cleared for Texas's September 14 season-opener at Boston College, almost six months from the day of his injury. The 1973 Southwest Conference rushing leader, however, was a fraction of his former self following surgery. Leaks's injury meant Campbell would shoulder most of the load in what proved to be, by Texas's standards, a pedestrian 8-4 season and a final No. 17 (AP) ranking. Campbell would be one of four Longhorns to notch First-Team All-Southwest Conference honors and was voted the league's Newcomer of the Year after rushing for 928 yards and 6 touchdowns on 162 carries.

Yet 1974 marked the first time in seven seasons that Royal did not win at least a share of the SWC title. Campbell helped wrestle a tie for the conference crown during his sophomore campaign, rushing for 1,118 yards and 13 touchdowns en

Earl Campbell poses with his Heisman Trophy, 1977

route to consensus All-American honors. The 10-2 season included a 38-21 comeback against No. 10 Colorado in the Bluebonnet Bowl. Campbell would be named the game's outstanding offensive player while his younger brother Tim was named defensive player of the game, lifting Texas to a No. 6 ranking in the final AP poll.

The 1976 season was a watershed year for Texas football. It would mark Royal's twentieth season in Austin and his seventh-ranked Longhorns would open at Boston College. But Campbell pulled a hamstring just before the opener and was limited to just 23 yards on five totes in a shocking 14-13 loss. Texas would need all of Campbell's pain-filled 208 yards, a career-high at the time, to stave off upset-minded North Texas, 17-14. The Tyler Rose contributed 91 yards on 27 carries in a bitter 6-6 tie against Oklahoma, but it was clear Campbell was ailing. He would be sidelined for four straight games, and Texas would lose three of them.

Throughout Austin, bumper stickers appeared with the simple plea: "Unleash Earl." Doctors cleared Campbell for the final home game against Arkansas, moved from October to the first Saturday in December. It was the third time in eight years that ABC Sports made Texas-Arkansas its college football regular season finale. With both teams limping into the contest with subpar records, it appeared that the third time was not the charm for the network. Then came the bombshell.

Late in the season, both Royal and Razorback coach Frank Broyles announced their retirements. Suddenly, the December 4 matchup became the swan song for two coaching legends. Campbell showcased his old form, rushing for 131 yards and 2 touchdowns to send Royal out a 29-12 winner. Royal would continue to serve as men's athletics director but was not asked to sit on the seven-member search committee to locate his successor. Royal's preference for his former defensive coach Mike Campbell is well documented. Instead, another of Royal's former assistants—second-year Wyoming coach Fred Akers—would be named Longhorn head coach at a December 15 press conference.

One of the first things Akers did, in essence, was recruit Earl Campbell. Akers informed Campbell that if he bought into the program by shedding at least 20 pounds, the first-year Texas coach would build an offense around his star running back. Akers would scrap the renowned Wishbone and install the I-formation, giving Campbell a lead blocker and a running start. Campbell could also count on 25 carries per game, maybe more. And maybe, Akers mentioned, the possibility of the program's first Heisman Trophy winner.

No. 1 TEXAS vs. No. 12 TEXAS A&M

November 26, 1977

College Station, Texas

Undefeated Texas was ranked No. 1 when visiting No. 12 Texas A&M the Saturday after Thanksgiving, but the Horns had dropped two straight to the Aggies. The home team took an early 7-0 lead following an eleven-play, 70-yard march. Curtis Dickey's run on a 7-yard pitch marked the first time all season Texas allowed an opponent to score on its opening drive. The Burnt Orange answered with a vengeance.

Campbell careened down the left sideline on a 60-yard scoring toss from McEachern. The only TD reception of Campbell's career came with 4:47 remaining in the opening frame. McEachern followed with a 9-yard touchdown pass to Johnny "Lam" Jones and then a 13-yard TD to Alfred Jackson. He also threw a 43-yarder to "Lam" Jones to set up another score in the first half. The Horns would score on five straight possessions to stake a 33-7 advantage.

The Aggies weren't done. Dickey's 50-yard KO return jumpstarted the A&M offense, setting up shop at the Texas 23. Fullback George Woodward scored six plays later on a one-yard run to pull the Aggies within 19 at intermission. By then, Campbell had tallied 80 yards on 5 carries, including a 59-yard run out of an I-formation sweep.

Campbell's four-yard TD run early in the third period made it a 40-14 contest, but Texas's kickoff carried just 25 yards into a stiff southerly wind; the shortened field resulted in A&M's four-play 38-yard TD drive. McEachern was guilty of his second interception of the afternoon, and the Aggies made him pay. The scoreboard read 40-28 following Woodward's second one-yard run.

Texas opened the final frame with Campbell stepping off 23 yards around right end for his final TD run of the regular season. A 37-yard TD toss to "Lam" Jones late in the fourth quarter was the final stake in A&M's comeback hopes.

The Game of My Life

By Earl Campbell

I think the game that solidified me as the Heisman favorite, and showed that I could play with the big boys, was when we played at Texas A&M in 1977.

It was the last [regular season] game of my senior year and we were undefeated. In my mind, [Oklahoma State's] Terry Miller and I were tied as the front-runners for the Heisman Trophy. Coach Akers brought up the Heisman when he came back [to Texas], but he and I didn't talk about it all that much the rest of the year. Coming onto the field at Texas A&M, Fred Akers told me that if I gave him anything with 200 yards, he would guarantee that I would win the Heisman. That day, I gained 222 yards against A&M. I was neck-and-neck with Terry Miller and Ken McAfee from Notre Dame. We had not beaten A&M in a while. We had lost to them two years in a row. When I was at Texas, we went 2-2 against the Aggies. We didn't beat Oklahoma until my senior year—we tied them my junior year—and, when we finally did, some said that was the game that won the Heisman for Earl Campbell. But the A&M game was the one that put me on the cover of *Sports Illustrated* for the first time. I didn't come out of that game thinking I had won the Heisman. The way I looked at it was I had done my job and that our team had done the best it could do. I don't think the Heisman Trophy belongs to me; I think it belongs to the entire team.

Coach Akers was in his first year as [Texas] head coach, but he coached me my freshman year as my running backs coach. He left, but there's no fault in a man trying to better himself. Coach Akers went to Wyoming to try to better himself. Frank Erwin and the Board of Regents decided to bring him back and give him a shot at Texas. When he came back, Coach Akers and I sat down and he told me the things he expected of me. He wanted me to be more than just a football player; he wanted me to establish myself as the leader. Coach Akers said that if I did what he said there could be the possibility that I would be the Heisman Trophy winner. I tried to do everything Coach Akers asked me to do.

Of course, I enjoyed my time with Coach Royal for three years. But I think one of the solidifying moments of my career was when Coach Akers put me and [Johnny] 'Ham' Jones in the I-formation. I think that's what did it. We were still running the wishbone before Coach Akers came back. I don't want to say that I wouldn't have won the Heisman if we had still run the Wishbone. I don't second-guess what coach Akers did, I don't second-guess what coach Royal did, and I don't second-guess what the good Lord was blessing me to do. I think it worked out kind of even.

I don't remember much about the [1977 Texas-A&M] game. I do remember that A&M scored first, and that we came back after I caught a touchdown pass. It might surprise people that this was the only touchdown I ever caught in college. That was more than thirty years ago. That's a long time. But I do know that the A&M game, to this day, is a very, very important game to us. That game and, of course, the Oklahoma game are the two important games. But after that game, my life has never been the same.

Of course, my life has never been the same since I came to the University of Texas from Tyler, Texas. I got a bachelor's degree in speech communications. I learned so much at the university that it would be very hard for me to say that just one thing changed my life. It would be wrong to say that it was only football that changed my life. These days, youngsters need to understand that when they come to this university, or to any university, they need to understand that the word says "student athlete."' You are a student first. I've thought about this over the years: Something has to be your No. 1 priority. I'm of the idea that academics is the first thing and the most important thing. God gives us the talent to do everything we do, in sports as well as academics. Athletes are typically known as those who don't care about their academics and then don't get a degree. An individual has to take it upon himself to want to be the best in both of them: academics and athletics.

[Laughing] If you live long enough, you're going to get old. You get to where you can't run or get into those same football stances anymore, even though you want to. But you still have to live. That's why I say academics is the most important thing. Football, basketball, and all that are very important, but academics is above that. You can play football, basketball, run track, and do it all. But the final word when you get to be fifty-two years old is going to be what you did academically. I can't run the football anymore, but I do want to be in business. I want to be productive. The first thing people look at when you get to be older is your college degree.

Very few people want to talk about academics. Most people just want to talk about what I did on the football field, but I think academics is the most important thing to me now.

Upon Further Review

Campbell's 222 yards on 27 carries against A&M represented a career best as well as the third-best rushing day in program history to that point. His four TDs tied the school's single-game record—a record Campbell himself had had set earlier in the season against Rice. Campbell also became the first SWC player to lead the nation in both rushing (1,744 yards) and scoring (114 points). By the end of 1977, his 4,443 career rushing yards stood at No. 4 all-time nationally, and he had created a Longhorn record that would remain unsurpassed for twenty-one years.

Texas would end a six-year nonwinning skid against Oklahoma in Campbell's final campaign despite losing its top two starting QBs to injury in the first half.

Campbell would score the game's only TD, a 24-yard draw, in what proved to be the difference in a 13-6 decision against No. 2/3 Oklahoma. Texas would follow with a 13-9 comeback win at No. 9 Arkansas the following Saturday. The win at A&M gave Texas a school-record eleven regular season victories and the outright SWC title, its twenty-first overall. There was little question, then, that Campbell was the Heisman front-runner.

The Downtown Athletic Club of New York was scheduled to present the Heisman on December 8 and, for the first time, there would be a prime-time national telecast of the ceremony. With hosts O. J. Simpson and actor Elliot Gould, the announcement was made at the end of an hour-long special: Earl Campbell, University of Texas.

Campbell had made no secret of the fact that he was ill-at-ease in front of a microphone, but the Tyler Rose broke the ice with these opening remarks: "When I was little and I got into trouble, my mom always told me to come tell her I was in trouble. Well, mom, I'm in trouble. I don't know what to say!"

Campbell had one collegiate game remaining. He capped his Texas tenure with 116 yards against No. 5 Notre Dame in the Cotton Bowl, but six Longhorn turnovers would be too much to overcome in a 38-10 heartbreaker.

Campbell's legend grew after the Houston Oilers made him their No. 1 pick in the 1978 NFL Draft. The NFL Rookie of the Year, Campbell was the League's leading rusher during his first four seasons (1978-81). He was named the 1980 NFL Offensive Player of the Year after running for 1,934 yards and 13 touchdowns on 373 carries. The five-time Pro-Bowler retired in 1986 after posting 9,407 rushing yards and 74 touchdowns during eight NFL seasons, including two at New Orleans. He was inducted into the NFL Hall of Fame in 1991.

He is now the owner of Earl Campbell Meat Products Inc., and has served as as a special assistant to the athletics director for student affairs at Texas.

Today, there is a nine-foot-tall statue of Campbell near the southwest entrance to Royal-Texas Memorial Stadium. It was dedicated in September 2006, the night No. 2 Texas hosted top-ranked Ohio State. It is a sculpted image from Campbell's younger days in Austin, and he wears jersey No. 20, long-since retired among Longhorn lettermen.

Chapter Nine

DONNIE LITTLE

Quarterback (1978-80); Wide Receiver (1981)

College freshmen are more likely to be history majors than history makers. Unless, of course, you're Donnie Little.

The Dickinson product was widely regarded as the Lone Star State's top high school quarterback when entering the University of Texas in 1978. Like most freshman football players, all Little wanted during the season opener was to get into the game. Then again, Little was not like most freshmen.

The game at Rice was quickly turning into a 34-0 Texas thumping when, late in the fourth quarter, head coach Fred Akers told Little to put on his helmet. Little was thrilled. He was raised just outside of Houston, and many of the hometown folks were on hand anticipating his collegiate debut. That's when Little heard it.

"I entered the game, I called the play in the huddle, I went to the line of scrimmage, and I was calling the cadence," Little recalled. "But then the Rice P.A. announcer said, '*The University of Texas is about to make history. Donnie Little will be the first African-American quarterback at the University of Texas.*' I'm in the middle of my cadence . . . "*Down!*" . . . and I'm listening to the P.A. announcer . . . "*Set!*" . . . . and I start thinking, "Wow, we're not even at home. This is an away game. This must be a big deal." . . . *"Hut! Hut!"*

"After the game, I reflected on it," Little said. "I realized it was bigger than I had imagined. We were on the road. I could understand if it was a home game that our announcer would have said it, but *their* announcer said it. A part of history? It was an eye-opener. I thought, 'Wow! What's to come?'"

The rest, as they say, is history. And part of that revisionist history was the shift in which Little was perceived publicly: he wasn't so much *Texas quarterback Donnie Little* but rather *Texas's black quarterback.* As such, the habitual pressure of playing quarterback at Texas was compounded by the fact that he would forever remain the program's first African-American starting quarterback.

"I came to realize that people put such high expectations on you just because of the color of your skin," Little recalled. "If you're going to play quarterback, you have to be Superman. You can't just hand the ball off. You're not supposed to fumble or throw interceptions. This was the fans' expectations because they were not used to African-Americans playing that position. When you're under the microscope, everything you do is scrutinized. There were questions about whether a black quarterback is intelligent, or could read defenses and call plays. Once you've disproved that stereotype, the question becomes whether you can throw. There is very little room to fail. It seems ridiculous now because everybody has an African-American quarterback. Back then, Texas had won without having to have a black at quarterback."

More recently, Texas had won largely because it fielded two of the most superlative running backs ever to play the game: All-American Roosevelt Leaks and 1977 Heisman Trophy winner Earl Campbell. But heading into the 1979 season, many expected Texas to diversify its offense with a dual-threat starting quarterback who just happened to be African-American.

It was, in more ways than one, a new day for Texas football.

No. 4 TEXAS vs. No. 3 OKLAHOMA

October 13, 1979

Dallas, Texas

Texas's ledger in the Oklahoma series during the 1970s stood at 2-6-1 when Little logged his first start in the bitter rivalry. The Sooners were ranked No. 3 in both major polls and in the top five for the seventh-straight year. The Horns were the lower-ranked team but listed as a 1-point favorite, the first time in six years that OU entered the game as an underdog.

Texas drew first blood on its second possession, driving 61 yards on ten straight running plays. The series stalled following a five-yard sack, but Texas managed a 37-yard John Goodson field goal. The Steer defense forced a second-straight Sooner

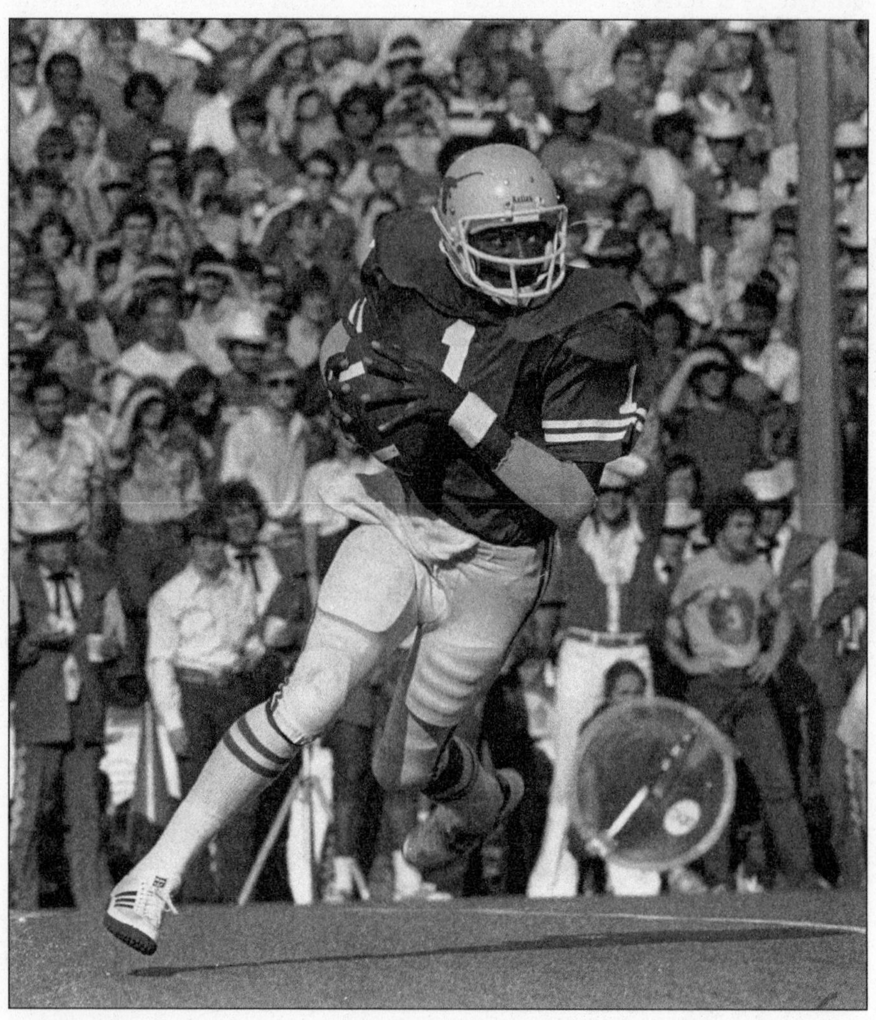

Texas' first African-American quarterback, Donnie Little (Photo courtesy of the University of Texas)

punt but, this time, punt returner Johnnie Johnson stumbled on the stadium's new Astroturf and misplayed Michael Keeling's 48-yard kick. The Sooners recovered the miscue at the Texas 16 and cashed in on a third-and-5 play-action pass.

The score remained 7-3 for most of the first half, thanks to a stalwart Texas defense that overcame a Little interception at the OU 17 and A. J. "Jam" Jones's fumble at the Sooner nine. Oklahoma picked up a first down following Jones's turnover and then threw a long-ball from its own 20 with 3:28 remaining. Defensive tackle Steve McMichael sidestepped Billy Sims's block and forced quarterback J. C. Watts into an errant toss. Cornerback Derrick Hatchett tipped the ball to himself at the Sooner 41 and followed a convoy of blockers to the 5-yard line. On third-and-goal from the two, Little connected with tight end Steve Hall in the corner of the end zone on a play-action pass with 74 seconds remaining until intermission. Despite three turnovers, Texas took a 10-7 lead into the locker room.

Texas opened the second half by driving to the Sooner 36 on seven straight runs but punted following a six-yard tackle-for-loss. Fullback Stanley Wilson dashed for 47 yards off left tackle on Oklahoma's next possession before Vance Bedford knocked him out of bounds at the Texas 28. Oklahoma's 37-yard field goal attempt, however, was wide-left. The Sooners forced a Texas punt, but tackle Bill Acker recovered a Watts fumble and returned it two yards to the Sooner 22. Texas could do nothing with the gift, turning the ball over on downs when stopped for no-gain on a fourth-and-one at the 13.

Texas's only sustained drive of the second half came on its first possession of the fourth quarter. Little got things started with a 14-yard completion to Les Koenning on third-and-10 before running back Rodney Tate collected 21 yards on consecutive runs. Little found Koenning again, this time for 18 yards to the Sooner nine. Texas settled for a 23-yard field goal after Jam Jones bobbled a late-pitch from Little. Oklahoma's attempt to respond was short-lived. Tackle Kenneth Sims threw Watts for a 10-yard loss before linebacker Chuck Holloway leveled Billy Sims in the backfield, forcing a fumble that Tim Campbell recovered at the Sooner 30. Texas parlayed the turnover into a 38-yard field goal to complete the scoring at 16-7 with 3:40 left.

The Game of My Life

By Donnie Little

If I had to choose just one game, it would be the 1979 OU game. Coaches always tell you, in a game like that, there will be only three or four plays that make the difference because both teams are well prepared, very competitive with each other, and similar in talent. The point is you have to capitalize on those opportunities when the opportunities come. That game was a growing-up game for me. There was something about the adrenaline and emotion. You're on television. In those days, it was one of the two, maybe three times you're going to be on TV all year. And this is national TV. The records were great on both sides. It was a recruiting advantage being on TV. Your family and friends were watching. It's a big rivalry. The stadium is packed, and you have half orange and half red. It wasn't even a conference game then. It set the standard for what your season was going to be for the rest of the year.

Going down the tunnel [to reach the Cotton Bowl field] definitely gives you goose bumps. You've got people on one side, screaming and calling you the worst names, and the other half is cheering for you. You definitely wanted to show up. You didn't want to have a lackluster performance. If you could play every game with the kind of intensity you have against Oklahoma, you'd be an All-American. There's no doubt about it. The deal is, you can't play with that kind of intensity every game. On a good day, I could have thrown it 60 yards. When you come through that tunnel and you're out there warming up, I could have thrown it 70 yards.

OU had the lead just before halftime, but we were deep in their end of the field. Our defense had just given us the ball with an interception and we wanted to punch one in and gain the momentum at halftime.

Our tight end was a junior named Steve Hall. We were in the red zone and getting ready to score. We called play-action pass in the huddle. When we broke the huddle, Steve was supposed to be on the left side, and a freshman tight end named Dewey Turner was supposed to be on the right. But Steve grabbed the freshman and told him to go to the left side. Steve went to the right side because the play-action pass was to be to the right side. I didn't have any clue that all this was happening. Steve told me after the game. Steve Hall scores the touchdown. That's the difference between a rookie and a veteran. The rookie did what the veteran told him. He went to the other side and blocked. Steve went out for the pass and caught it for the touchdown.

We couldn't do much, offensively, in the third quarter. In fact, neither team scored a touchdown in the second half. That's why our touchdown at the end of the second quarter was so important. Both defenses were outstanding. I knew if we could get at least one more field goal, and not shorten the field with turnovers, our defense was going to keep OU out of the end zone. I hit two or three passes in the fourth quarter. That set up a field goal. You don't always feel like a 6-point lead is enough, especially against Oklahoma, but I knew that our second field goal was really important [giving Texas a 13-7 lead].

Like I said, this was a growing-up game for me. Coach [Fred] Akers gave me the biggest compliment as a quarterback. He praised me for my knowledge of the game, grasping the offense and being able to read defenses, changing plays at the line. Fans don't always see that. You can't go into the huddle, call a play, go up to the line and just run it. OU scouted us. They'd seen we like to run to the strong side, so they'd over-shift and have more people over there than we could block. So, I'd call an audible. I used to think as a quarterback: "I just hate this. Anybody else could just go out there and run and have fun." The quarterback has to call the play, but that isn't enough. You're at the line of scrimmage and, oh boy, you notice they're showing blitz. You've got to scope it out, and you've only got 25 seconds to do all this. I would be mentally drained after the game. It was a cat-and-mouse.

J. C. Watts and I became good friends after that game. Everybody talks about how much we're supposed to hate OU and how much OU hates us. From a players's perspective, we're in their dressing room and they're in ours after the game. You're shaking hands and telling Billy Sims that he had a good game. Once the war is over, we're all human beings. We get along.

You learn from that game. Part of what you learned was that other schools got up for Texas the way Texas gets up for OU. It had nothing to do with what we did that year as a team; it was what people did before us. Texas was like a bowl game for other schools because Texas had dominated them for so long. You go into those games and you realize that everybody plays hard until you can give them a knockout punch. The longer you let them hang in there, the tougher they get. You had to learn why schools gave you their best shot. We stepped into those games thinking we were just playing these other schools, but our opponents were going on the history of what Texas had done in the past.

Upon Further Review

Little sported an 8-1 mark as Texas's starting QB heading into 1979's final home game. By then, Texas had posted impressive roads wins at No. 5 Missouri (in late September) and No. 5 Houston (in early November). The Longhorns were ranked No. 6 nationally and expected to accept a Sugar Bowl bid.

"I thought that we had finally arrived," Little said, "but then I hurt my arch against Baylor. That was disappointing. We were finally jelling as a team. They were starting to believe in me, from a quarterback's perspective."

The Horns won a 13-0 battle against the No. 17 Bears but may have lost the war as their top two running backs ("Jam" Jones and Rodney Tate) suffered season-ending injuries. A severely depleted offense dropped a 13-7 heartbreaker at Texas A&M, relegating Texas to the Sun Bowl for the second-straight year. A what-might-have-been season ended with a 14-7 loss to then-No. 13 Washington and a final No. 12 national ranking.

The 1980 season began with a 23-17 Labor Day collaring of No. 6 Arkansas, a game moved to primetime for an ABC Sports national telecast. Little's second season behind center included a win over No. 12 Oklahoma that may have been more impressive than the first one. In essence, he introduced the quarterback draw to the Longhorn playbook.

"Our game plan was that I would call two plays in the huddle and, at the line of scrimmage, I would call one of the plays according to what the defense gave me. We didn't take into account all the screaming when we were back in OU's side of the stadium. One of the things that happened in this game was that I stopped wearing a mouthpiece because my teammates couldn't hear me. I just took the thing off and played without it because I had to literally scream when we were in OU's territory. In football, if you talk to just one side [of center], defenses know that's where you're going. Defenses aren't stupid. You have to yell on both sides, even though you want teammates on just one side to know it's where you're coming.

"OU was in a 5-2 defense and, if we split our backs, their linebackers did that, too. So I told Mike Baab, my center, that if he blocked the nose guard to the right, I was going left. If he blocked him to the left, I was going right. Mike let him take the step he wanted to go. I took three steps back like I was going to pass. I figured that, if I made a move, it was just me and the safety. Coach Akers told me, 'I don't know what you did, but keep running it.' We didn't even have the quarterback draw in our playbook. That's how the quarterback draw at Texas was invented. Was the quarterback draw put in the game plan after that day? Absolutely!"

Little had improvised his way to 110 yards on 21 carries, leading Texas to a No. 2 ranking. A promising season, however, ended in a three-game tailspin, including a loss to North Carolina in the Bluebonnet Bowl. Little's two-year record as a starter stood at 16-8, an enviable mark at most schools but met with mixed reviews given the stratospheric expectations of the Longhorn fan base. As such, not all were surprised when Little asked if he could switch to wide receiver for his senior year.

"I was thinking about the next level," Little said. "There weren't a lot of black quarterbacks in the NFL then. Most likely, my best chance of playing in the NFL would have been at wide receiver. I'm not saying it was all about me. I thought the team could benefit from me playing receiver. We had a strong-armed quarterback named Rick McIvor. I was thinking that McIvor's strength was that he would throw the ball. I knew the routes, but I didn't realize how much running was involved. I knew the offense enough to where, if I had to come back at quarterback, I could run the team. It wasn't like I had to start all over."

Back-to-back wins against nationally ranked Miami and Oklahoma propelled Texas to the No. 1 ranking by mid-October 1981. But the wheels came off at Arkansas the following Saturday, 42-11. Texas rebounded with a 9-7 defensive decision at No. 8 SMU, but the Horns did not develop the type of passing attack that many expected with McIvor.

"I wish we had thrown the ball more," Little conceded, "but we were winning."

Then, McIvor was injured with Texas trailing Houston at halftime on November 7.

"There was some discussion at halftime of transferring me back to quarterback," Little recalled. "Coach Akers was for it, but then he said, 'Let's try Robert Brewer. Let's see how it goes.' If it didn't pan out, I would have gone back to quarterback."

Brewer salvaged a 14-14 tie and the team would not lose the remainder of the season, including a 14-12 comeback against Paul "Bear" Bryant's Alabama team in the Cotton Bowl. It resulted in a final No. 2 ranking, the program's best finish since the 1970 national championship squad.

But there was the matter of Little bringing closure to his collegiate career. Akers approached the senior during Texas's final home game when a 34-12 win against Baylor was no longer in doubt.

"Do you want to go back in and take a snap at quarterback?" Akers asked.

Decades later, Little concedes that he "wanted to"—but on that emotional afternoon, his mind was cluttered with what a single snap might imply for Texas's first black, and former, quarterback.

"I thought about throwing the ball into the student section, or walking to where my mother was and giving the ball to her. I was battling with it. At the time, I thought it would signify that they gave a black quarterback a chance—and it didn't work out. I didn't want that final play to say that I would be the last black quarterback at Texas. What I wanted to do is open up the door and say, 'There will be more.' It was so emotional, I couldn't go back out. I did not want to go out and take the snap. I understand, now, that coach Akers was giving me a chance to go out the way I came in."

Upon completing his eligibility, Little was offered a spot on the Atlanta Falcons developmental squad. Instead, he opted to play three years in the Canadian Football League at Ottawa before suffering a career-ending knee injury.

These days, Little is the married father of twin boys. He offices on the second floor of Bellmont Hall, tucked behind the stands on the west side of the football stadium where he made history as Texas's first African-American quarterback. As the development manager for the Longhorn Foundation and Longhorn Legacy, much of his work is public relations. Yet the most gratifying aspect of Little's vocation may be the opportunity to mentor young Longhorn lettermen who were just as anxious, or homesick, or eager to make their mark as he was in the fall of 1978.

"I constantly tell them that I'm human," Little concluded. "I'm going to fail, but the main thing is to get back up, try again, and do it in a different way. Because there is a God in my life, all of that is possible."

And so much more is possible for African-American student athletes at Texas than it was little more than one generation ago. The complexion of the environment has changed little by little and, in one significant respect, because of Little.

Chapter Ten

ROBERT BREWER

Quarterback (1981-82)

On the surface, you might say Robert Brewer was one of the most unlikely players to become a hero at the University of Texas.

At 5-11, 186 in his playing days in 1981 and '82, and as he likes to say modestly, "with my FIVE-OH time in the forty," Brewer was not the prototypical quarterback. He didn't have great arm strength, he didn't have great size, and no, he didn't have blazing speed. As a result, he never saw the field in a Texas uniform until his junior season.

But what he did have transcended the numbers.

Brewer had a fierce competitive streak that manifested in an intense, almost angry glare when challenged. He also learned early that to succeed he'd have to work his tail off. On trips to the beach at Padre Island as a teenager, while his buddies slept in, Brewer got up at dawn to run wind sprints in the sand with weights strapped to his ankles.

And he had football instincts. Brewer came from a now-legendary football-playing family from Lubbock, Texas. Robert was named after his uncle Bob Brewer, who in the 1940s started at Texas Tech as a freshman. Bob Brewer died tragically in World War II when his bomber was shot down over Austria. Bob Brewer's death at a young age devastated the Brewer family, particularly Robert's grandmother, Mamie, who did not get confirmation of her son's death until 1948, four years later.

But Brewer's father, Charlie, and his other uncle, George, carried on. Their success on the football field helped to pull their mother out of her terrible grief. Both starred at Lubbock High and had successful college football careers. Charlie Brewer quarterbacked the Westerners to a state championship in 1952 and also started for three seasons at Texas. George Brewer went to Oklahoma, where he shared the Sooner backfield with a guy named Darrell Royal.

So Robert was born into a rich football tradition. As a boy, he watched grainy, 16-millimeter movies of his dad's Longhorn games on the living room wall of their home in north Dallas. From the first time he could put on pads and play organized football, Brewer played quarterback. By early in his first year of high school, Brewer had taken over the starting quarterback job on the Richardson High varsity after the senior starter went down to injury. He never lost the position until he left for the University of Texas three years later.

Robert received a few scholarship offers, but not from his favorite team, his family's team, the Texas Longhorns. So he walked on.

By the middle of his junior year, Robert had played a few games in mop-up time during the 1981 season, but had not taken a snap when it mattered. After walking on, he almost walked away.

"We beat Oklahoma in the Cotton Bowl in 1981 and I didn't get to play," said Brewer. "Quarterback Rick McIvor had a couple of big plays and the team was No. 1 in the nation, and I told mom and dad that Sunday after the game, 'I'm out of here. This is it.' I wasn't going to quit during the season, but as soon as the season was over, I was done. I mean, we were No. 1 in the nation and after two and a half years in, I just thought, 'They don't need me around here.' I was going to just slip quietly into the night. But then Rick got hurt against Houston, and they put me in for the second half in that game."

UT's stay at No. 1 after the OU victory lasted all of one week, as the offense imploded against Arkansas the next week in a 42-11 defeat. The Horns rebounded with wins against SMU and Texas Tech. But in the Astrodome against Houston, Texas found itself down 14-0 at halftime after the Cougars capitalized on a pair of McIvor interceptions.

Head coach Fred Akers wanted to replace McIvor with former quarterback Donnie Little, though Little had been moved to receiver and hadn't played the position since the previous year. But offensive coordinator Ron Toman wanted Brewer, who got the call. Robert didn't find out until the second half had almost started.

Robert Brewer scores against 'Bama in the Cotton Bowl, 1982

"They told me right when we were buckling it up and walking back out," Brewer recalled, "which was perfect. And receiver Herkie Walls was right in front of me and saw Toman tell me, 'It's you, get ready,' and as Herkie was running out, he turned to me and said, 'You're not the second-string quarterback anymore, Brewer, so don't play like it.'"

He didn't. Brewer engineered 14 second-half points on two Raul Allegre field goals, a touchdown run by John Walker, and a throw to Walker for a 2-point conversion. That 14-14 tie began Robert Brewer's career at Texas.

Brewer started the next three games, wins over TCU, Baylor, and Texas A&M. Those wins earned the Horns the Southwest Conference championship and the right to face Alabama and legendary coach Paul "Bear" Bryant in the Cotton Bowl on New Year's Day, 1982.

No. 6 TEXAS vs. No. 3 ALABAMA

January 1, 1982

Cotton Bowl—Dallas, Texas

Bryant had become the winningest coach ever in college football that season, passing Amos Alonzo Stagg with 315 career victories. In the Cotton Bowl, his team led Texas 10-0 early in the fourth quarter, when Brewer turned in one of the most stunning plays in Texas football history.

Facing a third-and-10 at the Tide 30, Brewer surveyed the 'Bama defense and called time-out. The call was a quarterback draw, designed to beat the fierce Tide blitz that had already resulted in six sacks on Brewer. The play worked to perfection, as Brewer tucked the ball and ran untouched up the gut for a 30-yard touchdown.

The very next series, Brewer passed the Horns down the field on an 80-yard drive, leading to an 8-yard Terry Orr touchdown run with just 2:05 on the clock. Texas held on to defeat Alabama 14-12, giving it a final record of 10-1-1. Brewer was named the game's Most Valuable Offensive Player, and the Horns finished second in the country in the AP poll, behind only national champion Clemson.

The Game of My Life

By Robert Brewer

I had laryngitis three days before that game and I could not call the plays in practice. I had a bad case of cedar fever, so Carl Robinson and some other guys called the plays that day. Coach Akers always had me on a short leash anyway, so a couple of days before that game I didn't even know if I was going to start.

We had a Bible-study group that met on Tuesday nights in the dorm, which had started about a year earlier, and we had a chaplain come in on Friday nights before the football games. He would give a lesson and we would maybe share a comment or two, and it was always nice. The chaplain was named John Henderson.

But the night before the Alabama game, John had a problem with his car and couldn't make it. It was a really well-attended meeting, with maybe 25 guys in that room, so about 30 minutes into that meeting, we got word that John wouldn't be there. So here we are the night before the game, and you don't want to disturb any of your pregame rituals. But safety William Graham got up and said, "Why don't we just go around the room and share a little bit about what is on each of our minds and hearts and about what the group means to you."

Man, that turned into one of the most special hours of my life. We all just started telling each other what we all meant to each other and what we had done for each other, and it got to me. I have never told anyone about this, but I just started bawling. I'm not sure why, but I think it was because this group of guys was so special to me. Joe Shearin was there and William and several other guys, but also, looking back on it, I hate to admit it, but I think I was scared. But after I walked out of that meeting, I didn't feel another bit of pressure. The next day, I fell asleep on the bus going to the game.

I didn't get much sleep the night before the game. Pretty late, Coach Toman had come by after the Cotton Bowl party still in his tux and banged on the door, so he comes in and my roommate, Rick McIvor, was already in bed. So coach and I go into the hotel bathroom and go over the game plan. He left but I couldn't sleep so I went downstairs and Brent Duhon and Todd Dodge and a few other guys were playing cards so we sat up till about 3:30 or 4:00 in the morning. And the team had to get up for an early breakfast so I got maybe an hour's sleep, so I was tired.

But when we came out of that meeting the night before the game, there's something about it when you humble yourself in front of everybody . . . I had told the guys how much they meant to me and that I was going to do my best for them tomorrow, and William Graham said to me, "Robert, you believe in yourself." I said, "William, I believe God's with me, and I'll go out there . . . ." but William said, "Yes, God is with you, but he gave you the ability, so you go do it, you believe in yourself." He was a leader to me, he had started that group after going through some hard times of his own, and that really had an impact on me.

Then that night, we had a team dinner, but instead of going to the dinner with everybody, I just had this real strong sense that I just needed to get off by myself, kind of like the night before the battle. I was starving and I didn't want one of those wooden steaks they serve up, so I went to Shakey's and ordered a large pizza and got the sports pages, the *Dallas Times-Herald* and the *Dallas Morning News*. I sat there and read all the "pluses for Texas" and the minuses, one of which was quarterback—they gave the quarterback nod to Alabama—and I can remember really having a sense of peace and confidence. So that whole day before the game, I just had a good feeling. I got over the jitters the day before the game.

So I slept on the bus riding over and I woke up outside the Cotton Bowl. I started thinking about watching the Notre Dame-Texas games there growing up in Dallas, watching Don Meredith and Bob Hayes and the Cowboys, and it felt like home. It felt real comfortable even though it was going to be the bright lights shining and the big time.

Alabama got the opening kickoff and drove it past midfield on us and we stopped them, but they punted us down around our own five-yard line, so I ran out there and I'm like, "Let's get this first play over with." So I get in there and call the play, and right when we are breaking the huddle, the ref calls a TV timeout.

I've already got the play, there's no reason for me to run 40 yards back over to the bench. So I'm in the huddle, and all of a sudden I look between Mike Baab and Doug Dawson, and this guy named Warren Lyles, their All-American defensive tackle, has got his back turned to us. The 'Bama band is doing this really upbeat, jazzy tune and Lyles is just working his rear end back and forth, loose as a goose, and I remember my thought was, "Man, this guy has been starting for three years in the SEC and he's an All-American!" and I got this one little twinge of doubt again, and it was because of how totally loose that guy was—he was going, "I like this kind of party!"

But hey, let me tell you, our center Mike Baab wasn't worried at all. He was a great football player, Lyles's equal, he just hadn't quite gotten the recognition, but he wound up starting in the NFL for nine years.

Baab handled Lyles fine, but we hadn't been able to score any points going into the fourth quarter. I got sacked six or seven times because they kept coming with a safety or a corner or linebacker blitz. But our defense had been keeping it close, so we were still within striking distance when the fourth quarter started.

That whole fourth quarter was a series of minor miracles. On my touchdown run, we had a third-and-10 and I called time-out, which was the second one I had squandered that drive, and we were down 10 points, so the fans are all thinking, "That stupid . . . " And when I went over to Coach Akers, I could hear some of those catcalls coming at me. But I was thinking, 'Hey, they were going to safety blitz us again.' I saw their safety, Tommy Wilcox, sneaking up, and they were fixin' to do the same thing they had done all day. Had I not called time-out, we would have had a fourth-and-about-14 from a sack, so it was the right thing to do.

The thing was, because I was only four games in as a starter, I guess the coaches didn't want to have me checking at the line of scrimmage on pass plays. So the only thing they could really do was what they did, which was, out of necessity, call the quarterback draw. It was the only thing we could do to combat that outside blitz, without doing some kind of check with me at the line.

So when I got back from the sidelines to the huddle, Baab said, "What's the play?" and I said, "It's One," and he goes, "Oh, no!" And my buddy, Joe Shearin, jumped all over Baab. And then Bryan Millard didn't know what to do, so after jumping on Baab, Joe then told Millard how to block it. I told running back Rodney Tate and the receivers, "Just run to the sideline!"

The thing was, that play was put in for Donnie Little—who had beaten Oklahoma the year before on that play—not for me. He ran that play six or seven times in a row against OU in the fourth quarter in 1980.

So during the time-out, we tried to guess what defense they were going to be in. Well, coach Akers and the other coaches gambled that they would come back with the same defense. If they go back in a zone and I go back in and run the draw, it would've been fourth-and-8. So it was a big gamble.

So I called the play and I am walking up and am starting to go under center, and I went, "Oh, yeah!" You couldn't tell exactly, and I tried to act like I wasn't looking at him, but I saw that Wilcox was sneaking up again, and I could see that their safeties were walking outside a step or two so everybody was going to man-up. So I knew those linebackers were going to be gone because, since it was a passing situation, they were going to be man-up on the running backs, and our guys were going straight to the sidelines. So I'm thinking, "Catch the snap, don't get in too big a hurry backing up, *and don't trip*." And that's all it was. And it opened up and worked like a charm.

If it had been some other slug at defensive tackle, he may have still been in the middle mucking things up. But Warren Lyles was such a good football player that he went hard up the middle and Baab just took him past me. So I took off and I remember that the only thing I could see were those little high school band uniforms up in the stands coming at me, and then it just got totally quiet, and then it went pretty crazy on the sidelines.

Then after the touchdown, I was so excited I ran over by Coach Akers and I pointed at him, and I regret that to this day. All I was doing was saying, "That was a great call," but it looked on TV like I was telling him off, and a ton of people asked me that—for a couple of years after that, I bet four or five hundred people asked me that question. They would say, "You made that call, didn't you? You were telling Fred I told you that would work!" I guess that's what everybody wanted to believe, but that wasn't it. What I was saying was, "That was a great call, coach." It just didn't look right. I meant it to be complimentary to him.

Then we held and the next series, we had to cover 80 yards with only about 6 minutes left on the clock and we hadn't done much offensively all day. But after that touchdown run, that whole stadium went upside down and there was a feeling not of *if* we scored again, but *when*. Saying we knew we were going to win is a little strong, but there was no lack of confidence in our huddle, with anyone.

But we faced a third-and-10 on our own 20-yard line. We had thrown incompletions on first and second down, but tight end Lawrence Sampleton and I both had told the coaches earlier that the corner route was open, but we had not gotten to it. So they pulled it out and signaled it in on third down. I remember watching the guys on the sidelines signaling the play and formation and I remember that feeling of going, "Yes—this is going to work!" I didn't really throw a great pass, but I wanted to make sure I didn't overthrow him or underthrow and get a pick, so I threw it high and outside, and Lawrence caught it for a 37-yard gain. So there was another minor miracle.

So there's a first down—game over if we don't get that one. And then the next one, I threw an out route to Lawrence and I misread the coverage and the Tide had a guy named Benny Perrin, No. 23. He was all-conference and played in the NFL. I thought he was in cover three and he rolled up in cover two, and I threw the out route to Lawrence and Perrin broke on it outside. I actually underthrew the ball and Lawrence adjusted and made a great catch or Perrin would've intercepted it. Lawrence caught the ball and broke a tackle, then he broke another tackle and rambled for about another 20-yard gain, so now we're down pretty deep in their territory.

After that we knew. Donnie Little also made a great catch on a ball I overthrew on that drive, and Herkie Walls had a huge catch also, a 15-yarder against Jeremiah Castille who also had a long NFL career. I hit Herkie on the run—that was probably the best pass I threw all day—and he was so fast. So we scored on a run by Terry Orr and hung on to win.

The day before the game we had a neat meeting between the teams where they had tables with eight or ten people with alums and players, and I sat with Alabama's starting running back. But right at the next table, right smack behind me, was Paul "Bear" Bryant. And when I recognized that, I started listening to his conversation and looking at the back of his neck—it was all leathery and John Wayne-looking with creviced skin, and when he talked, it literally sounded like a thunderstorm way off in the distance. I looked down after that and about half my meal was on the ground in front of me because I was so mesmerized by coach Bryant!

But as far as the game, you know, it's weird when you are playing against a team like that, you don't have any contact with the coach—it's all kind of like smoke, it's mythical. But we ran out for pregame warm-ups and then when we went back to the locker room, there he was, leaning against the goalpost, both when we went down and came back. When we went down I remember thinking, "Wow, there's Bear Bryant!" It was a classic scene, like a poster with him against that goal post. So it was total reverence and respect going out for warm-ups, but on the way back I felt like he was maybe trying to intimidate us, still leaning on that goal post. But I was feeling really good being back at home in Dallas, playing in the Cotton Bowl, so I didn't feel intimidated. And by the way, he did have the houndstooth hat on! It was golden . . .

But that game was just so special for me, for so many reasons. To play against Bear Bryant, of course. But after the game, Roger Staubach, who I had idolized growing up in Dallas and who was working the game for CBS, broke through the crowd to congratulate me. And I was a bit of a historian growing up, and I knew my dad had played in a high school state championship game in that very stadium thirty years earlier to the day—January 1, 1952—against Baytown in the Cotton Bowl. And the score of that game was 14-12. And my dad was the most valuable player of that game.

Upon Further Review

Following the Cotton Bowl victory, Robert Brewer started all of the 1982 season at quarterback for Texas, as the Horns went 9-2 and earned a trip to the Sun Bowl against North Carolina, a game Texas lost 26-10. But five days before the bowl game, Brewer suffered a broken thumb in practice, robbing him of a chance to lead his team one more time in the postseason.

Brewer and receiver Herkie Walls hooked up that '82 season to become one of the most explosive passing tandems in school history. Brewer's 1,415 yards passing with 12 touchdown throws in 1982, including an 80-yarder to Walls for a score against Baylor, were school records at the time. He finished his career at Texas with a 13-2 record as a starter.

Today, Robert lives in Austin with his wife and two younger children, and is a financial planner for Merrill Lynch. His oldest son, Michael, is a quarterback at Texas Tech University. As the years have gone by since his playing days at Texas, Brewer's perspective has shifted.

"I kind of shut that game out and moved on," Brewer says of the days and years following the Cotton Bowl. "In football, I had to do that in spring training and into that next season, but in my life, too.

"But now I think it's good to go back and revisit the good times in your life as well as the bad. And one thing I get out of the experience of that game is that, boy, when things are going tough in your life, you can rely on your faith—whatever faith a person might have—you've got to get on your knees and ask God, 'What are you trying to do with me?'

"But also, now that there's some time and space since those days, I've learned that it really wasn't about me at all. It was about my family and my friends. That game wasn't just a gift to me; it was a gift to my grandmother and my mom and my dad, all of us, because of a lot of things we'd been through. That's the lesson of it. It's not about you. It's about the people in your life that you love and care about and how the things you do can have an impact on them."

Chapter Eleven

JERRY GRAY

Defensive Back (1981-84)

The University of Texas celebrated its centennial year in 1983. Students who graduated that year received a diploma with the official centennial seal embossed in the lower left corner. The Texas Longhorn football team wore the same seal on their right shoulder pads.

But the celebration wasn't limited to seals and ceremonies. On the gridiron, the Longhorns gift-wrapped a perfect 11-0 record in the year of 1983, and fielded perhaps the most dominant defense in the history of the program. Following that season, the Longhorns had seventeen players taken in the NFL draft, still a school record. Only an agonizing defeat to Georgia in the Cotton Bowl on January 2, 1984—to this day one of the most painful losses in school history—kept Texas from a certain national championship.

Jerry Gray started at safety on that Texas team, earning All-America honors in the process. He followed it up with another All-American campaign in 1984. During each of those '83 and '84 seasons, Gray turned in a pair of spectacular plays against Auburn that vividly exemplified not only his own talent, but the almost invincible nature of the Texas defenses of that era.

Gray had signed with Texas in 1981 out of Lubbock Estacado High School where he had played quarterback. He knew he would line up at defensive back in college, so when it came time to choose his collegiate destination, Gray naturally took a hard look at Texas.

"I was recruited pretty much all over," recalled Gray, "by Notre Dame and all of the West Coast schools, but two of the things that got me about Texas were,

I ran track down there my sophomore and junior years in the state track meet, and got a chance to see a great place. The campus was incredible, I loved the weather, and then I saw how they were putting out All-American defensive backs. They have a history of putting out great DBs."

Indeed, particularly during the 1970s, the decade preceding Gray's arrival in Austin, Texas had been blessed with an abundance of defensive backfield stars, many of whom would go on to stellar careers in the NFL.

"Johnnie Johnson, Ricky Churchman, Derrick Hatchett, Raymond Clayborn, Bill Bradley, those guys were before me," said Gray, "and then when I got there, we had the Mossy Cades, myself, then later Bryant Westbrook. It's been a great school for producing defensive back talent."

Gray would play as a true freshman in 1981, the year Texas won the Southwest Conference and defeated Alabama in the Cotton Bowl. But his greatest contribution that season may have been his ability to learn from the experienced veterans in front of him, guys who taught him about what it would take to be successful at a program like Texas. What he learned would help him be a leader as an upperclassmen for the guys coming up behind him.

"When I got there they had William Graham, who was a senior and a really good player," said Gray. "We had Bobby Johnson who was Johnnie's brother, then Mike Hatchett who was Derrick's brother, and then Vance Bedford was at corner. Those guys taught you and set the standard for how defense was supposed to be played at the University of Texas."

After that Cotton Bowl victory over the Crimson Tide on New Year's Day, Texas turned in a 9-3 season in 1982 that ended in a 26-10 Sun Bowl loss to North Carolina, a game that starting quarterback Robert Brewer missed after breaking his thumb just days before the game.

The Longhorns had earlier suffered back-to-back midseason losses, the second derailing their chances to repeat as conference champions. Despite the disappointments, the '82 season saw a young defense grow up, and set the stage for the domination that was to follow the next season.

"It really started back in 1982," Gray recalled of the evolution of that great Horn defense of '83. "We went up to Dallas to play Oklahoma, which was my first game playing that season. I had injured my knee in two-a-days. We lost to Oklahoma and Marcus Dupree, and then the next game, SMU came to Austin and we lost to Eric Dickerson and Craig James. That was the first time I had ever lost two

Texas' two-time consensus All-American safety, Jerry Gray (Photo courtesy of the University of Texas)

games in a row, even going back to high school. But then after that, we won the next six games in a row."

Gray believes the experience of battling against but ultimately losing to the Sooners and the Pony Express taught the young guys what it would take to reach the next level. "It wasn't a bunch of yelling or anything like that," he said. "Our defense was young, but we kind of jelled right then, and then it carried over to the next year. We were juniors and sophomores that became seniors and juniors. I think winning 11 in a row my junior year was a byproduct of what happened my sophomore year. We played against really good teams. Oklahoma was really good at that time, and then you go up against Dickerson and James and those guys go 11-0-1 that same year."

The Longhorns finished the 1982 season hovering around the top 20, but the pollsters saw enough in the team to rank them third in the nation entering the next season. The Horns wasted no time proving that the scribes knew their stuff.

No. 3 TEXAS vs. No. 5 AUBURN

September 17, 1983
Auburn, Alabama

Texas opened 1983 on the road, traveling to play fifth-ranked Auburn in front of 73,500 fans. The Tiger's ground-gobbling offense featured running backs Bo Jackson, Lionel James, and Tommie Agee running out of the Wishbone, with quarterback Randy Campbell pulling the trigger. Auburn had already beaten Southern Mississippi easily, so Texas entered the game facing an opponent that had a tune-up game under its belt, and without quarterback Todd Dodge who had been injured. None of that mattered.

The Horns jumped on Auburn quickly, scoring on three straight possessions to take a 17-0 lead. The first score came on their second possession of the game, an 84-yard drive that took sixteen plays and ate up 7:57 minutes of clock, culminating with quarterback Rob Moerschell's 1-yard touchdown run. The Horns had converted four third-down attempts in the series, the last one coming on a 20-yard pass from Moerschell to Terry Orr that went to the Auburn six.

Following a 66-yard punt return by Jitter Fields to the Tiger 23, Texas then tacked on a 37-yard Jeff Ward field goal to take a 10-0 lead. Following a spectacular one-handed, circus interception by Jerry Gray at the Texas 10 the next series, the Horns broke the Tigers' backs with an 80-yard bomb by Rick McIvor to Kelvin Epps that made it 17-0. Epps hauled the ball in at the 37 and raced to the end zone, just avoiding a leaping tackle attempt by a Tiger defensive back. Texas would make it 20-0 on a 32-yard Ward field goal just 17 seconds before halftime.

Auburn managed to scrape out only two first downs and 51 net yards against the bone-crushing Texas defense in the first half, and never crossed its own 46. Before finally scoring on Bo Jackson's 1-yard run with 1:33 to play, the Tigers had crossed midfield only twice, once courtesy of a 23-yard interference penalty on Texas. Jackson managed a paltry 35 yards on 7 carries for the day, and said afterwards, "I feel like I have been stampeded by a herd of cows." Auburn coach Pat Dye called the game "an embarrassment." For the Longhorns, it was a work of art.

The Game of My Life

By Jerry Gray

It wasn't difficult to prepare to play Auburn that first game. We had beaten Alabama in the Cotton Bowl and Alabama was a good team from the SEC, and we came into the season ranked in the top five just like Auburn. They had Bo Jackson and Tommie Agee, so we knew they were good, but we had already played against Eric Dickerson and Craig James, so playing those guys helped prepare us for that '83 year.

That was one of the first times that I had played on grass, so you go into Auburn, the thing that you see, is there was a hedge all the way around the field, then a fence, and then the fans. So there was no track around that football field, so it was really, really close. You could tell that it was a big game, and their fans were incredible because it was really loud, all the time.

And for me, that's how you play football. You don't worry about, "Who can we play at the beginning of the year to get a win." With Fred Akers and the athletic director at that time, they prepared you to be the best team in the country every year. Because we didn't play a lot of teams that weren't ranked. You went out and played Penn State at the Meadowlands my senior year, we played Auburn my junior and senior years along with Oklahoma, then you put Penn State in there my senior year with tailback D. J. Dozier. So these were our nonconference games, where we had Auburn, Oklahoma and Penn State, and then we had to play the conference schedule.

So the school prepared you for life after football because it taught you a lot about the tough times—you go on the road and you learn that you can win anywhere. And that was one of the reasons why football was really good for me, because it really wasn't a shock when you got in front of sixty, seventy, eighty thousand fans that weren't for you.

We really didn't know what to expect going into the season, but when we went to Auburn and beat them 20-7, we knew we could be a really good defense. From then on, we just kinda jelled from there. All of the talk was about Bo Jackson and the speed and that type of stuff, but I don't think they had played a team with the type of speed that we had, especially on defense. We were really, really good on defense. Our defensive ends were 4.5 guys, and our corners were 4.3 guys. So they didn't know us and we didn't know them, but we knew how fast we were.

Again, the thing that helped us was going against the Jameses and Dickersons the year before. That prepared us to go against Bo Jackson and their option team. Dickerson and those guys were really, really good from their freshman year to their senior year. They could put two backs in the backfield, or reserve one guy and the other could come in and get 1,600 yards, so after seeing those guys, we weren't afraid of who we were going to be playing against at Auburn. The question was just whether we were going to execute the defense to win the game.

From Leon Fuller my freshman year to David McWillliams all through my year of graduating, we had really good defensive schemes. Basically, with the option, the safety was going to run the alley and take the pitch, and the defensive end could do one of two things: He could either come down and take the fullback or he could take the quarterback, depending on the stunt we called on the line, and then if the ends took the quarterback, then the linebackers would have to take the fullback, and then you could switch it. The free safety was the guy who was responsible for the pitch just about all of the time. Then you had to understand how to read uncovered linemen. And I was able to take some of the things I had learned playing quarterback in high school and flip it, to where I could say, "If the quarterback did this, how would I defend it playing free safety?"

That year I led the team in tackles, and we were the No. 1-ranked rushing defense in all of football that year, so being on the line of scrimmage, you couldn't allow many breakaway runs. You were also responsible for the pitch, you had to stop the pass, and you had to be in the run front. With the speed that we had, the coaches weren't afraid to put us in those positions to make those plays.

On my interception, they were coming down the line on the option. I read the lineman firing out, but what they were really trying to do was reach, so you knew it wasn't a run. I saw the quarterback come off of the line, so I turned and ran as fast as I could and I know they were doing the same thing, and it just so happened I put my right hand up and caught the ball one-handed falling backwards.

At the time you don't think of those things as being great plays. You just say, "Hey, this is what my job is, to protect the middle of the field, don't let them get touchdowns, don't let them make big plays." And you look back and say, "Man, that was a great play," but at the time, you're saying, "OK, I was doing my job."

One thing that didn't really tick us off, but it surprised us, was that we had never played any SEC teams besides Alabama, but when we played Auburn, they ran off the field after the game and nobody came over to shake our hands. We didn't know if that was their tradition or what. We were used to playing in the Southwest Conference and when the game was over, you go and shake the guy's hand and you go on. We were playing in their backyard, so we just didn't know if they ran off because they had lost the game or because it was their tradition. We were trying to figure out what was wrong—I don't think the head coach shook coach Akers's hand or anything.

But Bo Jackson came over to our locker room, and I think that was the start of the friendship that he and I have now. You could tell the kind of class that he had, because he knew that wasn't the way they were supposed to be acting. It was a game, it was competition, but you know what, after the game, you shake a guy's hand and you move on. One of the things that lets you know about a guy like Bo Jackson is that he came over and it was, "Hey look, sorry about that, that's just the way we are, but I'm apologizing for the rest of the team."

Upon Further Review

After dominating the No. 5 team in the nation on its home turf, the Horns moved up a notch to No. 2, a position they would occupy throughout an entire undefeated season. In the process of compiling its perfect 11-0 record, Texas defeated three teams ranked in the top ten in the country, holding Auburn to 7 points and knocking off eighth-ranked Oklahoma 28-16 and ninth-ranked SMU 15-12. The Horns trailed only the Mike Rozier-, Turner Gill- and Irving Fryar-led Nebraska Cornhuskers, who held onto the No. 1 spot the entire season.

After thrashing Texas A&M 45-13 to close out the regular season, Texas claimed the Southwest Conference championship and the right to play seventh-ranked Georgia in the Cotton Bowl on January 2, 1984. A victory, and Texas certainly would have claimed its fourth national championship, as later that evening, Nebraska suffered a shocking loss at the hands of the Miami Hurricanes.

But the Longhorns, despite another suffocating performance from its defense, could only muster three Jeff Ward field goals of its own heading into the last minutes of the fourth quarter. With 4:35 to play, Georgia punted from its own 34. The Horns' Craig Curry couldn't hang on to the 43-yarder, and Jitter Fields, standing behind Curry, also lost the handle. Georgia recovered at the Texas 23.

After a couple of runs made it third and four, Bulldog quarterback John Lastinger took an option keeper around right end, found a seam, and took it to the end zone, despite taking a shot from Jerry Gray at the goal line. Replays appear to show a Bulldog lineman grabbing the ankle of Longhorn outside linebacker Mark Lang, causing Lang to trip over backwards, but no penalty was called. When Kevin Butler hit the extra point, Georgia had dealt Texas a stunning defeat, despite scraping together only 215 yards of offense on the day.

"The game was heartbreaking," recalled Gray, "especially to the seniors who couldn't play anymore, the way it happened. Georgia knew they couldn't drive the ball, we knew they couldn't drive the ball, but then a fluke dropped punt gives them the ball inside the 20-yard line, so they go 10 yards and win 10-9. If you look at that game, they knew and we knew and most everybody in the country knew that if they got the ball on the 50, there was no way they were going to do anything with it. I don't mean to be arrogant, but that's how dominating that defense was. Every time we touched the football field we were saying, 'Hey look, our job is, no matter where they get the football, they're not going to score.' That was the mindset that we had."

Rather than be crushed by the stinging defeat, Texas regrouped in the off season and came out smoking again to start the 1984 campaign. First up again were the No. 11 Auburn Tigers and their Heisman candidate Bo Jackson. In a more high-scoring game than the previous year, Texas this time knocked off the Tigers by a score of 35-27, aided in part by a play by Jerry Gray that is to this day one of the most talked-about plays in Texas football history.

Jackson took a pitch and went left and headed upfield before cutting back to his right and racing for the sidelines. Despite Jackson's tremendous speed, Gray turned on some jets of his own and caught Jackson, hauled him down and separated Bo's shoulder in the process. Jackson gained 53 yards on the play, but Gray saved a sure touchdown, and the Horns secured an 8-point victory.

"In thinking about that play, it reminded me of my senior year in high school," Gray said of his tackle of Jackson. "We're at the track meet and I was running anchor with three sophomores on the mile relay. I had come in third in the 400, but I knew that there were three other guys counting on me to get us to the state track meet. I got the stick with the lead and there were two other guys who had just beaten me in the 400 that passed me on the backstretch. So I am thinking, 'If I get third, they don't go to the state track meet in the mile relay.' Well, coming home, something inside me said, 'Hey look, this is what you gotta do,' and I happened to run my best time ever, which was a 46.1. If I had run that in the 400 I would have won by a long shot, but at the time, it was what I had to do."

"So that was the same thing that happened in the game. The play came down and they pitched the ball to Bo Jackson and he cuts back and I overran it. I had committed outside because most of the time I had seen Bo Jackson outrun guys, he was a hit-the-sideline-and-stay-that-way runner and not a cut-back guy. So I am thinking he is going to outrun us to the sideline, but instead he cuts back. So I had to cut back and turn also, and the good thing was, there was nobody blocking me, which gave me the chance to get my speed up. I knew how fast Bo Jackson was, and people say, 'Well Jerry, where'd it come from, how did you catch him?' Number one, it was just will and determination and saying, 'Hey look, these guys are counting on me to be their leader.'"

Despite making what turned out to be a game-saving tackle on Jackson, Gray realized he had derailed Jackson's chances to win the Heisman Trophy that year, and it bothered him. "I knew he was a front-runner for the Heisman because of what he had done as a sophomore, so that caused him to miss his whole junior year," Gray recalled. "So I called down to the hospital and talked to him and apologized to him, because I know how important football is. I didn't really know how he was going to take it, but he was joking around as he always was and told me, 'You don't have to be sorry because that's football.' But you could tell the character of the guy at the end of his sophomore year when we played up there. That let you know the type of guy you were dealing with."

So what could have been a bad situation resulting in hard feelings between the two players resulted in a situation where now Gray and Jackson consider each other friends. "Today, I can pick the phone up and call him or we'll see each other in the airport and say 'Hi,'" said Gray. "Those are things you get for life because you know that here is a guy that had the same type of attitude about football that you had. A lot of guys don't have that. They come in and say, 'What can I take from football?' and then leave. Bo Jackson's attitude was, 'What can I give football?' God blessed him as a two-sport player, and I think if he had not gotten hurt on the play against Cincinnati in baseball, he would have been a Hall of Fame running back."

Texas destroyed Penn State 28-3 in its next game at the Meadowlands in New Jersey and carried a No. 1 ranking and 3-0 record into its game against Oklahoma, which ended in a 15-15 tie. The Horns won their next three and stood 6-0-1 and ranked third in the nation before losing four out of the next five games to finish the regular season, then getting blown out by Iowa 55-17 in the Freedom Bowl, a game many saw as signaling the end of an era for Texas football. The Longhorns would not win another conference championship for six years.

Says Gray of that 1984 season, "After we lost the Cotton Bowl to Georgia, what people didn't understand was that we came back the next year and we actually went 6-0-1, tying Oklahoma, so I don't think it was a bad deal for us to get over the Cotton Bowl loss, I think we just didn't get it done like we did the year before in the Southwest Conference. We went and beat Penn State, we beat Auburn, and we tied Oklahoma and went from No. 1 to No. 2. Although we tied OU 15-15, we had a chance to win that game a whole bunch of times."

Gray believes the loss of so much senior leadership played a role in the team's disappointing finish in 1984. "Unlike my sophomore year," stressed Gray, "where we bounced back from losses to win six or seven in a row and then went eleven in a row in '83—we didn't do that my senior year. Then, we had graduated a lot of seniors so now we had juniors and sophomores playing, and you're trying to teach those guys, 'Hey look, this is how you play dominating football, this is how you win games.' When do you seize the moment of understanding how to dominate when you are young? And that's one thing I learned when I was playing behind William Graham and those guys, because my focus was on how can these guys play great defense, so when I get my chance, I don't want to screw it up for the next guy. I think it becomes more important because you are always thinking about how it is going to affect the next guy, compared to just yourself."

The Los Angeles Rams drafted Gray in the first round of the 1985 draft, and he played in Los Angeles through the 1991 season. He played in the Pro Bowl each year from 1987 to 1990, and was named the game's Most Valuable Player in his last appearance. He was the NFL's Defensive Back of the Year in 1989. Gray played three more seasons with the Houston Oilers and Tampa Bay Bucs before retiring after the 1994 season. In 1995, Gray began his coaching career with SMU, before serving four years with the Tennessee Titans. Prior to joining the Washington Redskins as their defensive backs coach, Gray spent five years as defensive coordinator of the Buffalo Bills, and later also coached defensive backs for the Seattle Seahawks.

"Coaching was a natural fit for me," said Gray. "I enjoy it and I don't look at it as a job; I look at it as something I would do for free, and it just so happens I get paid for it. That's the way I approach football, because to me, if you played in this league, then you have something to give back. If you don't give it back, then I think you are selfish."

After leaving Seattle, Gray became the Longhorns' defensive backs coach in January of 2011, but less than a month later, he left to become the defensive coordinator of the Tennessee Titans. The quick move came as a surprise to many Texas fans. After making the decision, Gray said it was the hardest decision he'd ever had to make, but that a chance to be a defensive coordinator in the NFL was something he couldn't pass up.

As for the possibility that Gray might someday return to Texas as a coach with the Longhorns, a hope of many Longhorn fans, he certainly is open to the possibility. "I think at this point, Texas has got a terrific coach," Gray emphasized. "[Mack Brown] is doing a fantastic job. He knows my heart. We've had heart-to-heart conversations. If that opportunity comes available to where they say, 'Hey look, we're looking for a guy to come and lead the University of Texas after Mack Brown again hopefully wins them another national championship and retires,' to me, that would be great. People don't really understand how you can really get the goose bumps like you did when you were a freshman. It's the same that happens when you get a chance to go back to your school and you say, 'Hey, this is where I actually started. If one of these days the University of Texas ever came open and they said to me, 'Jerry, do you want to come back and coach here?' I would say, 'Yes.' I watch the men's basketball team, the women's team, baseball, I watch Texas every chance I get, not just football. I have friends from Texas all over. The University of Texas means a lot to the people who have actually played there and the students who have been there. Every chance to go back, I always go."

Chapter Twelve

PETER GARDERE

Quarterback (1989-92)

Pete Gardere's career as a 1951 Longhorn defensive back lasted all of one play. He was darn lucky to survive a broken neck in Texas's opener against Kentucky, but his first collegiate tackle was career ending. He would not letter at Texas, although his father did—barely. The 1922 leather-headed Longhorns included one George P. Gardere who suffered a season-ending broken jaw in his only year to letter during the pre–face mask era.

It meant that Peter Gardere, a 1988 Houston Lee graduate, had the rare opportunity to become a double legacy at a traditional football program. It's just that Texas had lost much of its luster, stumbling to a 31-26-1 mark in the five years since the undefeated 1983 regular season. By then, Gardere had established himself as a soccer star, a baseball standout, a solid punter, and a decent passer who eventually flourished when Lee varsity coaches installed the run-and-shoot offense. The likes of Notre Dame, Penn State, Michigan, and Texas A&M expressed interest in Gardere and, of course, so did Texas.

Longhorn coach David McWilliams's first season was a rollercoaster ride. The 1987 Longhorns stumbled out of the gate at 2-3, including thumpings at the hands of No. 5 Auburn and top-ranked Oklahoma. But the 16-14 win at No. 15 Arkansas marked the first time Texas had ever won on a game's final play. A Bluebonnet Bowl win against Pittsburgh eased the bitterness of a fourth-straight loss to Texas A&M. The Horns' first top-twenty final rating in four seasons (No. 19 in the coaches' poll) suggested the program was headed in the right direction.

When Gardere decided to head to Texas, it was generally believed his talents were best suited as the team's primary backup quarterback. Many expected Shannon Kelley (who married Olympic gold medalist Mary Lou Retton), or Mark Murdock, or Donovan Forbes, or Jason Burleson (later converted to fullback) to emerge as McWilliams's first great quarterback. Gardere was typically perceived as a tad smaller or a step slower than a prototypical Division-I signal caller. His strengths lent themselves toward the rollout game, but there was some question about the kind of offense that first-year coordinator Lynn Amedee would install in 1989.

In time, Gardere would be regarded as cut from the same cloth as former Longhorn quarterbacks James Street, Randy McEachern, and Robert Brewer: It wasn't pretty, but all they did was win. Gardere's career record of 25-16 indicates that, when he wasn't winning, he did just enough to stave off demotion. Yet there is one mark of distinction that sets Gardere apart from all Texas quarterbacks who went before him and from all who followed in the decades since. Indeed, it is the very achievement that forever established Gardere in Longhorn lore as "Peter the Great."

The Horns were coming off a 4-7 stinker in 1988, the program's worst showing in thirty-two years, while the 1989 squad was lucky not to be 1-3 heading into its annual grudge match against Oklahoma. McWilliams's third Texas team opened with a 3-touchdown setback at Colorado before leveling SMU in its first season back from an NCAA "death penalty" suspension. For the first time, Joe Paterno and Penn State visited Austin and came away with a late 16-12 decision on a blocked punt returned for a touchdown.

McWilliams shuffled three quarterbacks throughout September, searching for someone, anyone, to jumpstart a young team that would field just one All-Southwest Conference performer (wide receiver Johnny Walker) in 1989. He simply had to settle on a starter before facing the Sooners, and redshirt freshman Gardere was given the nod against lightly regarded Rice on October 7. It was a night to remember but, from a burnt-orange perspective, for all the wrong reasons. No game, in recent memory, against the Owls had been decided on a late and controversial officiating call. Texas trailed 30-24 with less than 4 minutes remaining, but Gardere had engineered one last drive. On fourth-and-goal from the four, McWilliams called time-out to discuss *how in the world* Texas could avoid an inexplicable loss to a team that had not won in Austin for nearly a quarter century.

Peter Gardere led Texas to a SWC championship in 1990

Gardere recalled: "Coach McWilliams told me, 'Whatever you do, throw it or run it, but get your ass to that pylon. I don't care what you do.'"

Gardere ran right, was hit by a couple of Rice defenders and dove for the goal line just as he was tackled.

"I rolled over [following the tackle]. I knew I was going to disappoint the coach if I didn't score. I was more concerned about him getting on my ass. First of all, it was Rice. We should have been kicking their butts. We were behind, so I was thinking, 'God, I've just got to get in there.'"

The officials decided that, by god, he had. Touchdown, Texas. The record will forever read Texas 31, Rice 30, but Rice fans on hand that night insist Gardere was stopped short of the goal line.

"I still catch a lot of grief today from Rice people," Gardere acknowledged.

The narrow escape did little to soothe Longhorn partisans who feared that, in a week's time, Oklahoma would extend its mastery over their team for a fifth-straight year. Yet Gardere was not dubbed "Peter the Great" for his 1-3 mark against Texas A&M. His lofty title stems from his 4-0 record against Oklahoma. Indeed, the redshirt freshman became a case study in the way the Texas-OU game immortalizes its victors.

TEXAS vs. No. 15 OKLAHOMA

October 14, 1989
Cotton Bowl—Dallas, Texas

The 1989 Texas-OU game marked a changing of the guard in the ancient rivalry. McWilliams was still looking for his first series win while, for the first time since 1973, someone other than Barry Switzer wore the head coach's headset on the Sooner sideline. First-year OU coach Gary Gibbs saw his team trail 7-0 after Gardere connected with diminutive wide receiver Tony Jones on a 7-yard fade. Gardere converted a third-and-15 from the 15 with his 19-yard scramble just before Sooner defensive end James Goode was ejected for striking Longhorn lineman Ed Cunningham with his helmet on that opening possession for the Horns. Gardere hit all five of his passes, for 55 yards, on the eleven-play 80-yard drive.

Sooner tailback Mike Gaddis knotted the affair on Oklahoma's opening series with his 62-yard TD run. Gardere was sacked on consecutive snaps to force a punt, but then fortune smiled on the Longhorns. Mical Padgett got his hands on punt returner Otis Taylor's mid-air fumble and rumbled 44 yards down the left sideline for the score. Texas's charmed life extended for one more snap: Wayne Clements's

PAT attempt was blocked, but he alertly gathered the bounding ball and tossed it to tight end Curtis Thrift for an unscheduled 2-point conversion. Texas held an improbable 15-7 lead at the end of the opening frame.

A shell-shocked Sooner team was shut out during the second period while Clements contributed a pair of field goals, the first from 42 and another from 49, to stake a 21-7 halftime lead. Despite losing Gaddis to a knee injury, Oklahoma would get untracked in the third quarter, starting with quarterback Tink Collins's 41-yard TD pass that put the exclamation point to a nine-play, 83-yard drive to make it 21-14. Late in the quarter, the Sooners faced a fourth-and-1 at the Texas 10. Lance Gunn forced a desperation option pitch to Ike Lewis, who was buried by Anthony Curl.

Oklahoma forced a Texas punt to begin the fourth quarter, setting up J. D. Lasher's 44-yard field goal to draw the Sooners within 21-17. The teams would exchange punts, but safety Jason Belser intercepted Gardere's second-and-nine attempt. It was Gardere's first pick of the afternoon, but the Sooners operated from their own 49. Ted Long fumbled at the end of a 26-yard reverse, but the Sooners recovered at the 25. OU had outgained Texas 222-67 in the second half when they faced another critical fourth-down attempt, this time needing two yards at the Texas three. The Sooners called their final time-out just before Collins went under center and handed off to Lewis. Curl celebrated after stopping Lewis off right guard, but the measurement indicated a fresh set of downs by the very nose of the football. Lewis's one-yard plunge on the next pay gave Oklahoma its first lead of the afternoon, 24-21, with 3:42 left.

Texas had notched just five first downs in the second half when taking over at its own 34. Gardere's first down completion to Jones along the right sideline went for 9. He then went downfield to Walker on a run-and-shoot play, good for 16 more. Gardere went back to Jones on the right sideline, this time for 8. Running back Chris Samuels moved the chains on a 2-yard draw, setting up first-and-10 at the 30 with 2:28 left. It also set up one of the game's biggest plays.

Unblocked strongside linebacker Frank Blevins crashed the middle on a stunt, throwing Gardere for a 10-yard loss. But backup defensive end Corey Mayfield, subbing for the ejected Goode, would hit Gardere late before rolling him across his body, drawing a 15-yard roughing penalty. Clements's 2-point play in the second period meant Texas needed only a field goal to tie but, on second-and-10 from the 25, Gardere went for the jugular. Oklahoma came hard with a corner blitz and Gardere looked to Walker on the hot route. He hit an outstretched Walker, who had a step on safety Charles Franks, at the goal line. Touchdown, Texas!

Gardere had completed all five of his passes on the winning march. Oklahoma reached the Texas 42 but, with no time-outs, the game ended on a Collins sack. Texas fans stormed the field and tore down the goal post in the north end zone following the team's first series win in six years.

The Game of My Life

By Peter Gardere

The funny thing is I'd never attended a Texas-Oklahoma game as a spectator when I was growing up. I came to a couple of games in Austin but that was about it. I had never experienced the Texas-OU game, but I'd always heard about it. Shannon Kelley, who was a Texas quarterback from Houston and kind of my mentor when I got to college, had always told me about it. He said if there was a game to start, it's got to be the OU game. The coaches played crowd noise at the stadium when we practiced that week in Austin. They played the OU fight song in the locker room. When I was a redshirt, I had to play the [OU] quarterback on our scout team. It was Charles Thompson, whom I actually became good friends with. We had certain outfits that we wore. [Defensive tackle] Brian Jones, who redshirted the same year I did, came out to practice wearing the OU helmet. He was the scout team running back. You knew, then, that this was different.

I had only started one game, the Rice game the week before, so the 1989 Oklahoma game was basically my first start. We try to treat every game the same, especially quarterbacks. But every afternoon, from two o'clock on, I had to meet with the press and deal with that before practice. It was such a pain for me. Here I was, starting my first game, and there was so much else going on, and I had to do all these interviews. But there's something about the OU game and the Texas A&M game. Those are the rivalry games.

You go into the game and, all of a sudden, there's the whole atmosphere that you've always heard about: the state fair, the tunnel, the fans divided down the middle of the stadium. Part of what helped me the most is I didn't know what to expect. When you go down that tunnel and all those people are yelling, and the [Oklahoma] RUF/NEKS are shooting off their guns, it's overwhelming. I give a lot of credit to [defensive] coach [Leon] Fuller and Coach Amedee because they were prepared and they knew what to expect. Coach McWilliams's job was to get us fired up and to make us understand that it's not the end of the world if we lose, but that we want to win. That's why he was such a great coach to play for. He knew what it was like to be a player in this game. You knew you could count on him. You know he was always going to be there for you, whether you won or lost.

We had a good team, but had a lot of people who got hurt that season. We had a strong defense, and thank goodness, because it was a struggle the whole game. The defense kept us in every one of those OU games when I played. It's a crazy game. It's one of those games where you never know what's going to happen. It was a defensive struggle, but we had some early success. We clicked in the first half, and then we stalled. We didn't get the things done that we needed to do [in the third quarter]. They probably made some good adjustments defensively. [Laughing] I just don't remember what they were.

It was late in the game. Time was running out, but we still had a chance. Oklahoma obviously didn't want to give up any long plays, and I'm sure their coaches told their defense not to let our receivers get behind them. Our coaches told us to just take what the defense gave us. We hooked up on a couple of short routes and the receivers made some great runs after the catch, which really helped in the last drive down the field.

The play before the [winning] touchdown was actually more important because Oklahoma got flagged for roughing the passer. I had been sacked, but the guy grabbed me and rolled me over again. He probably wasn't expecting me to be just 175 pounds. I was probably a lot lighter than he expected.

We were on the 25-yard line. Here my teammates are looking at a [redshirt] freshman in the eyes and wondering, "Can he do this?" Deep down, I was wondering the same thing.

They had a blitz on. We had built-in hot routes. We called a 'dig' route with two [receivers] on the front side and two on a crossing route. We had a drag route with the tight end and a post route to Johnny [Walker]. Johnny was my blitz route, or my hot route. I saw this guy coming off the end and he had a clear shot at me. He went more towards knocking down the ball than trying to tackle. I threw it up and Johnny made a helluva catch. I didn't put enough air under it so he had to go up and get it.

Coach McWilliams was very relaxed and very laid-back. He treated every game the same and he was very even-keeled. I think Gary Gibbs was more of a John Mackovic type, where he feels the pressure and he wears it on his sleeve. Gibbs was the Oklahoma coach for six years, and I beat them four years in a row. I was responsible for him getting fired, or at least a big part of it.

Upon Further Review

The Texas-Oklahoma rivalry is a historically cyclical series; each team takes turns whipping the other for an extended period of time. The 1989 upset ended Texas's 0-4-1 skid against the Sooners while launching an 8-2-1 upswing in the Longhorns' favor. Gardere would direct half of those wins and become the only Texas quarterback to go 4-0 against Oklahoma.

Incredibly, Gardere's second win against Oklahoma in 1990 was a virtual carbon copy of the first. Once again, Sooner safety Charles Franks surrendered the game-winning touchdown pass in the final 2 minutes—against the same route, no less. This time the completion went to Keith Cash to upset No. 14 Oklahoma, 14-13. It was part of undefeated Southwest Conference campaign that fed off of the 17-13 season-opening win at No. 21 Penn State and included an emotional 45-24 shellacking of a No. 3 Houston team that had bullied the Horns for three straight years. Texas claimed the league title with a 23-13 win at No. 25 Baylor before holding on against No. 17 Texas A&M, 28-27. The No. 3 Horns had an outside shot at the national championship but were blindsided by No. 4 Miami, 46-3, in the Cotton Bowl.

Eight Longhorns were selected in the 1991 NFL Draft.

"We lost a lot of talent and we didn't have a lot of experience my senior year. We had a new offensive line; we had new receivers and a new secondary. You can go on and on. Nothing beats experience."

As such, Texas got beat more in 1991 than boosters could stomach. The Horns got past No. 6 Oklahoma on Bubba Jacques' late fumble return for a touchdown, but the young and injury-riddled team fell to 5-6. Just one year removed from an outright conference title, McWilliams's tenure ended with his third losing season in four years. Gardere would play for his third offensive coordinator when Texas hired Illinois head coach John Mackovic.

"The personalities between McWilliams and Mackovic were so different," Gardere said. "McWilliams was very even-keeled while Mackovic was very intense. Mackovic wasn't a players' coach. He had a great offense, but going from McWilliams to Mackovic was like oil and water."

Mackovic conducted interviews and outlined his expectations with individual players during spring training.

"He told me he didn't care that I was a three-year starter," Gardere said. "He said I was going to have to earn my position every day in practice. It was an added pressure. Every practice, we charted every pass that we threw, even if it was against air. I was tight every practice, but I always ended up being the starter."

Gardere's senior year ended with a 6-5 mark, highlighted by a 34-24 win against No. 16 Oklahoma. His collegiate days behind him, Gardere knew that any shot he had in the NFL would be as a punter. He initially signed as a free agent with Seattle.

"I was out of my league," Gardere recalled. "I hadn't kicked in five years. I never kicked in college. If I had one regret, that may be it. So there I was in Seattle, entering training camp. I'm a punter, so I didn't get to practice with the whole team but maybe 15 minutes a day. Most of the time I was snapping to the quarterback. They made the kickers and punters snap it, too. It was a demoralizing experience to go from taking 'em to giving 'em, to go from being a quarterback to having a quarterback with his hands under my butt."

Following his release, Gardere spent three seasons playing for two different teams in the Canadian Football League. It was while playing for the Sacramento Gold Miners that, ironically, Gardere was teamed with Charles Franks, the very Oklahoma DB he had burned in consecutive seasons with game-winning passes.

"I'd always give Charles a hard time," Gardere smiled. "I'd say, 'Why couldn't you cover us? You knew it was coming.' We knew that was a play people would remember. But then he and I would watch the Texas-OU together on TV."

Gardere eventually auditioned for the New Orleans Saints but "knew it was time to hang it up" after his father died of cancer. He returned to Houston to ease his mother through the loss before finding his way back to Austin.

"It was pretty easy for me to let go of football," concluded Gardere, currently employed by an Austin residential and commercial real estate development company. "I knew I wasn't the typical quarterback that anybody was looking for. I wasn't tall enough, I wasn't big enough, and my arm strength wasn't as good. You have to be in touch with reality and know that when it's your time . . . it's your time."

And knowing, of course, that part of his time was "great."

Chapter Thirteen

BRIAN JONES

Linebacker (1989-90)

By the late 1980s, the Southwest Conference had planted the seeds of its own destruction. Rampant cheating by member schools, culminating in SMU's receipt of the only death penalty ever meted out by the NCAA in 1987, gave the conference an outlaw reputation. Out of nine SWC schools, only Baylor, Rice, and Arkansas escaped NCAA probation during the '80s. Water-cooler stories of cash payments, car purchases, and out-of-control boosters overshadowed talk of who would start at tailback or replace that shut-down corner who had gone to the NFL. As the conference rap sheet lengthened, the list of top prep athletes who bolted the state of Texas to play their college football lengthened with it.

One of the players who left was a blue-chip linebacker from Lubbock who had bled Texas orange since he was a kid. Linebacker Brian Jones came out of Dunbar High School in 1986 heavily recruited, but the plan all along was to sign with Texas, just like another Lubbock native and one of his heroes, Jerry Gray, had done six years earlier.

"Coming out of high school, Texas recruited me and I'd been to Austin," recalled Jones. "I was in Boys State and stayed on campus so I'd seen the campus and met with the coaches, so it wasn't imperative that I take a recruiting visit. I knew I was coming [to Austin]. I had always wanted to be a Longhorn. I had watched Jerry Gray make spectacular plays against Auburn two years in a row, one where he goes up and snatches an interception and the other he runs down Bo Jackson and messes him up, so I was thinking, 'I'm comin' baby!' But then SMU got the death penalty, then A&M goes on probation, then TCU, Texas is being investigated, so it was crazy at that time. The Southwest Conference was in disarray."

Jones visited Notre Dame as well as Iowa, the state where he was born. He was recruited by Vince Dooley and flew from Atlanta to Athens in a helicopter on his recruiting visit to Georgia. TCU's Jim Wacker made a home visit and nearly frightened Jones into signing up with the Frogs. "Coach Wacker was so excitable," said Jones, laughing. "He came in banging on the furniture and I was like, 'Where do I sign, coach!' He was hilarious, but he was great."

Jones also got pitched by Terry Donahue of UCLA, and got starstruck on his visit to Tinseltown. "I went to UCLA and that was like a whole 'nother world," Jones said. "I still remember my trip to Los Angeles; it was December the 6th, 1985. It was cold and windy when I left Lubbock, but it was sunny and 70 as soon as I landed. The linebackers coach picked me up and we took a tour of Beverly Hills, went by the *Beverly Hillbillies* mansion where they filmed that—the whole thing was like a fairy tale. That night I went to a Prince concert, then a basketball game at Pauley Pavilion Saturday night. And UCLA was hot at that time; they'd been to the Rose Bowl and they spent a lot of time recruiting me. They were always in Lubbock at my basketball games or whatever—it was flattering."

Flattering enough that Jones signed with the Bruins in 1986. After playing as a true freshman, Jones had back surgery and only played three games as a sophomore. He began to think about returning to Texas.

"I loved LA," said Jones. "You couldn't beat the social life. I had friends, people were nice, and I played as a freshman and made freshman All-American, but I always wanted to be a Longhorn. The coaches knew it and Coach Donahue tried to do everything to keep me there, but I always wanted to be a Texas Longhorn, even though we were getting our butts kicked back then. I would watch the UT games even when I was at UCLA. So that spring my sophomore year I decided to transfer. And it was funny because coach McWilliams had recruited me in high school for Texas, then he got the Texas Tech job, and by the time I transferred he was back! So I enrolled at Texas for the fall of 1988."

When he arrived in Austin, Jones sat down with head coach David McWilliams, who had an important question for his new arrival. "Coach McWilliams asked me, 'What number do you want?'" related Jones. "I said, '60'. It was braggadocio at that time. My mouth thought I was better than I was, so I said, 'Gimme 60, coach, why not? I'll be the first black to wear number 60.'" Look, when I grew

Brian Jones directs the defense against Houston, 1990 (Photo courtesy of the University of Texas)

up, my week began and ended with Texas football, the Longhorns and the Cowboys. So when the Longhorns lost I was crying.

"But I knew the history of the number 60. I didn't think I was worthy of it, but it meant a lot to me and I had a lot of pride. When I asked for that number, I sensed some hesitance on the part of coach McWilliams, but he was fine with it. He had recruited me, so he knew me. I was a blue-chip athlete coming out of Lubbock Dunbar and was a freshman all-American at UCLA, so he was comfortable giving me the number. But especially my junior year, I didn't come close to living up to it. And Mr. [Johnny] Treadwell was always coming by practice, so wearing that number and then seeing the guy who started it, that was some pressure!"

When he arrived, the Longhorns had just come off a pretty good season in 1987, going 7-5, including a win over Pittsburgh in the Bluebonnet Bowl. But that '87 campaign was bookended by losing seasons in 1986 and 1988, something almost unthinkable in Austin. When he arrived, Jones didn't much like what he saw.

"When I got there, we started to hold people accountable," he asserted. "We had a saying in West Texas: there are guys who are 'riders and eaters.' You ride the Greyhound bus to the game and eat the chicken fried steak afterwards, and that's all you do—you don't produce and you're not an asset to the team. And when I got to Texas, we had a whole bunch of riders and eaters. I don't take credit for turning the team around. I was a good athlete, but I'm not saying I was better than the guys there. Texas had good athletes; they just weren't producing."

Jones sat out his first year at Texas in 1988, but made his presence felt fast with his play, and more importantly his attitude, on the practice field.

"My first year at Texas I sat out and I ran scout team and I was killing guys," recalled Jones. "I talked smack and they hated me. But that's how I play football; that's fun to me. It's nothing personal; I just like to talk noise. But we had a bunch of guys that really didn't belong, and they thought we were going to win just because we had 'Texas' on the front of our jerseys, which was bull. And I had been around first-class athletes at UCLA, and not just people who played for the Bruins, but people who trained there across the athletic spectrum. You had superstars like Jackie Joyner-Kersee, FloJo trained there, Magic Johnson played pickup games at Pauley Pavilion, so I'm seeing all these cats, and then when I get to Texas, we got DBs who are fatter than me! These guys had *guts*; you gotta be kidding me! And then *I* proceeded to get fat! So we had a lot of riders and eaters and we had to weed those guys out. So yes, we had fights, but it takes that sometimes. You gotta hold each other accountable. I love that sign they have in the UT weight room—THE PRIDE AND TRADITION OF THE UNIVERSITY OF TEXAS WILL NOT BE ENTRUSTED TO THE WEAK OR TIMID—that's right!"

The Horns went 4-7 in 1988 and followed that dismal season with another one in 1989, as Texas went 5-6 with Jones starting at middle linebacker. But that '89 season gave Texas's fans hope, as the team beat Oklahoma for the first time in six seasons and followed that up with a win over 5-0 Arkansas at Fayetteville. The team narrowly lost to Penn State at home 16-12, on a blocked punt in the fourth quarter. More importantly, a nucleus of great players that would form the core of the team was taking shape, a core of players with talent and heart who would stage a dramatic turnaround in 1990.

That 1990 season saw Texas open on the road at State College, Pennsylvania, taking on Joe Paterno and Penn State before 85,973 screaming fans in Beaver Stadium. The Horns carried a ranking of No. 23 into the game, but expectations among the fans and media weren't high against the No. 21 Nittany Lions. In a grinding, physical football game, the Horns overcame a Penn State touchdown on the game's first possession, and held on for a 17-13 victory. The "Shock the Nation Tour" had begun.

"Penn State in '90 was one of my favorite games," said Jones, "because they ran the opening kickoff back to our 1-yard line, and their first play is an ISO, so I hit Sam Gash who played in the NFL a long, long time, and I get a stinger and my whole left side goes numb! But you got to stay out there, man. You can't go to the sideline. Luckily, I had gotten my first stinger when I was ten years old in Pee Wee football, so I was used to the sensation!

"So they take the opening kickoff to our 1 and I get a stinger on the first play, and then on third down they score, but even then, we weren't demoralized. We knew we had 'em; we knew we could play with these guys. We were just such a totally different team in 1990. The off-season program we'd gone through was phenomenal and we went up there with a lot of confidence.

"That game was big-time college football. The weather was gorgeous; it was a physical game because it was Penn State—that was three yards and a cloud of dust. The crowd was loud, it was packed. It was Penn State football, it was big time, baby! They had barely beaten us the year before in Austin when they had Blair Thomas, who was a No. 1 pick at running back, and when we went up there they had Leroy Thompson who was drafted by the Pittsburgh Steelers, so they were still a good football team. But we just outphysicaled 'em. We just went toe to toe with them and made some big stops. They went for it once on fourth down and inches, and we stopped them. It was just a hard-hitting football game. It was fun! Then after the game, they gave Keith Cash the credit for my slogan—'Shock the Nation!' Let's get this corrected! I'm a huge Muhammad Ali fan—'I shocked the world!' So I had been saying that all preseason, quoting Ali, and Cash was on the floor with me in the dorm, and he ended up getting credit for it!"

Texas lost a heartbreaker to eventual national co-champs Colorado at home the next game, 29-22, after leading 19-14 entering the fourth quarter. The Horns would then reel off victories against Rice, Oklahoma, Arkansas, SMU, and Texas Tech, climbing to No. 14 in the national rankings. Next up would be a Saturday-night showdown with the hottest team in America, the third-ranked Houston Cougars and their gun-slinging quarterback, David Klingler.

No. 14 TEXAS vs. No. 3 HOUSTON

November 10, 1990
Austin, Texas

In this day and age of run-of the-mill, run-and-shoot offenses, it is almost hard to imagine how revolutionary, and unstoppable, the Houston offenses of the late '80s and early '90s were. Andre Ware had won the Heisman Trophy in 1989, and the Cougars had throttled Texas by the scores of 60-40, 66-15, and 47-9 respectively the three previous seasons. In 1990, Houston entered the game with Texas with an 8-0 record, and had put up 162 combined points in the three previous games against SMU, Arkansas, and TCU.

But when the Cougars arrived at Memorial Stadium that night for the nationally televised tilt with Texas, they found the stadium crackling with electricity. Most players and fans who were there that night claim it is the loudest they have heard the famous old stadium to this day. With their frenzied crowd behind them, the Horns destroyed Houston and its aura of unstoppability behind a punishing, physical rushing game, the accurate passing of quarterback Peter Gardere, and a blitzing, bone-crushing defense that time and again pounded Klingler into the turf. Texas led the game 45-10 well into the fourth quarter, before a couple of late, face-saving touchdowns by the Cougars made the final margin a deceptive 45-24.

The Game of My Life

By Brian Jones

I remember before the Houston game, Eric Metcalf, who was in the league at that time with Cleveland, and Tim McCray, a former tight end who had hurt his neck, were reading me the riot act, cussing me out, saying, "Boy, you guys better not get embarrassed out there you sorry so-and-so," because Houston had been kickin' our tails the last few years, and they were No. 3 in the nation at that time. We were saying, "Don't worry, we got it, we got it," but I remember that like it was yesterday, walking out for warm-ups and having Eric and Tim just giving it to me!

What I loved about that whole week before the game was Coach Leon Fuller saying, "We're not changing anything." Because what would happen when you played the run and shoot, pretty much everyone would junk what they traditionally do, their base defense, and put in more DBs. We said to hell with that, we're gonna do what we do best. We're gonna go out there and we're gonna play man defense. We may substitute an extra DB now and then, but we're not gonna have six or seven DBs out there. He moved me around. I was in the middle, I was on the outside, and my main function the whole game was to stick with that little bowling ball, Chuck Weatherspoon. That was it. Wherever he went, I went with him. That was the game plan right there —we were gonna play man. And I blitzed a ton in that game. But I loved the confidence we got from Coach Fuller. Because that means a lot. It starts at the top. He said we're not going to change anything, we're going to go out there and do what we do best, so for all of that week, the confidence was there.

We knew what Houston was capable of doing—they had kicked our rears the year before and it was like a track meet; I couldn't even breathe I was so out of breath in that game. And the year before that it was 60-40, so we knew what was coming. But defensively, we just had that confidence, thinking, "Hey, we're not scared of you, we're going to play man defense." And the funny thing was, everyone adopted our strategy after that game about how to beat them. No one was throwing six or seven DBs out there anymore. But we had really good athletes, and coach believed in us, and that's what you want—someone that believes in you. And Coach Fuller and Coach McWilliams believed in us and they said, "We're going to do what we do best." We had a great secondary and we had the boys up front to put pressure on them. James Patton, Tommy Jeter, Shane Dronett, and Oscar Giles—every one of those guys played in the NFL. Our secondary was great with Lance Gunn and

Stanley Richard, and Mark Berry and Grady Cavness at the corners, and Anthony Curl, and Boone Powell at linebacker with me.

I remember getting on the sideline and it was the loudest I had ever heard that stadium. It was in the second quarter and we had just gotten a turnover and I was sitting over there with Stanley, and I said, "Man, we are going to whip their butts." We knew early! I knew before the game, actually. You gotta visualize it before it happens—I'm big on that—and I knew before the game we were going to win. All that week leading up to the game, we were saying, "We're not going to change anything, this is what we're going to do, and we got this down!"

Houston was solid on defense, but our boys on offense, Peter Gardere and the Cash brothers and Butch Hadnot, they really got it going. But the bottom line was we were tired of getting our asses kicked. I say it on my TV show all of the time, but at some point, as a man, you get tired of getting beat on. It's like with the bully at school—at some point, you have to stand up for yourself and say, "I'm not going to take this anymore." It was the same thing with A&M later on that year, and it was the same thing with Houston.

I was talking to Klingler the whole game! Always! You gotta talk noise! "It's going to be like this all day, baby!" You gotta talk trash. He'd just look the other way or smile or something.

But what stands out the most is just the game plan. We had a saying when I was at Texas: — "Real men play 'man'—man-to-man defense." We had that saying and that belief and we took pride in that. Our defensive backs took pride in that. We had come in that Sunday or Monday before the game and we were thinking we were going to have to junk everything and throw some elaborate defense at them, like we had tried against them the previous years. But the key was to put pressure on them and we were able to with the guys up front and moving me around. The same as with the spread offenses today—you've got to be able to put pressure on the quarterback with your four down linemen. If you can manhandle them up front, you've got a good chance of winning.

Upon Further Review

Following the rout of Houston, Texas knocked off TCU and Baylor to clinch its first Southwest Conference championship since 1983, but it still had one more score to settle, this one against the hated Texas A&M Aggies, winners of six straight against the Horns.

Texas fell behind 14-0 early and looked ready to fold again, but Peter Gardere's 50-yard run from scrimmage and his 7-yard pass to Keith Cash tied the score at 14 going into halftime. In the second half, the teams traded touchdowns, the final one coming by the Aggies with just a couple of minutes remaining. Rather than play for the tie, A&M elected to go for two. Crashing up the middle from his linebacker spot, Jones forced Aggie quarterback Bucky Richardson to toss the ball deep to his right to running back Darren Lewis. Texas corner Mark Berry flew to the ball, spilling Lewis far short of the goal line. The Horns would march the ball all the way to the Aggie 2-yard line before the clock expired, giving them a 28-27 win and a final 10-1 regular season record. More importantly, they'd kept their hopes alive for a realistic shot at a national championship with a win in the Cotton Bowl on January 1.

"What really stands out about the A&M game," said Jones, "was that they had just scored a touchdown and we were up 28-27, and they were going for two. And we go to the sidelines and Coach Fuller says, 'What do y'all want to run?' Here we are, a minute left in the game, they had just scored, he's making the big bucks, and he's asking us what we want to run! But that's how he was, and I loved that. He would always take your input. So I said, 'Let's run a mad dog blitz'—that was our number one blitz; that was me up the middle, and he said, 'OK, go do it,' just as calm as that. That was him, man, that was Coach Fuller, and I loved that. He was excellent. He made me such a much better football player in one off-season. So he said go run it, and I blitzed and forced Bucky Richardson to pitch early, and Mark Berry made the tackle and stopped them short."

Texas faced a Miami team in the 1991 Cotton Bowl that did not want to be there, and it showed. Fueled by bad blood that had been brewing since an altercation earlier in the week involving Texas's giant offensive lineman Stan Thomas, the Hurricanes came in angry. They taunted the Texas players as they came down the Cotton Bowl's famed tunnel, and proceeded to knock out the Horns return man, Chris Samuels, on the game's first play. Things got worse from there, as the Hurricanes routed Texas in a game that to this day stands as one of the worst moments in Texas's proud football history. Miami played with reckless abandon, embarrassing a very good Texas football team, 46-3. The Texas offense, dominated up front by the 'Cane front four led by Russell Maryland, did virtually nothing all day. By game's end, the Hurricanes had almost as many penalty yards, 202, as the Horns did in total offense, 205. The "Shock the Nation Tour" had come to a truly shocking end.

The loss toppled Texas, which had entered the game ranked No. 3, all the way to a final ranking of twelfth in the AP poll.

In looking back at the Miami fiasco, Jones doesn't think the problem was a lack of preparation. "We had so much fun in Dallas," recalled Jones of the pregame festivities. "But we practiced hard, the preparation was great, and we had some of the best practices we had all year. And then—sometimes you get out there and things just don't click. I thought defensively we played OK. I've gone back and watched the tape of that game at least ten times, as painful as it is, and defensively, I thought we did all right. But you can't keep your defense on the field the whole game. They had a lot of talent as Miami always does, but, we could play with them, and what I hate about that and what I regret is that huge opportunity we lost, because even though Colorado beat us that year, we would have been in the hunt for a national championship had we won.

"So the preparation wasn't a problem; we prepared and practiced hard and I felt confident going into that game that we could play with them. Looking back, though, when we came out of the tunnel and they were waiting on us and started talking all of that trash, I wish we'd have started a fight. That would've really helped us, I think. Looking back on it, maybe that would have gotten the guys fired up. But I was fired up and I thought the rest of the team was, too. But we were not intimidated at all taking the field—we were a good football team, we were confident, we had traveled to the Northeast and won, we had beaten all of the people who had beaten us in the past, so we thought we could play with them. And we kept holding them to field goals. But you can't keep your defense out there. But I was cool with the preparation; I didn't think anyone was afraid of them, I certainly wasn't, but you look at the turnovers—eventually you run out of gas . . . "

The Miami game was the last of Brian Jones's career at the University of Texas, but his football career was far from over. The Los Angeles Raiders took Jones in the eighth round of the 1991 NFL Draft, and he played eight years in the NFL, including stints with the Indianapolis Colts, the Miami Dolphins, the Raiders and the New Orleans Saints.

Following his football career, Jones returned to the Texas campus, and in the spring of 2000, he received his degree in corporate communications. He has put it to good use, working various jobs in the Austin media, including several years as the Longhorn Sports Network's sideline reporter for Longhorn football games and the host of *Longhorn SportsCenter* with Mack Brown and Rick Barnes. More recently, Jones has worked for CBS Sports Network's *Inside College Football* as a college football analyst.

Among Longhorn fans, Jones will most likely be remembered as a key part of the Texas team that did shock the nation in 1990, and for now, as the last Texas linebacker to have worn the famous number 60 for the duration of his career. "I thanked coach McWilliams for having the confidence in me to give me that number," Jones said, "but he knew I loved Texas. I always had and I always will. But I really wasn't thinking so much in terms of being a trailblazer, because I was the first black ball player to wear number 60—I just wanted to go out and win because it was *Texas*—the Burnt Orange, baby! I just loved it!"

Chapter Fourteen

JAMES BROWN

Quarterback (1994-97)

If James Brown had been standing anywhere else along the Texas sideline on October 1, 1994, his Longhorn legacy may never have been established.

On that sun-splashed afternoon, No. 16 Texas was in a down-to-the-wire contest against No. 4 Colorado. Midway through one of the most eagerly anticipated home games in recent memory, a hush fell upon Austin's sold-out Memorial Stadium. Starting quarterback Shea Morenz lay on the turf, clutching his knee. The San Angelo product was Texas's prize recruit after coach John Mackovic was hired in December, 1991 to restore the once-proud program. Following 6-5 and 5-5-1 campaigns, the Longhorn faithful ached for revival. Many had anointed Morenz, generally considered 1992's top national prep quarterback, as the program's savior. Now, those hopes were being assisted to the sideline. Mackovic immediately turned and searched for the nearest available quarterback.

There stood redshirt freshman James Brown.

The Beaumont product enjoyed a noteworthy high school career but, like backup John Dutton, remained in Morenz's shadow. Almost as formidable was the program's lingering shadow as one that was slow to start African-American quarterbacks. The issue resurfaced when, fourteen years after Donnie Little became Texas's first black quarterback, rival schools told Brown told that his chances of starting in Austin were slim.

"People told me it was a racist school that wouldn't have a black quarterback," Brown recalled. "I knew that wasn't true. I knew that I was going to be quarterback at Texas."

He just did not know how happenstance his first collegiate start would be. The extent of Morenz's injury, that afternoon, was unknown. All Mackovic knew was that a nationally televised game was on the line and the clock was ticking. Mackovic still needed a signature win at Texas against a highly ranked opponent. For now, he just needed a quarterback.

"I was just the closest person to Coach Mackovic against Colorado because I was the guy with the clipboard," Brown said. "The other quarterback, John Dutton, was somewhere else. He was on the headset talking to the coach upstairs. I had always thought John and I were equal on the depth chart. Neither one of us had any game experience. I guess no one ever thought Shea would get hurt. He was this All-American guy. I just happened to be close to the coach at that one time. Coach Mackovic grabbed me and said, 'Get in!' I ran my fake and handed the ball off well. I came back to the sideline and Mackovic said, 'You did good.' It was just one play, but I think that made me the second-string quarterback in his mind at just that moment."

It was also the moment that one of the most remarkable careers in Texas football history was launched. By the time he was done, Brown would guide Texas to three straight conference titles and rewrite school record books for passing offense. For the moment, he was still the backup—but with an asterisk. Everything that week hinged on Morenz's knee. Texas would drop a heartbreaker that day to Colorado, 34-31, on a last-second field goal. However, the Horns had little time to lick their wounds. The annual border war with archrival Oklahoma was just days away.

History dictated that Brown would view the tilt between the nationally ranked programs as a highly partisan bystander. Only one player in the storied archives of Texas football [Andy White, 1966] had debuted as a starter against Oklahoma. The 18-9 Longhorn loss that year meant that no Texas player had ever beaten the Sooners when debuting in the Red River rivalry.

Until now.

No. 15 TEXAS vs. No. 16 OKLAHOMA

October 8, 1994

Cotton Bowl—Dallas, Texas

Offensive coordinator Gene Dahlquist modified the Oklahoma game plan just in case Morenz was unable to play. Early on, Dahlquist called for a number of short passes intended to boost Brown's comfort level. Brown's first completion went to FB Juan Kemp in the left flat for a 4-yard gain.

The Horns' dynamic James Brown scrambles for yardage, 1995

Oklahoma drew first blood, however, scoring early in the second quarter on Jerald Moore's 23-yard run. Brown threw an early interception, but was otherwise coolly efficient to finish the first half 11-of-13 for 85 yards. Yet four Texas drives would stall in Sooner territory. Oklahoma threatened just before halftime, driving 72 yards to the Longhorn 26. That's when cornerback Bryant Westbrook intercepted QB Garrick McGee. The turnover was the game's turning point, Mackovic later recalled, because another Oklahoma score just before intermission would have changed the complexion of what remained a 7-0 toss-up.

The Horns opened the second half with an 80-yard drive, resulting in Phil Dawson's 19-yard field goal. After Texas forced a punt, Brown led the team on a 15-play drive deep into Sooner territory. On-second-and-goal from the 9, Brown dropped back to pass. He looked left before scrambling through a gaping hole on the right side of the line. He vaulted over a Sooner defender and dashed into the end zone, giving Texas its first lead with 17 seconds remaining in the third quarter.

Oklahoma tried to regain the momentum with trickery on its next possession, but Westbrook intercepted a halfback pass. His 27-yard return set Texas up at the Oklahoma 6. Brown connected with TE Pat Fitzgerald from 2 yards out on a play-action pass to extend the Longhorn lead to 17-7 with 13:05 left in the contest.

The final book on Brown's debut game stood at 17-of-22 passing for 148 yards and one touchdown, while adding 51 rushing yards and another touchdown on the ground. Yet, for all of his offensive wizardry, the 1994 Texas-Oklahoma game lives in Longhorn lore because it came down to one of the most crucial goal line stands in program history. Texas led 17-10 with 43 seconds remaining, but Oklahoma faced fourth-and-goal at the Longhorn three. The Sooners ran a "slip draw" misdirection play. Working under center, McGee appeared to run an "option right" but then handed back to RB James Allen. For a second, Allen appeared to have a clear path into the end zone. But NG Stonie Clark had seen the handoff when a gap momentarily opened between two offensive linemen. Linebacker Robert Reed turned the play inside, redirecting Allen toward a collision with the 343-pound Clark. The two met just outside the goal line.

Clark won.

Allen fell to the turf, just one foot shy of pay dirt. The game-saving tackle, forever known as "The Stop" among Longhorn fans, became *Sports Illustrated*'s choice as college football's Defensive Play of 1994.

The Game of My Life

By James Brown

During the [Oklahoma] pregame, we all thought Shea was going to play. He was on the bicycle trying to get warm, even though he didn't practice all week. I thought they were just saving him. Throughout the week, I never thought I would start the Oklahoma game. But, on game day, Shea didn't go out for pregame warm-ups. He went in for a little extra treatment. The rest of the team went out for warm-ups. We came back in and did our team prayer. After the prayer, Coach Mackovic said, "By the way, fellows, James will start today." A couple of guys were like, "Yeah, yeah! That's what you want. Let's go."

I didn't have time to get nervous. I didn't have time to have any bad thoughts. Since I was a freshman at the time, I hadn't learned about the mystique of the game. And that probably helped in that game. I didn't have time to think. I just went out with the knowledge that I had and played the best that I could with the short notice that I had up to that point.

I think the coaches might have told Shea a little bit sooner that he couldn't go. After that, they came and talked to the team. I wasn't expecting it at all. Maybe that's what made me good that day. I just went out and ran the plays the best I knew how. We kept it simple, but I think that's good football when you run simple plays. I was a cocky guy, really. I think all football players are cocky, but a team usually adheres to its coach's personality. All the guys on the team wanted to be cocky. A lot of guys liked my winning attitude. We just wanted to play and have fun.

I threw an interception early. It was against a Cover-Two defense, and I got lazy. I don't like throwing interceptions. After that first interception, I said to myself, "Okay. That was a stupid read. I saw the Cover-Two. I'm better than this. I don't have to throw an interception to these guys." After that first interception, [wide receivers] coach Cleve Bryant called me over and said, "Calm down, James. You're better than that. You saw the Cover-Two. Why did you throw it?" I said, "I just wanted to throw a deep pass." I learned a lot that game.

After that mistake, I had a good game. I settled down. I just took what they gave me. I threw a touchdown and ran for a touchdown. We had a lot of third-down conversions that game. It was my main goal to focus on third downs. I threw a lot of balls to the flats. When I couldn't find a receiver, I took off and ran. I'd rather get five yards running than throw an incomplete pass or an interception.

I wasn't the All-American [high school QB] in the huddle; I was the redshirt freshman. So, I said, "Guys, help me out." Chad Lucas was our fullback and he was a big help to me. During the Oklahoma game, a lot of the reason I was so good was because Chad would tell me where the blitz was coming from. I was a freshman who had never played, and I didn't get sacked that game. I had Chad back there talking to me.

I think my solid play that day got everybody involved. Everybody wanted to have some swagger. When you think about it, everybody who plays for the University of Texas was probably the best at his position in the state of Texas. Then they got to college, and it was like they got their drive taken away to fit in [Mackovic's] system. I think I gave that drive, or swagger, back to all the players. Even [Blake] Brockermeyer said, "I'm glad you're playing. I like it when you're in the huddle."

The game came down to [Oklahoma's] final drive. They had fourth-and-goal from our three. I was on the sideline thinking, "Man, it would be nice if we win this game. I started the game, so it would be nice to win it. But it's not in my hands." They [OU] called time-out and ran this trick play. For a second, it looked like Oklahoma was going to score. But our nose guard Stonie Clark made the stop. After we won, I was excited. I mean, I was! It was a nationally televised game. ABC Sports came up afterwards and interviewed me on the field. I knew my family and everybody back at home was watching.

It was just a blessing and a great catapult for my career. It was just a blessing. It was just a whirlwind. I had a chance to start, and we had lost to Oklahoma the year before. No one thought we would win. All the fans got behind me. The Oklahoma game is *the game* to win at the University of Texas. I'm thankful that I was in a position to be able to start in that arena. With that being my first college game, I didn't have to look up to anything. It was the pinnacle. The media here made it seem like it was the biggest feat in the world. After that Oklahoma game, I had the confidence to win every game.

Upon Further Review

Texas's surprising win vaulted the team into the Top 10 in the coaches' poll with a visit to Rice on the horizon. It had been twenty-nine years since the Longhorns dropped a contest to the Owls, but the announcement that Morenz would return to the starting lineup was met with mixed reactions.

"I read a few of the newspapers after the Oklahoma game," Brown said. "I knew the fans wanted me to play. Personally, I didn't care if I got the start against

Rice. I was still in a whirlwind. But, naturally, I wanted to play. I came to Texas to play."

The game was waged on a Sunday night in a monsoon, but paled in comparison to the storm that hit Mackovic's program following the stunning 19-17 loss to the Owls.

"Naturally, fans were upset," Brown said. "They asked, 'Why didn't you put James Brown in?' Mackovic didn't like other people running his program."

Brown and Morenz began to split time, but the Horns would drop two of their next three games in blowout fashion. Mackovic's career mark at Texas stood at 16-14-1, and the Longhorn fan base was howling. By late-1994, it was apparent that Morenz was not completely healthy. Mackovic handed the offense to Brown for the final home game of the season, resulting in a 48-13 thumping of Houston.

"Mackovic would run different plays for me than he ran for Shea," Brown recalled. "He would run easier plays for me. We had a play where I'd run a half-roll: I'd either roll right or roll left about half way. I either threw an 'out route', or I'd pump the 'out' and throw it long. I'd have a backside guy running a postcurl. It's a simple route. I think the 'out route' is the best route in football because it's a timing route. I'd throw the ball before my receiver even breaks, and the DB just doesn't know. I was pretty good on that route. If the DB breaks on that route, I'd throw the out-and-go. I threw three or four touchdowns on that route against Baylor. By the eighth game of the season, I was the starting quarterback. We beat Baylor, 63-35, won a share of the Southwest Conference championship and ended up going to the Sun Bowl."

The 35-31 comeback against Mack Brown's North Carolina team resulted in a No. 18 final finish in the AP poll for Texas. Morenz would trade in his cleats for a baseball career, and was drafted into the New York Yankees farm system. Brown would return for the 1995 swan song of the Southwest Conference.

"If Shea had stayed, I think I would have been a better quarterback," Brown concedes. "I didn't have any competition. I actually think I got worse as my career went on rather than getting better."

Even if Brown regressed, Texas would capture the final SWC title in 1995 under his watch. He would then lead Texas to the inaugural Big 12 Conference championship the following season with a stunning 37-27 win over Nebraska in the Big 12 Championship Game. Brown would earn Honorable Mention All-Big 12 honors that season but completed his eligibility following an injury-riddled 4-7 campaign in 1997. Mackovic was reassigned even as Brown finished his career as the leading passer in program history with 7,638 yards. It is a mark surpassed only by Major Applewhite and Colt McCoy following Brown's tenure.

Ironically, Brown followed offensive coordinator Gene Dahlquist to Scotland and signed with the former NFL Europe.

"Learning [Mackovic's] system helped me throughout my professional career because it was a pro-style offense," Brown said. "I knew all the terminology and all the reads."

Still, Brown remained a backup under Dahlquist. Brown was traded to Frankfurt where, as a starter, he guided the Galaxy to a World Bowl Championship.

Brown became the running backs coach at Lamar University when the school revived its football program in 2011.

Chapter Fifteen

DAN NEIL

Offensive Lineman (1993-96)

Dan Neil made first-team on the *Dave Campbell's Texas Football* 1991 Super Team as a blue-chip offensive lineman. Once at Texas, he earned all-conference and All-American honors in 1995 and 1996, and went on to play for two Super Bowl champions his first two seasons in the NFL. But his head coach at Texas had to be convinced to offer him a scholarship.

"The year before I came to Texas they recruited five offensive linemen," explained Neil, "the famed 'Class of Beef,' so I was the only lineman they recruited. I found out later that coach John Mackovic came in and saw I was the only lineman on their board so he said, 'OK, let's take this Neil guy.' But after he visited me at my house, he wasn't too keen on me because he thought I was too small. But as it transpired, when I committed to Texas, they only had two or three verbal commitments and then after I committed, not because of me but because of the timing, all of these other guys committed, like Shea Morenz, Lovell Pinkney, and Mike Adams, and it turned into a pretty good class. But I just decided I wanted to go to Texas because that's where I was happiest and fit in and because it was close to home and my family could come see me play. But it kind of took some convincing for Mackovic to take me."

It didn't take much convincing for Mackovic to get Neil on the field once he arrived. After redshirting in 1992, Neil started at guard for Texas from 1993 through 1996, and played on three straight conference championship teams, including the last-ever Southwest Conference champions and the first-ever in the Big 12.

But despite the championships, Neil's coach at Texas, John Mackovic, became a lightning rod for controversy and criticism. Mackovic coached five seasons at Texas, and bookended the championship seasons with campaigns that saw the team finish 5-5-1 in 1993 and 4-7 in 1997, after which he was fired. The conventional wisdom held that Mackovic cared only about offense, and that he wasn't much concerned with the defensive side of the ball. Dan Neil thinks that criticism is unfair.

"I don't think it's fair to any coach to sit there and say that they recruit offense only," said Neil. "Now I think every coach has their baby, be it offense or defense, but every coach also understands that you have to play well on both sides of the ball. Mackovic was an offensive guy, so he did focus more on offense than he did on defense, but he knew how important defense was. But I think maybe that translated through the recruiting process to the recruits, that 'they don't play defense at Texas,' which wasn't true, but they hear that and sometimes I think guys backed off because of it."

Still, to go along with the offensive firepower that saw guys like Ricky Williams, James Brown and Priest Holmes come to Texas, the Mackovic era also produced some of the best defensive players in Longhorn history. "We had great defensive talent at that time," asserted Neil. "We had Bryant Westbrook, Chris Carter, Tre Thomas, we had Casey Hampton, we had Tony Brackens, so we had players on that side of the ball, too. The truth is, 1983 was the highest number of draft picks ever for Texas, then our year in 1997 was the next most and then in 2005, so we had the same amount of draft talent they had on the '05 national championship team. We had a top five pick in Bryant Westbrook, so we had comparable talent."

That talent led Texas to a 10-1-1 regular season mark in 1995 and a berth in its first ever Bowl Alliance game, where the team lost to Virginia Tech in the Sugar Bowl after news broke that an impostor, thirty-year-old Ron Weaver, had been playing under the name Ron McKelvey and claiming he was twenty-three.

The Horns returned most of their starters the next season, and entered the year in the top ten. After blowing out Missouri and New Mexico State to start the season, the Horns vaulted to No. 6 in the nation. On September 21, Texas welcomed No. 9 Notre Dame to Austin for yet another in what had become a classic series between the two storied programs. In 1995, the Irish had routed Texas 55-27 in South Bend. This time, in Austin, the Horns were primed for revenge.

Jumping out to a 14-3 lead in the second quarter, Texas looked positioned to seal the deal. But Notre Dame fought back and took a 17-14 lead into halftime. Texas took a 24-17 lead on a 1-yard run by Ricky Williams with just under 11 minutes to play, but with less than 3 minutes left, Notre Dame's Autry Denson tied

Priest Holmes cuts behind the block of Dan Neil for a 61-yard touchdown against Nebraska, 1996 (Photo courtesy of the University of Texas)

it at 24 with a six-yard run on fourth-and-goal, after Irish linebacker Lyron Cobbins intercepted a tipped James Brown pass. After the Horns' next series stalled, a Texas punt netted only 22 yards, and Notre Dame set up shop at its own 43 with just 59 seconds left.

Ron Powlus guided the Irish 35 yards to the Texas 22 with only five ticks remaining. With 83,000 Texas fans creating an ear-shattering din, true freshman kicker Jim Sanson, who had almost quit the Irish team in August and who had been nicknamed "Foul Ball" by coach Lou Holtz for his many practice misses, lined up for the kick. Sanson calmly stroked it through from 39 yards out with no time left, and Notre Dame had beaten Texas for the fourth time in a row dating back to the 1971 Cotton Bowl.

The loss was devastating. A demoralized Longhorn team proceeded to lose three out of the next four ball games, giving a team that was on the cusp of the top five earlier in the season a shocking 3-4 record.

But after the fourth loss, to Colorado in Boulder, the team came together. After a players-only meeting, the team determined to fight its way to the title game for a winner-take-all contest for the Big 12 championship. They did just that. The team won four straight games, including a 51-15 total destruction of Texas A&M, and found themselves sitting atop the conference's South division, with only the mighty Nebraska Cornhuskers standing between them and an improbable Big 12 championship.

TEXAS vs. No. 3 NEBRASKA

December 7, 1996
St. Louis, Missouri

And the Huskers were indeed mighty in the mid-90s. Under coach Tom Osborne, Nebraska had won national championships in 1994 and 1995 with undefeated records, and entered the game against Texas ranked No. 3 in the nation with a record of 10-1. The Huskers had lost only two games in four seasons as they traveled to St. Louis. The Horns, meanwhile, came in with a four-game winning streak, but the overall 7-4 record was hardly intimidating. The odds makers weren't impressed, making Texas a 21-point underdog.

But the week before the game, Texas got a huge spark from its play-making quarterback James Brown, inadvertent though it was. In answering a reporter's question about the 21-point spread, Brown threw it back at 'em. In a confident but not boastful way, Brown said, hey, the Longhorns just might win the game by

21! The media, looking for a storyline, took off with it in a dead sprint. Headlines across the region that week screamed that Texas had a new Joe Namath, a brash quarterback who dared to *predict* a 3-touchdown Texas victory. Never mind that Brown had not actually predicted a win—he gave his team a shot of confidence.

Whatever he said, once the game started, Brown backed up every word. On the game's first drive, he completed all four of his pass attempts and by the end of the first quarter, Texas and Nebraska stood tied at 7-7. Priest Holmes scored his second TD out of three on the day with a 61-yard run on a counterplay in the second quarter, but the Huskers tied it on a 23-yard run by DeAngelo Evans, before Phil Dawson put Texas up by three at halftime by a score of 20-17. Texas trailed Nebraska 27-23 in the fourth quarter when, with only 8:53 remaining, Brown hit receiver Wane McGarity on a 66-yard catch and run that put Texas up 30-27.

Then, with only 2:53 left, Texas faced a fourth-and-inches from its own 28. John Mackovic had a decision to make: punt the ball back to Nebraska and let his tired defense try and preserve the victory, or keep the ball in the hands of the guy that had dared to believe he and his teammates could do the impossible. The coach called on quarterback James Brown to do his thing.

The call was "Roll-Left." After faking a handoff inside to Priest Holmes, James Brown did just that. The Huskers, with ten guys in the box, blitzed them all, and they bit hard on the fake. Tight end Derek Lewis never hesitated before sprinting up field past the onrushing Huskers, and Brown found him with a soft toss 10 yards behind the nearest Husker defender. Lewis cradled the ball in at the Texas 44 and raced 45 yards to the Husker 11 before being dragged down. When Holmes danced in from the 11 behind a clearing block from Dan Neil, the Horns went up 37-27 and sealed one of the biggest upsets in that era of college football.

The Game of My Life

By Dan Neil

We were loose going into the game. You have to look at the context of the whole season and what had transpired. We knew we had talent because the year before, we had won the Southwest Conference and wound up losing the Sugar Bowl, but we were a very good team, and we had most everybody coming back, so we knew we would be a good team in '96, too.

We had Ricky Williams, who was a sophomore, so we knew he was going to be even better, but we struggled early on, losing to Notre Dame in a close game, and we would have been out of any championship race, but this was the first year of the Big 12, and the South was weak that year. Oklahoma wasn't very good, while A&M was the team to beat.

We went up to Colorado that year with our backs against the wall and we put a lot of emphasis on having to win that football game. And we went up there and played a very good game but ended up losing. So we were very dejected. When we got home, we called a players-only meeting and talked as players. We said, "Look, as bad as we have played this year, we can still win this thing if we can get to the championship, because it's a winner-take-all, one-game shot." So we knew we had to win all of the rest of our games. And from that Colorado game on, we just started playing a lot better football. Each week we played better until the last week, when we had A&M at home.

They were still A&M then and were the team to beat, a very good team. And before that game, I remember that it was kind of eerie. It was the quietest locker room I had ever been in and ever was in. No one said a word. Everyone was just kind of sitting around. A coach came up to me later and said, "We thought for sure we were going to lose when we came in the locker room, we thought no one cared, that every one just wanted to get the season over with." But then we went out there and just blew their doors off. It was the best football we had played all year. We were just starting to peak.

So we get into the Big 12 championship against a team that had lost only one game in three years, so no one thought we had a chance, and we were picked to lose by 21.

But what solidified that game for us was that we had a team meeting on Monday before the game, and Coach Mackovic got up in front of the team and told us, "Don't give them any blackboard material; tell them we're just happy to be in the game and give Nebraska their due."

But our quarterback, James Brown, was talking to a reporter who asked him about being picked to lose by 21, and James wasn't being arrogant or cocky, but he said, "You know what, *we* could win by 21. We've got a good team, too," and of course the press just ran with it, saying he *predicted* we would win by 21. We all knew that wasn't what he was saying—we knew what he was saying was, "I believe in my football team." When we realized that our quarterback, a leader on our team and a guy we all liked and got behind because we knew how hard he played, truly believed in us, I think that right there was what our team needed to say, "You know what, if he believes, maybe we *can* win this game. Why not?"

We had also just put it on A&M like nobody had put it on them in a long, long time, and we were playing the best football we were capable of playing, so we thought, "We are going to beat these guys." So we had that feeling prior to the game. We were very relaxed, realizing that we weren't even supposed to be there, and that we had an opportunity that a lot of teams don't have. And if it had been any other year than the first year of the Big 12, we wouldn't have been there. So we were thankful for the opportunity, but we also knew that we could go out and do it.

Nebraska has some of the classiest fans in college football. Before the game of course they were cheering for their team very loud, but after the game they showed respect for us. We stayed in the hotel which was very nice and quiet and we were treated well; nobody bothered us. We got watches so we were really excited—when you are in college you don't have any money, so to get those watches was really great. But we were just excited being there. We knew that win, lose, or draw, we were making history given that it was the first year of the Big 12, so it was really great to be there.

In the stadium in St. Louis, there was one little pie-shaped sliver in the corner that was orange, and the rest of the crowd was red. So practically the entire stadium was Nebraska fans. Texas fans never thought we would be there or they thought if we did get there we would get blown out, so there literally was just a sliver of Texas fans and the rest was all red.

The game was back and forth, but we realized after a quarter that we could play with these guys, that they weren't as good as everybody said they were. We had played teams that were just as good and probably better. They were living a little bit off of the reputation of the Tommy Frazier years, when they *were* really good. And I hate saying that because it takes a little luster off of the win, but it is true.

We had a good game plan. We never asked James just to drop back and set up in the pocket. We rolled him out, we moved him around, we kept Pat Fitzgerald in to do some blocking—he was a better blocker than he got credit for—plus, he was such a threat catching the football and he had a few big catches, so they couldn't bring everybody, they had to cover that. So Mackovic did a good job trying to force them to only rush four guys, and then we did a good job moving around and trying to get on those four guys in protection. As an offensive line you try to find their best rusher, the guys you are going to worry about and you account for them; you don't just leave somebody one-on-one. You do that by turning your protection, you do it with backs, with tight ends, and we mixed all of that up a little bit. You talk about

Priest Holmes—I tell you what, nobody on the field wanted to get hit by that guy with a block—he would knock your head off. So that's what we did. We got after them physically. I don't think they expected us to be as good and as physical as we were. So I think that played into it. I don't think they were as good as advertised, and I think we were a little better than advertised.

Priest Holmes scored on a 61-yard counterplay to the right in the second quarter, and I was the right guard so I blocked down and we pulled the left guard and tackle. We were a pretty good counter team, and I remember lying on the ground and seeing Priest break through the hole and he was gone. That was as big as it gets. It was a seesaw game where you had to fight for everything you got, so that was a big play. And I can point to you on the field to this day where it was and where he went. Ricky Williams was hurt and not at full speed that day so we ended up using Priest a lot. He just got off that day, he was flying, as we expected. The players voted him Player of the Game.

Then it came down to the fourth down call late in the game. As I always tell people, if you knew Coach Mackovic, there shouldn't have been any surprise that we threw the ball. When it comes down to the game being on the line, he is going to throw the football, and that's what he did there.

And Nebraska had no clue, which is understandable, because the call really made no sense with Priest having the day he had and having a quarterback with James's ability to run. You'd think that we would just give it to Priest. He was built perfectly for this type of run and he had done it so many times. And we felt very confident lining up and running against these guys. And of course as an offensive lineman, my first reaction is, "Why aren't we running the ball?"

But I knew what we were going to do, and when I heard the play and that it was going to be up to James, I was fine with that. We all had a lot of confidence that James could get us that one yard. I can't say enough about the kind of player James was. James was a hard-nosed guy. He was a linebacker in a quarterback's body. He would never back down from anybody, and as a player, we all respected him. And he was a good football player, too.

It went back to what had happened the week before when James said he thought we could win by 21. James was the one getting the ball with the whole game on the line, and you knew that's the way he wanted it—"Put the game on my shoulders and I'll carry everybody." He wanted it and he knew he could do it, so I don't think anybody doubted that we were going to get the first down. We just knew he had to sell the fake and we would get it.

Our defense had played very well this day, but we knew that this game had been back and forth, it was a physical football game with two teams just trading punches, so we knew if Nebraska got the ball back, we couldn't ask the defense to go out there and stop them. No defense could stop Nebraska that much—they were too good of a team. And we needed one yard, one first down to put the game away. Of course we wanted to go for it; we knew we had to. And I give credit to Mackovic because he knew we needed to win this game *now*. And we had nothing to lose. And obviously, at that time, it was the perfect call. We broke their back on that call. A little league team could have scored on them after that because they were just stunned. They couldn't fathom what had just happened to them.

After that touchdown, the whole stadium was silent except that little sliver of Texas fans. When the game ended, Mike Adams was carrying a Texas flag, but the Nebraska team was a very classy group of guys and came over to shake our hands.

Nebraska reflected their coach very well. They were a quality program with quality guys, and I would put Texas in the same category. So there was no trash talking, just a hard-nosed game. Looking back, I really enjoyed that game because I always thought trash talking was ridiculous. Just line up and play hard football and when it was over, shake hands and earn each other's respect, and that's completely how that game played out.

After the game, going out to the buses, there were just red shirts everywhere and people congratulating us and telling us "great game"—the Nebraska fans are just really classy people. But that's how football is supposed to be played.

Upon Further Review

The Horns' 37-27 win over Nebraska earned Texas the right to face Penn State in the Fiesta Bowl, Dan Neil's last game as a Longhorn. After leading at halftime 12-7 and being tied at 15 midway through the third quarter, Texas gave up 23 unanswered points to lose 38-15.

"We thought this trip was going to be a vacation," recalled Neil, "and we got out there and we were doing two-a-day practices! At one point I thought there was going to be a mutiny because guys were so upset. We were working hard, but I think the two-a-days are what put guys over the edge. I wanted to win the game, but I wasn't too happy about that either."

Neil developed a newfound respect for Penn State coach Joe Paterno after facing his team in the Fiesta. "I always got kind of upset when I heard people say Joe Paterno was too old, that the game had passed him by," exclaimed Neil. "Watching the film of Penn State, I was very impressed with the defense. They were a very complicated defense and they could execute it. They had a blitz package and we spent the whole month working on this blitz package, and we go out there in the first half, and they don't run one of those blitzes. They do a completely different blitz package. So we were leading at halftime but we definitely weren't in control of the game. So we go in at halftime to handle these blitzes we'd been getting, and we go back in the second half, and they do a completely different blitz package, the one we had spent the past month working on, but we had just got done switching. So our heads were swimming that entire game. Talent-wise, they couldn't touch us, but they were very well coached and they played well."

Texas won the Big 12 championship that year, but finished with an 8-5 record and barely cracked the top twenty-five, finishing up with a final ranking of twenty-third in all of the major polls.

Following his senior year at Texas, the Denver Broncos took Neil in the third round of the NFL draft. He joined a Broncos team that had played in and lost four Super Bowls going into the 1997 season. They were quarterbacked by one of the game's all-time great players in John Elway, who was nearing the end of a legendary career. Denver went through the 1997 regular season with a 12-4 record and, as a wildcard, made it all the way to Super Bowl XXXII, where they beat the defending champion Green Bay Packers. The next season, the Broncos won the Super Bowl again, this time defeating the Atlanta Falcons.

"As I tell everybody, the missing link for the Broncos was a Texas player!" Neil said, laughing. "It was an interesting time for me because I had just won three championships with Texas and had had a lot of success. I knew Denver was good, but I knew nothing about them because they weren't a team I thought was going to draft me. And I went there and I didn't realize how good we were. There were two or three Hall of Fame players on that field. So I was just in awe of everything and didn't play much my first year."

But Neil stuck with it, and by the opening game of his second year, he was starting at guard for the defending Super Bowl champs, a position he kept for the next seven seasons. "There's a huge learning curve," said Neil of that rookie season with Denver. "It's not only learning how to play football; it's learning how to be a pro. It's a difficult transition and I struggled mightily with it. There were a lot of adjustment factors for me. For example, I remember the first time I got in the huddle with John Elway. I'm going, 'There's John Elway!' I remember skipping school to go home and watch the draft when he got drafted. Of course I never told him I was twelve years old at the time! All of that factored into my first year, plus we were such a good team. I was just trying to keep my head above water. And I wasn't ready to play physically, mentally, or in any way, shape, or form. We ended up winning the Super Bowl and I had a good time, but it all happened so fast, I didn't really understand what it meant. And then when we won again the next year, I honestly thought this was pretty easy!"

After almost not making the team his second season, Neil got his break and made the most of it. "My second year, I played terrible in training camp," recalled Neil. "I was getting progressively worse. Finally, they had a journeyman lineman in front of me that they cut and we didn't have many guys left. So they kept me just because I was a third-rounder and they didn't want to cut me and count their losses just yet. So another guy got hurt so going into the last preseason game, they said, 'You're the guy.' I played alright, then went into the next week and started, and then started for the next seven years."

Dan Neil retired from the NFL after the 2004 season, having played his entire eight-year career with Denver. Today, he lives back in Austin with his wife and three children. After a stint on the air in local Austin sports talk radio, Neil has settled into a career in the insurance industry.

Chapter Sixteen

MAJOR APPLEWHITE

Quarterback (1998-01)

The day had come when Major would meet Major.

The introduction, though inevitable, was no less surreal. On that frigid November 2000 afternoon in Tuscaloosa, with arguably the most heated rivalry in college football as its backdrop, an All-Conference University of Texas quarterback became acquainted not only with a former Alabama All-America running back but also with his namesake.

Major Applewhite, meet Major Ogilvie.

Already, Applewhite had begun to make a name for himself as a record-setting Longhorn signal caller. It was during a bye-week in Texas's schedule when Applewhite would meet, at the Alabama-Auburn game, the renowned Crimson Tide letterman for whom he was named.

"It was very strange," said Applewhite. "It's unique to meet someone named 'Major' who's not in the military."

Applewhite's parents were die-hard Crimson Tide fans despite their Louisiana upbringing. When their son was born in the summer of 1978, the Applewhites's devotion to Alabama was enough to name him after one of its star athletes. It's all part of the region's frenzied football following that needs little explanation south of the Mason-Dixon Line. The fact that Applewhite's father was a close friend with former Alabama QB Terry Davis only cemented the relationship between team and fan.

"Ogilvie came to Alabama toward the late 1970s," Applewhite continued, "and Dad liked the name 'Major.' He went with it."

Applewhite can empathize with the fact that the November 2000 introduction was no less strange for Ogilvie.

"He's meeting me, and he's probably thinking that somebody has named their child after him. It goes full circle. You play at Texas and, all of sudden, there are Little Majors. You're getting pictures in the mail of Little Major because someone has named their child after you. You realize how important football is to Alabama fans, and to Texas fans, when they name children after you. You realize how much you're a part of their family. That's what they do on weekends; they talk about you, and they talk about your coaches. It's just part of their life. It's part of the culture."

The cultural experience came full circle for Applewhite when he served as Alabama's offensive coordinator for the 2007 season. Alabama actually recruited Applewhite one decade earlier when he was a Baton Rouge high school quarterback, but never offered a scholarship. Texas, LSU, Texas A&M, and Mississippi State were the primary suitors, and the freckle-faced redhead eventually opted for the Longhorns. Applewhite was part of the first class that head coach John Mackovic signed following Texas's 1996 Big 12 Conference Championship upset of No. 3 Nebraska. By then, the sixth-year Longhorn coach had developed a reputation as an offensive think tank, but was also perceived—by some—as cerebral and aloof.

"I actually enjoyed Coach Mackovic's cerebral approach to everything," Applewhite said. "I did not know him as a person, but I liked the offensive strategies that he brought with him."

Applewhite redshirted during what would be a disastrous 4-7 season in 1997, including a 66-3 debacle at home against UCLA. At season's end, Mackovic was shown the door. Texas went in search of its fourth head coach since legendary Darrell Royal retired in 1976. The quarterback situation was also in flux. Senior James Brown had just completed his eligibility while backup Marty Cherry left to pursue a modeling career. Heading into the 1998 season, there were three scholarship quarterbacks on campus, but none had started a collegiate game. Texas would also announce in early December the name of its new head football coach, plucking a candidate from a storied basketball university to revive the fortunes of a traditional football power.

His name was Mack Brown.

One of the first things Brown did was convince Ricky Williams, the NCAA rushing leader as a junior, to return for his final year. The Texas defense needed an

Major Applewhite guided the Longhorns to a 9-3 record in coach Mack Brown's first season at Texas

infusion of talent, but that would take time. The more immediate concern was naming a starting quarterback, and Brown tabbed senior Richard Walton for the September 5 home opener against New Mexico State.

"I just wanted to be competitive following my redshirt year because there were just two backup quarterbacks," Applewhite said. "I wanted it to be clear in their [coaches'] mind that I'd been working hard to have the opportunity to be the second-team quarterback."

Applewhite logged mop-up duty in a 30-point win over NMSU but had worked himself into a position where he was just one heartbeat away from the starting job. And it all changed in a heartbeat. Applewhite was suddenly thrust into the lineup during the fourth quarter at No. 6 UCLA when Walton suffered a season-ending hand injury. The reward for a 49-31 loss in southern California was a visit to No. 5 Kansas State. Now, a redshirt freshman QB was directing the Texas offense.

"That's probably the best Kansas State defense they've ever had," Applewhite recalled, as the Wildcats rolled to a 48-7 shellacking of the Longhorns.

Texas would then post four consecutive wins, including a 34-3 thumping of a less-than-vintage Oklahoma team. Applewhite settled in at quarterback and Williams continued his assault on the NCAA career rushing record. Williams's school-record 350 rushing yards against Iowa State, as well as his decision to honor 1948 Heisman winner Doak Walker by donning Walker's jersey number against OU, garnered the type of media attention that thrust him into the thick of the Heisman race. Virtually overlooked in Williams's record-setting run is the fact that Texas actually amassed more yards through the air [2,931] in 1998 than it did on the ground [2,212]. Senior Wane McGarity established himself, statistically, among the top five receivers in program history, with 1,087 yards on 58 receptions that season.

"People were playing Ricky with nine-man fronts," Applewhite recalled. "We threw a lot of stuff over the top of coverage. We practiced it every day, and that's why we were good at throwing the deep ball. If you want to be good at the deep ball, you can't just show up on Saturdays and hope you're going to be successful with it."

Yet, it would be a toss to McGarity—covering all of 2 yards—that would be the difference-maker at perennially sold-out Memorial Stadium in Lincoln, Nebraska. It would come with just 2:47 remaining on an overcast Halloween afternoon. During his pregame oratory, however, Brown had tried to convince his troops they would still be in the game at that juncture.

"I believe in you guys," Brown affirmed. "You deserve to be here. You belong here."

Now, it was time for his young Texas team to prove it.

TEXAS vs. No. 7 NEBRASKA

October 31, 1998
Lincoln, Nebraska

Texas was not only facing its third top-ten team of the season, but it was also visiting two-time defending national champion Nebraska, a team that boasted college football's longest active home winning streak [47]. The Cornhusker roster was dotted with players who keenly remembered their 37-27 upset loss to Texas just two seasons earlier in the inaugural Big 12 Conference Championship game. It was such a daunting scenario that ESPN commentator Lee Corso's midweek prediction was that Nebraska's Blackshirt defense would knock Williams out of the mismatch.

But Texas scored on its opening possession, courtesy of tight end Derek Lewis's 16-yard TD grab that put the exclamation point on an eleven-play, 68-yard drive. The Horns forced consecutive Cornhusker punts and grabbed a who'd-a-thunk-it 10-0 early second-quarter advantage following a 36-yard Kris Stockton field goal. Quarterback Eric Crouch replaced starter Monte Christo on Nebraska's second possession of the second quarter. A suspect Longhorn defense held the Huskers in check during the first 30 minutes of play, limiting the home team to a 27-yard field goal as time expired on the first half.

Nebraska rallied with 10 unanswered points in the third period, capped by Crouch's 38-yard touchdown run. The momentum had clearly shifted to the Huskers' sideline when Texas, now trailing 13-10, faced third-and-10 from its own 19. Applewhite called the play in the huddle: Max 222 Pump, a four-wide set in which little-used WR Bryan White would run a slant-and-go on the outside. It would be the final play of the third quarter.

White's 76-yard catch-and-run down the right sideline was the longest reception of his career. It spotted Texas a first-and-goal at the five as the quarter ended. It would also set up one of the most dramatic final frames in Texas football history.

The Husker defense stiffened, and the Horns settled for a 19-yard Stockton field goal. Nebraska responded with a 57-yard march, attempting just two passes in eleven plays, to reclaim a precarious 16-13 lead with a 42-yard field goal. There was 8:24 left in the ballgame when the decisive Texas drive began on its own 15.

The Horns moved the chains with Applewhite's nine-yard completion to Ryan Nunez on third-and-2. He followed with a first-down completion to McGarity, this one good for 14 yards. Yet, a false start penalty, a 6-yard sack and an incompletion resulted in an improbable third-and-21 conversion attempt from the Texas 35. Cornhusker coaches instructed the punt return unit to get ready while the call from the Longhorn sideline was for a Three Vertical route. For the second time in as many possessions, White saw the precious pigskin float his way. This time, White's 37-yard grab put Texas in prime real estate at the Nebraska 28.

From there, Texas turned to its battering ram. Five Williams rushes, plus a Husker personal foul, culminated in a critical third-and-goal from the two with 2:54 remaining. The Horns called time-out. From the coaches' box high above the chilly field, offensive coordinator Greg Davis called for a sprint-out with Williams in motion. WR Kwame Cavil was the primary target but was quickly blanketed by a pair of Blackshirt defenders. Applewhite dropped back, hoping to buy a few extra seconds for his receivers. That's when he saw McGarity tight roping the goal line across the middle of the field. Free safety Mike Brown, who would post a career-best 18 tackles that afternoon, crushed Applewhite just as he released the ball. Yet McGarity's shoestring TD grab in heavy traffic gave Texas a 20-16 lead.

Nebraska had one last opportunity, taking over on its own 23 with 2:35 remaining. After a first-down run put the Huskers near midfield, a 4-yard loss and two incompletions forced a Nebraska punt with just under 2 minutes to play. Williams's 11-yard burst up the middle on the second play of Texas's final possession sealed the upset.

The Game of My Life

By Major Applewhite

I don't know if there was a game that was definitive of my career as much as the era in which I was playing. Texas was a traditional program that was restoring itself as a winner again. The game that stands out as definitive for our program was when Coach Brown had just come in 1998, and we won that first big road game at Nebraska. To me, that meant so much. It was so big, not only for Coach Brown as a first-year head coach, not only for momentum in recruiting, but it was also a statement about the Southern Division of the [Big 12] Conference versus the Northern part of the Conference. It was also a big statement for Ricky and the publicity toward what he was doing. In so many ways, he solidified the Heisman that day in Lincoln. That game was big for us. It substantiated Coach Brown as someone who could win in this conference. It was also an opportunity for some to believe in a freshman as a quarterback even though he had great players around him.

There was some confidence among the upperclassmen because they had beaten Nebraska in the [1996] Big 12 Conference Championship. At the same time, there was the thought in the back of everybody's mind that Nebraska had that forty-seven-game home winning streak. This was the same Nebraska program that had the bloodletting against Florida in the Orange Bowl two years prior. It still was "Nebraska" in peoples' minds. It wasn't the 2002 and 2003 version of Nebraska. It was still the mid-90s, Tommy Frazier kind of Nebraska: maybe not talent-wise, but perception-wise. That's what our players were thinking, so it was kind of a mixed bag. We wanted to go up there and do something special. It would be a lie to say we went up there with complete confidence that we were going to win the game. There was some nervousness, at least on my part.

It was one of those things, as a college football nut, that I was excited to be a part of. Whether it's the Big House or the Horseshoe, or the Swamp or Death Valley, it was just one of those places that you're fortunate the schedule lines up during your years of eligibility. It was exciting for me to play at a place like Nebraska, what with the tradition of their program. I mean, it wasn't Disneyland. We weren't taking pictures and just happy to be there. There was a game to win. But it was one of those deals where we knew if we won, this is a lot sweeter than winning on the road anywhere else.

As we came out for pregame, the fans were roped off by a yellow rope. They were saying, "Good luck! Good luck today, guys!" I thought, "OK. That's a little strange." We went into the halftime leading 10-3, and they were saying, "Great effort, guys. You're giving us a great game." Before the game, I thought that type of kindness might be sarcasm and arrogance. At halftime, I thought, "This is not sarcasm. These are salt-of-the-earth, good people who really want to see you give their team a good game." Don't get me wrong—they want to beat your tail.

Undoubtedly, Bryan White had the two biggest plays of that game outside of Wane McGarity's touchdown catch at the end. We ran four-wides on Bryan's first catch. We ran a slant-and-go on the outside, and he ran a perfect slant-and-go route. I'll never forget it. It was a Max 222 Pump. We pumped him and he turned the corner like a top. He made a great play and set up a score. Then on a huge third-and-long from our 35, he made a real tough catch on the outside. That was a Three Vertical route. That was Menu Nine for us. We had a ten-play Menu. I remember [offensive coordinator] Greg Davis telling us at the "install meeting" where the ball typically goes on that play. In six previous years, the ball had gone outside just one time. Well, in seven years, it had gone out there twice. In other words, it was the second time that a ball had been thrown to that particular receiver on that specific play. It was very rare for the ball to go that receiver. And Bryan was open on that play. That catch set up a field goal that tied the game.

Nebraska answered with a field goal. On that [winning touchdown] pass to Wane, we were going to line up with two receivers to the right. It was a sprint-out by design. We wanted to motion Ricky out of the backfield so we could show that we possibly could get isolated with him one-on-one. [Fullback] Ricky Brown was blocking at the edge because it was Sprint-out Right. The inside receiver, or the No. 2 receiver in that case, was Kwame [Cavil]. He was to run a flat [route]. The outside receiver, or the X-receiver, was Wane. He was to run a 12-yard curl. As I sprinted out, they jumped coverage on Kwame. He was the No. 1 progression on that play. When they jumped Kwame, I tried to drift to gain depth and get some space to throw the ball. Wane sat in the hole. I was about to pull the trigger but a guy came with the flow of the play right into his window. Wane did exactly what he was supposed to do as a wideout. As the adage goes, when one window closes, another one opens. Well, this window closed and another one opened. He slid further into the middle of the field, and there was a little spot to put a dead ball in there. It was one of those deals where either he was going to catch it or we were going to tie it, 16-16, with a field goal. I was thinking, "If there is a play to be made, make it. If not, bail that sucker out in the back of the end zone. Let's go into overtime." But there was a little spot, and he made a helluva catch. He made a great adjustment on his route. All the little details: He did a great job of getting both hands underneath the ball, securing the catch, and making it evident, holding the ball up and showing it to the official. And then I got blasted right at the end of it.

[Safety] Mike Brown came and just put his helmet square underneath my chin. It snapped my head back and I fell on the back of my head. When I got up, I was woozy as all hell. I really didn't know what was going on. I just remember our left guard Ben Adams coming over and slapping the hell out of my head. He was saying, "Great job!" I said, "No, no, no, no, no! Don't touch me. I can't see." He said, "Quit being a wuss." He was a lineman and had no time for my shit. I remember that part of it before going to the bench. Our trainer tried to take me into the locker room. I said, "You can't! I mean, c'mon. We had talked all week about breaking this streak. You can't take me into the locker room."

When the game ended, the ovation that I saw from the Nebraska fans was for Ricky and how he played. He ran for 150 yards that day. He basically came in there and won the Heisman. He won it on a national stage against a top-ten team.

I remember flying back to Austin that night. It was Halloween, and I went out with my girlfriend Julie, who is now my wife. Everybody was dressed up in Halloween costumes. That was the last night of anonymity that I had. Before then, I could walk down the street and nobody would say anything. I was just an average college Joe Blow. Nobody gave a flip. All of it sudden, it built. We kept winning. Ricky was in the Heisman race, and we were on every sports network because of what Ricky was doing. When you have a guy who's going to win the Heisman Trophy, you're going to have every media outlet in the country at your school. All of us players were tagging along behind him as far notoriety, but the Nebraska game was when it all changed.

Upon Further Review

Applewhite would complete 14 of 26 passes for 269 yards against a Blackshirt unit ranked among the top twenty in total defense. The 20-16 shocker at Lincoln was the signature win that Mack Brown needed to jumpstart his program. The momentum from that afternoon carried Texas to its first New Year's Day bowl victory in sixteen years.

"We all began to believe we were better players than what we were," Applewhite said. "So much of the time that's what happens: You start playing better than what you really are and from where your talent really is. We ended up winning five of six games. Baylor, Nebraska, Oklahoma State, and Texas A&M were all fourth-quarter wins for us. We lost a fourth-quarter game at Texas Tech, but four of the five we won. It was one of those deals where confidence, a different kind of esteem, and a new coach will help you get over the hump."

Applewhite was named Big 12 Freshman of the Year and then Big 12 Offensive Player of the Year during his sophomore campaign. He would rotate with highly touted sophomore QB Chris Simms during the first half of the 2000 season before coaches named him the sole starter on October 14 at Colorado. Texas would finish the regular season with six straight wins, but Applewhite was sidelined for the remainder of the year when he suffered a leg injury at Texas Tech three weeks later.

As a senior, Applewhite would remain Simms's backup in a season in which Texas's only loss during the 2001 regular season was a 14-3 setback against No. 3 Oklahoma. Applewhite would replace Simms in the Big 12 Conference Championship game, trailing Colorado 29-10 midway through the second quarter. Applewhite nearly erased the 19-point deficit, but the Texas rally fell short, 39-37. The loss sent Texas to a second straight Holiday Bowl, this time against No. 21 Washington. Applewhite's first start of 2001 would also be the last game of his career.

Behind a school-record 37 of 55 passes for 473 yards and 4 touchdowns, Applewhite would help engineer what was then the biggest comeback in Longhorn history. Texas's 47-43 thriller resulted in the program's first eleven-win season since 1983.

Applewhite signed a free agent contract with the then-defending Super Bowl champs New England Patriots in April of 2002, but he decided during the off-season that his skill level lent itself more to becoming a collegiate coach than a highly successful professional player. He remained in Austin and served as a Longhorn Graduate Assistant through the 2005 Rose Bowl win over Michigan. He became the quarterbacks coach at Syracuse in 2005 before accepting the offensive coordinator's position at Rice the following year. In early 2007, at age 28, Applewhite became one of the youngest offensive coordinators in the history of Alabama.

Less than one year later, Applewhite returned to Austin when he became Texas's running backs coach. He was promoted to co-offensive coordinator in January 2011.

Again, a piece of Applewhite's life had come full circle.

Chapter Seventeen

RICKY WILLIAMS

Fullback (1995-96); Tailback (1997-98)

Ricky Williams's decision to return to Texas for his senior season began with a Snickers bar.

John Bianco, head of Texas Football Media Relations, usually keeps a handful of the product in his desk drawer. So it was not uncommon for Williams to drop by Bianco's office for a chat and, of course, a candy bar.

"I would come up to his office nearly every day," Williams recalled. "John would keep Snickers in his drawer. I would get his Snickers and we'd sit and talk."

It was a casual setting for idle conversation, sandwiched between Bianco's duties and Williams's balancing act between football and school. But there was plenty to talk about on this particular day in late 1997. The Men's Athletic Department, in the wake of a disappointing 4-7 football season, was searching for its third head coach in eleven years. John Mackovic was on his way out and, for the most part, so was Williams.

After all, Williams was college football's leading rusher his junior year with 1,893 yards, as well as the winner of the Doak Walker Award, which honors the nation's top running back. Williams was projected as a top-five pick in April's NFL Draft; the immediate direction of the Longhorn program, however, was anyone's guess.

"I was 80 percent sure I was going to declare for the draft," Williams said.

But as Williams rummaged for a Snickers bar, Bianco observed that something even sweeter was within his grasp: a legitimate shot at breaking Tony Dorsett's NCAA career rushing record. The mark, which had stood for twenty-one years, was something Williams had not fully considered until Bianco opened the current NCAA record book. Dorsett ran for 6,082 yards during his days as a Pittsburgh Panther en route to the 1976 Heisman Trophy. Williams's three-year total stood at 4,155. He quickly did the math.

"At that moment," Williams said, "I went from being 80 percent sure I was leaving to where it was about 50-50."

He would not reach a final verdict until he met Mack Brown, hired from North Carolina after transforming a downtrodden football program at a basketball school into consecutive top-ten finishes. Texas fans generally welcomed Brown's affable persona and homespun folksiness, and, indeed, Williams's initial encounter with Brown made quite an impression.

"After talking with Coach Brown," Williams said, "it went back up to 80 percent that I was going to leave."

Say *what?*

"He mentioned something to me about cutting my hair," laughed Williams, who sported attention-grabbing dreadlocks during his Texas tenure. "That turned me off right away."

The head coach and the star player would meet again. This time, instead of nitpicking about Williams's hair, Brown picked his brain.

"He asked me what I thought about the team and what the team needed to get over the hump. I gave him my honest opinion. I told him that, in the past, we had focused too much on offense. I don't think we ever played good enough defense. The next day, he started implementing some of the things that I said. We started moving some reserve players from offense over to defense. I told him that some of the players were not very disciplined. He started being harder on us. He got us into the best shape that we had been in. I had never had the experience of a coach asking for my opinion. I started to like him. The more time I spent with him, the more I looked forward to playing for a guy like him. We had lunch one day, and I told him I was staying."

As a senior, Williams ran for 215 yards and a school-record 6 touchdowns in UT's 66-36 season-opening romp against New Mexico State. Texas would then travel to No. 6 UCLA, an early litmus test for the team's collective psyche. The Bruins' 66-3 annihilation of Texas in Austin one year earlier was the beginning of the end

Ricky Williams sets the NCAA all-time rushing record on this electrifying 60-yard TD sprint against the Aggies, 1998

for Mackovic. The home team jumped to a 35-3 first half lead, but Brown delivered a halftime warning: The final 30 minutes would determine which players would make the trip to Kansas State the following Saturday. The Longhorns scored on their opening series of the third quarter and played competitively before falling 49-31.

"We didn't play well in the first half," Williams said, "and we were getting beat pretty bad. After halftime, I just decided I was going to go out there and have fun. By the end of the game, I had 160 yards and 3 touchdowns."

The road grew tougher when Texas traveled to No. 5 Kansas State. Senior QB Richard Walton suffered a season-ending wrist injury against UCLA, and now redshirt freshman Major Applewhite would log his first start. The Wildcats boasted one of college football's premiere defenses and the Horns were never in it, falling 48-7. What's more, Williams suffered a leg injury and was held to 43 yards on 25 carries. Texas was 1-2 and several pigskin pundits declared that Williams's Heisman campaign was over.

"I had a bad quad sprain against Kansas State and I wasn't sure if I was going to play the next week," Williams recalled. "I went home and rented *Blazing Saddles*. I sat down, had a good laugh, put the game behind me, and got 300 yards the next week, and 300 more yards the next week."

Williams careened for 318 yards and 6 touchdowns in a 59-21 thumping of Rice before turning his attention to the Big 12 Conference opener against Iowa State. But, for Williams, the rest of the season became deeply personal.

The day after Texas dispatched the Owls, Williams learned that Doak Walker had just died. Williams was crushed. He had established an immediate friendship with Walkers family after winning the award named for him ten months earlier and dedicated the rest of the season to honoring Doak. Williams placed a No. 37 decal, Walker's jersey number, on his helmet just before the Iowa State game. That night, he rushed for a school-record 350 yards, eclipsing by 8 yards the mark Roosevelt Leaks had set twenty-five years earlier against SMU. Williams set five school records during the 54-33 win against the Cyclones, and then set his sights on Texas's annual border war against Oklahoma at the Cotton Bowl. Williams's thoughts, however, remained with Walker.

"The Cotton Bowl is known as The House That Doak Built," Williams said. "I asked Coach Brown if I could wear No. 37 for that game, and I was able to."

Williams ran for 139 yards and 2 touchdowns as Texas distanced itself from the Sooners in the second half, winning 34-3. Afterwards, the Longhorns presented Walker's children and their families the game ball in a locker room ceremony.

"It was very emotional for me after the game," said Williams. "Doak's family came in, and I took my jersey off—my bloody jersey—and I gave it to his family to honor Doak Walker."

In a touch of irony, the 1998 season represented the golden anniversary of Walker's Heisman Trophy year at SMU. Now, Williams was back in the thick of the Heisman race. Following a 30-20 win against Baylor where Williams rushed for 259 yards, Texas would face its third top-ten team in seven weeks when it traveled to No. 7 Nebraska. The Cornhuskers were defending national champions and owned college football's longest active home winning streak at forty-seven games. In a back-and-forth affair, Applewhite's 2-yard completion to wide receiver Wane McGarity on third-and-goal gave Texas the lead for good, 20-16, with just 2:54 remaining. Yet, as the teams left the field, a sold-out Memorial Stadium applauded Williams's 150 yards on 37 carries by chanting, "Heisman! Heisman!" Brown was so moved by the classy gesture, and his program's signature win, that he called Darrell Royal from the dressing room.

"That's what college football is all about," Royal commented.

Texas got past Oklahoma State, 37-34, on a Kris Stockton field goal as time expired but lost in the closing minutes at Texas Tech, 42-35. It cost Texas a shot at the Big 12 South title, but there was still plenty of incentive on the Longhorn sideline: a shot at the program's first New Year's Day bowl in eight seasons and a chance to avenge the previous year's loss to Texas A&M.

On November 27, it wasn't just the eyes of Texas but all of college football that focused on Darrell K Royal-Texas Memorial Stadium. A virtual Who's Who of college football, including career rushing leader Tony Dorsett, gathered on a soggy morning to watch the Horns battle the Aggies in Austin for the final time of the twentieth century. But that's not why they were there.

Ricky Williams was just 62 yards shy of the NCAA all-time rushing record.

TEXAS vs. No. 6 TEXAS A&M

November 27, 1998

Austin, Texas

After the teams traded punts to begin the game, Applewhite threw an early interception, but Texas got the ball in Williams's hands on its next series. The thirteen-play, 51-yard drive resulted in a 22-yard Kris Stockton field goal, but Williams was responsible for 42 of those yards with 9 carries. The Horns forced an Aggie punt, and Texas operated from its own 20 with 2:58 remaining in the opening frame.

On first down, Williams collected 4 yards up the middle, and the scoreboard in the south end zone quickly reflected the yardage he still needed to break the all-time rushing record. Eleven yards separated Williams from out-distancing every other running back in college football history. Applewhite's sideline pass to McGarity, good for 16 yards, gave Texas a fresh set of downs at its own 40.

Still . . . *11 yards!*

The call from the sideline was "L King Zin 53."' It was a simple isolation play over left guard that Williams had run effectively throughout the season. Applewhite handed off to his big back who followed fullback Ricky Brown's lead block. Williams evaded linebacker Warrick Holdman, slipped past the line of scrimmage and found room to roam. He cut left along the Aggie sideline and headed south. Strong safety Rich Coady had a beeline on Williams, but ricocheted off the hell-bent-for-history tailback as Williams lowered his shoulders. The Longhorn sideline erupted with Dorsett leading the cheers: "Go! Go! Go!"

For Williams, it was as if time stood still. He knew the record was his; the only question was whether he would score. Williams cut right at the 12-yard line. There was one man to beat. Jason Webster still had a shot at Williams, but McGarity's downfield block slowed the Aggie cornerback just enough as Williams neared the promised land. Webster grabbed at Williams's jersey just outside the goal line, but Williams plunged into the end zone and into the record books.

The 60-yard run spotted Texas a 10-0 lead and Williams was immediately mobbed by his teammates. Play was halted as Williams was presented with the game ball during an impromptu ceremony. There was 1:45 left in the first quarter, and a national television audience had just witnessed what it had tuned in to see. But there was still quite a bit of football to be played between the two ancient rivals.

Williams fumbled on his next carry, and the Aggies recovered on the Longhorn 19. Randy McCown's sideline pass to Derrick Spiller on third-and-11 from the 20 put A&M on the scoreboard 6 seconds into the second quarter. Texas answered with a thirteen-play, 58-yard drive that led to a 24-yard Stockton field goal. The Longhorn defense forced a three-and-out and Stockton tacked on 3 more points following a fifteen-play, 47-yard march. His 49-yarder gave the home team a 16-7 halftime lead.

McGarity set a school single-season record with his 57th catch—it was a 10-yard reception on Texas's opening series of the third quarter—but the eight-play drive ended when Stockton was wide right from 50 yards out. The Longhorn defense forced another three-and-out before Applewhite connected with Kwame

Cavil on a 26-yard screen to the A&M 16. Stockton would misfire on a 28-yard attempt, again wide right.

It was a scoreless third quarter, and Williams recovered his own fumble at the Longhorn 27 on his first carry of the final frame. A pair of up-the-gut rushes netted 15 yards for Williams before he barreled over right end for 38. On third-and-5 from the 10, Applewhite connected with Cavil on a slant to give Texas a 23-7 cushion with 9:46 left in the game.

Just as quickly, the game turned for the Aggies.

Needing a spark, McCown went up top to Chris Cole on first down. The reception covered 55 yards as the Aggies set up shop at the Longhorn 8. A delay of game ruling hurt the Farmers, who settled for a 30-yard Russell Bynum field goal. Protecting a 23-10 lead, Texas needed to drain the play clock with 8:29 remaining. But Williams fumbled on the first play of the drive, and the Aggies were back in business at the Longhorn 16. The McCown-to-Spiller combo worked again, this time producing a 17-yard scoring toss over the middle. Suddenly, it was anybody's ballgame at 23-17.

An emboldened Aggie defense forced a three-and-out before Jason Webster returned a Chris Robertson punt 35 yards to the Longhorn 24. McCown converted a critical third-and-6 from the 20 with a 16-yard sideline pass to Matt Bumgardner. McCown's next third-down attempt, this time from the Texas 1-yard line, fell incomplete. Texas A&M called its second time-out. A record crowd of 83,687 was in full-throated hysterics when McCown lined up behind center and then carried over from the one. A hush fell over the partisan Burnt Orange crowd. The Aggies had taken their first lead of the game, 24-23, with just 2:20 remaining.

Texas had seen a 16-point lead evaporate in little more than 7 minutes and, now, after two short completions faced a critical third-and-2 at its own 31. Applewhite's 6-yard toss to tight end Derek Lewis breathed new life into the Longhorn drive. Seconds later, Applewhite would contend with another third-and-2 and, this time, connected with Bryan White for 4. The Horns were at midfield with less than 50 seconds left. Applewhite hooked up with McGarity for 7 yards on first down, setting the table for Texas's biggest completion of the day. Applewhite's sideline pass to Cavil accounted for 25 precious yards. Then, on second-and-5 from the 14, Williams's final carry in Austin was a 7-yard rumble over left end.

The Aggies called their final time-out with 9 seconds remaining to try to ice Stockton. A field goal would be a game winner, but Stockton had misfired on his previous two attempts. This time, though, Stockton split the uprights from 24 yards out. The 26-24 thriller was Texas's third triumph against A&M in four meetings and put the Horns in the Cotton Bowl. It also put Williams atop the charts in another offensive category: His 295 all-purpose yards that day were enough to break the NCAA all-time mark. Remarkably, he did it without ever returning a kick.

The Game of My Life

By Ricky Williams

No matter who we're playing, I've always had the fantasy that somehow the other team is going to stop me and that I'm going to have a horrible game. The thought crossed my mind the day we played A&M and I was going for the rushing record. I remember trying to stay loose that morning on the bus ride from the hotel to the stadium. I was sitting with Wane McGarity, and we were listening to Snoop Dog's. I was just trying to stay loose and focused. I got to the field house and went through my routine. I have a routine that I go through before every game. I go out on the field early and try to get loose and relaxed. I started thinking that *anything* could happen in a rivalry game against Texas A&M. You just never know what's going to happen. It doesn't matter what kind of season either team is having, but A&M was very good that year. You don't know if they're going to play lights out, or not. I had had great success against them in my career, so I was just thinking that I hoped they wouldn't shut me down on that day. [Laughing] That would have sucked.

During our previous home game, Oklahoma State held me to less than 100 yards. They had a great [defensive] game plan. They put nine in the box all day, and we won by throwing. Even in that game, there was a little hitch pass that I caught and took to the house. But you're thinking that something like that might happen again against A&M. I was trying to stay loose that morning and stay within the moment. I was trying to enjoy my last home game. I knew it was the last time I was going to be around the guys at home. I was thinking that beating A&M would be a great way to end my career.

The record came on a lead-isolation play. We had run it a lot all year, and we had done a very good job running that play. I kept looking up at the scoreboard because they kept showing how many more yards I needed. I looked up, and I needed 11 yards. I didn't think too much of it because it was only 11 yards. Then we ran the Iso play. For me, it was like the whole play happened in slow motion. Our fullback Ricky Brown had a good block. It was enough to get me through the hole. I came up and I saw a defensive back coming up to hit me. I decided to get low and he bounced right off of me. The next thing I realized I was in the open field. Another guy had an angle on me, but I saw Wane McGarity coming full speed. He got a great block and I got into the end zone. That's when I realized, "Oh my god! I got the record on a 60-yard run."

I can't even put it into words. What made it so special is that I felt like I shared it with my teammates, with Wane who was my best friend on the team, and the fans. I jogged from the end zone to the sideline; I couldn't wait to see coach Brown and Tony Dorsett. There is a tradition that as you get close to breaking a record, you want the person whose record you're breaking to be there. Tony Dorsett's record had stood for twenty-two years. No one had come close to it. I had seen Tony Dorsett play, so it meant a lot to me that he would be there. He and Earl Campbell are good friends, and Earl helped get that done where Tony would be in Austin the day I had a chance to break the record. Having Tony Dorsett on the sideline to share that moment made it even more special.

That whole season, I felt like I was in the zone. It felt different than the first three years because coach Brown put the team on my shoulders. Mackovic would never have done that. I really felt like it was my team. Usually in football, you throw the ball if you're trailing in the fourth quarter. But I remember when we played Baylor, we were down and they gave me the ball three times in a row and I got all the way down the field and we scored. For me to be able to carry the team like that in the fourth quarter and win like that is special. The fact that a head coach trusted me had a big effect on me.

I'm the kind of guy who, when I hit a plateau, I don't look back and say "wow."' Instead, I look forward and ask where I can take this. It was a great game, but we barely won the game. I had 259 yards and some really nice runs but I fumbled twice. If I hadn't fumbled twice, I might have had 350 yards and really took it to the Aggies. In fact, they took a late lead. We came back and kicked a field goal to win. The thing I loved about Coach Brown was that, no matter what was going on, he was still the same guy. If we were up by 50 points, or trailing, he's still going to tell us to get back out there and stay focused. I think that really helped me, especially in the A&M game. Coach Mackovic's demeanor would definitely change according to the score.

The coaches did a good job of keeping us focused. I really enjoyed it. I was into it. I had so much fun that year, but one of the things that Mack worried about was that things would get out of hand. He wanted to make sure I was comfortable and that I was protected. They also had to come up with ways where I wasn't getting so much attention that it was no longer a "team" thing.

The Heisman Trophy never crossed my mind. I'm the kind of guy who either doubts something 100 percent or I know something 100 percent. Basically, I knew the Heisman was mine. It was just a feeling I had all season. I knew I was going to win the Heisman. In my mind, I didn't have to break the rushing record to win the Heisman. For me, it was more of a matter of *how* I was going to break the record. But I never would have expected it to be on a 60-yard run.

Upon Further Review

The Trophy that Williams assumed would bear his name officially became his on December 12 at the Downtown Athletic Club in New York City. He also became the first two-time winner of the Doak Walker Award and Texas's first player to win unanimous first-team All-American honors in consecutive seasons since Jerry Gray (1983-84). Williams capped his collegiate career with a UT bowl game record 203 yards rushing and 2 touchdowns in a 38-11 Cotton Bowl win against a Jackie Sherrill-led Mississippi State team. It was Texas's first New Year's Day bowl victory in sixteen years, giving Williams 6,279 rushing yards during his Texas tenure. All told, Williams finished his career with 46 school records and 21 NCAA marks.

It was such an impressive resume that the New Orleans Saints traded their entire draft in 1999, as well as their first- and third-round selections in 2000, for the right to select Williams with the fifth pick. Professional football, however, would be a rollercoaster ride for Williams. He raised eyebrows when he hired rap star Master P's agency No Limit Sports to negotiate his contract and then occasionally conducted interviews while wearing his helmet. But Williams would rush for 3,129 yards and 16 touchdowns in three seasons with the Saints, the franchise's first player to rush for 1,000 yards in consecutive seasons.

The Saints were still searching for an elusive winning season when they fired head coach Mike Ditka and traded Williams to the Miami Dolphins in 2002. That season, Williams led the NFL in rushing with 1,853 yards and was a Pro Bowl selection. He followed that up with 1,372 yards for Miami in 2003.

"I had fun in 2002 when I led the League in rushing," Williams said, "and it was pretty fun before then. Then it started to get not so fun."

Williams had tested positive for marijuana shortly after he joined the Dolphins, and in 2004, the NFL levied a four-game suspension against him for another infraction of its drug-abuse policy. Then, one week before 2004 training camp, Williams announced he was retiring from professional football.

"I didn't have an identity outside of being a football player," said Williams. "So, I went on a journey to find out who I really am."

His "journey" included training as a yoga instructor and attempts to come to terms with a social anxiety disorder and depression.

"I thought if I was rich and famous and all the girls loved me," Williams said, "then I'd be happy. It didn't turn out that way."

Williams has gone on record stating that his use of marijuana was essentially to treat his symptoms, asserting that it had fewer side effects than his prescribed medications.

Miami finished 4-12 during the first year of Williams's retirement, resulting in coach Dave Wannstedt's resignation. In 2005, first-year Dolphins coach Nick Saban said he would welcome Williams back to the locker room. Williams served his four-game suspension, reimbursed the organization a percentage of his signing bonus and ran for 743 yards and 6 touchdowns on 168 carries.

Then, in February 2006, it was announced that Williams had violated the League's substance-abuse policy for the fourth time. He was suspended for the entire season, but was allowed to play for the Toronto Argonauts in the Canadian Football League on the condition that he return to the Dolphins in 2007. One month after his CFL debut, Williams broke his left arm and missed the next two months of the season. His only season in the CFL saw Williams rush for 526 yards and 2 touchdowns on 109 attempts.

Williams's return to the NFL was contingent upon weekly drug tests and he was reinstated in October 2007. He returned to play in a November 26 Monday Night Football game at Pittsburgh. Players were ankle-deep in mud following heavy rains but, on Williams's seventh carry, linebacker Lawrence Timmons stepped on Williams's right shoulder while chasing Williams's fumble. The next day, it was revealed that Williams would miss the remainder of the season with a torn pectoral muscle.

The four previous seasons had been, by any measure, tumultuous for Williams. His customary role as the featured running back appeared to be in his rear-view mirror until the 2009 season. That's when Dolphins starting running back Ronnie Brown suffered a season-ending injury. Suddenly, Williams was back in the lineup. He reached 1,000 yards rushing with one game left in the 2009 regular season, setting a new NFL record for the longest stretch between 1,000-yard seasons at six years.

Williams retired from the NFL in 2012 following a one-year stint with the Baltimore Ravens. His final game pushed him past the 10,000-yard mark for career rushing. Williams was just the twenty-sixth player in history to reach that plateau and actually finished with 602 more NFL rushing yards than Earl Campbell.

In April 2012, Williams became the only player other than Campbell to have a statue built in his honor on The University of Texas campus.

Chapter Eighteen

NATHAN VASHER

Strong Safety, Cornerback (2000-03)

Few knew what to make of Nathan Vasher when he reported to Texas as a lanky, 170-pound freshman in the summer of 2000.

The Texarkana product excelled at both cornerback and wide receiver as a prepster but was overshadowed in a recruiting class boasting Roy Williams, B. J. Johnson, and Sloan Thomas.

"When we recruited him we really weren't sure where he would play," head coach Mack Brown said. "That was the [recruiting] year that there were so many great receivers. We thought we could play him at safety and still play the nickel position but, then, he grew into the cornerback position."

There would be plenty of growing pains. For some, the issue wasn't simply where Vasher should play but *if* Vasher could play at this level. It was the first day of August Camp when Vasher so badly misplayed a one-on-one drill that he literally fell down, the victim of a simple juke at the line of scrimmage. Split end Roy Williams incredulously turned to a teammate and asked, "They gave *that guy* a scholarship?"

Vasher understood the early misgivings. He harbored them himself.

"Roy Williams and I were in the same recruiting class," Vasher said, "but Roy was this highly touted, Odessa Permian great. At first, I wasn't everything I was supposed to be cracked up to be. I was falling everywhere. I was nervous playing against these guys. But that made me a better professional player because

I had faced those guys for four years at Texas. I competed against Roy, Sloan, and B. J. in practice. Once I got to the game, it seemed like anything less than Roy Williams was easier."

Vasher started three games his freshman year as a nickel back for a secondary that posted an NCAA-leading 88.3 pass efficiency rating. That season, he saw action in eleven games at cornerback while serving as a backup punt returner. Vasher would add nearly ten pounds of muscle to his 5'11" frame during the off-season in Texas's strength-and-conditioning program. He was penciled in as the starting strong safety and top returner when spring drills were scheduled to begin Tuesday, February 27.

It was a practice session that never happened.

The day before would forever change the lives of every Texas coach and player numbered among the 2001 squad. It had nothing to do with football.

Longhorn coaches convened Monday morning to conclude final preparations for spring training. The fourth year of Brown's tenure promised to be his best. Nearly all of the players were his own recruits and the program was poised for what was expected to be its first top-ten finish in nearly twenty years. But later that morning, at the Texas Department of Public Safety headquarters in Austin, instructor Lance Coleman received a call from the DPS office in Bryan.

There had been a fatality on U.S. 79; the sole occupant of the vehicle was a young man wearing a 1999 Big 12 South Division championship ring. The truck had Louisiana license plates registered to Marc Pittman, the father of twenty-one-year-old Longhorn defensive lineman Cole Pittman.

"It was the worst day of my coaching life when I got the call from the highway patrol," Brown said. "They thought they had identified Cole, but they wanted us to send a picture to be certain. I also needed to call Cole's dad and talk to him."

Texas's annual spring football media conference that same morning had been on the calendar for weeks, and Coleman arrived just before it concluded. There had been a positive identification. Louisiana State Troopers were already en route to talk to Marc Pittman. Brown immediately sequestered himself in his office to try, as best he could, to console the Pittman family through a long-distance call from Shreveport. When Brown emerged, players had already gathered for a team meeting that they assumed would be strictly about spring football. Now, Brown searched for the words that would bear terrible news to a group of very young men.

"Spectacular" Nathan Vasher led the Horns over North Carolina in 2001
(Photo courtesy of Will Gallagher)

Initially, Brown took Stevie Lee and Phillip Geiggar out of the room—both Longhorns played high school ball with Pittman at Shreveport Evangel Christian—to inform them privately before facing about 120 players.

"We had eighteen- to twenty-two-year-olds looking us in the face and asking 'Why?'" Brown recalled. "'Tell me why this happened. He was here yesterday. He was a buddy of mine. Now he's gone. Tell my why.'"

While words are inadequate in the context of an unspeakable loss, it was important to make a distinction between "moving on" and "moving forward," Brown said.

"We're always going to remember Cole Pittman, so we're not 'moving on.' We're going to think about this every day. You can 'move forward,' but you keep Cole in your heart.' [Pause] I've got a picture of Cole in my office. I look at it every day."

Coaches and several players attended Cole's funeral in Shreveport on Wednesday while the UT Men's Athletic Department held a memorial service on Thursday. Just before the service, the team walked through the football stadium where Pittman's picture was displayed on the JumboTron. Marc Pittman was there and spoke briefly to the team. Then, those assembled turned to face the larger-than-life image of Cole Pittman and sang "The Eyes of Texas."

"I just can't imagine a family losing a child after going through that," Brown said. "I really pray for those who have had it happen."

Players would wear a decal of Pittman's initials on their helmets throughout the 2001 campaign. Pittman's football locker would remain as it was for the duration of his scholarship. It was decided that his No. 44 jersey would not be worn by a Texas player until after his eligibility would have been completed following the 2002 season.

In addition, the September 8 home game against North Carolina, with 83,106 in attendance, was dedicated to Pittman. Just before kickoff, Pittman's family, surrounded by coaches and players, was presented with a T-ring—given to all Longhorn football lettermen who earn a degree—and a framed No. 44 jersey.

The contest had one other underlying significance. It marked the first time that Brown's former North Carolina program had traveled to Austin since he arrived in 1997 to restore the Longhorn tradition. It also signaled the first time Nathan Vasher faced a quality opponent as a full-time starter.

NO. 4 TEXAS vs. NORTH CAROLINA

September 8, 2001
The "Cole Pittman Dedication Game"

The tone for Vasher's record-breaking day was set early with his 14-yard return to near midfield after Texas forced a North Carolina punt on its opening series. The Tar Heel defense forced a three-and-out but, on UNC's next possession, Texas defensive end Cory Redding stepped in front of quarterback Ronald Curry's slant pass and returned it 22 yards for the pick-six. Redding's first career touchdown, a somersault into the end zone, spotted Texas a 7-0 lead 4:56 into the ball game.

Inspired, the Texas defense forced another Tar Heel three-and-out. This time, Vasher collected a John Lafferty punt and dashed 59 yards to the 5-yard line. It set up quarterback Chris Simms's 1-yard sneak on second-and-goal to give the Horns a 14-0 lead. The Tar Heels immediately responded with a nine-play, 77-yard drive, capped by Curry's 20-yard scoring run on a quarterback draw. The teams would trade punts but, this time, Vasher fumbled at the Texas 17. Carolina cashed in two plays later with a 9-yard run, tying the score at 14 with 2:20 eclipsed from the second quarter. Freshman Dusty Mangum would boot a pair of field goals, from 36 and 49 yards out, to give Texas a 20-14 halftime lead.

Early in the second half, the Horns could do nothing with a Quentin Jammer interception after Simms was thrown for an 8-yard loss. Despite another three-and-out from the Tar Heels, it was still anybody's ball game when Texas took over at its own 11 following a 5-yard Vasher punt return. Simms launched a twelve-play drive with a 9-yard completion to Roy Williams. The big play, though, was Ivan Williams's 31-yard rumble over left tackle. An 8-yard completion to flanker B. J. Johnson set up a first-and-goal from the 7. From there, freshman running back Cedric Benson put the finishing touches on the 89-yard march when he tallied the second touchdown run of his career. The 2-point conversion attempt failed, but Texas led 26-14 with 2:25 remaining in the third quarter.

The Longhorn defense forced another three-and-out. Roy Williams collected 25 yards on a reverse, setting up Mangum's 51-yard field goal to extend the lead to 15. It quickly became a 31-14 contest when Curry was sacked for a safety on North Carolina's first snap of the final frame. Two possessions later, Darian Durant would check in as the Tar Heel QB. After moving the chains with an 11-yard completion on first down, a holding penalty and an 8-yard sack would doom the Carolina drive.

Despite Vasher's early success, his most recent return had resulted in a 7-yard loss. This time, though, Vasher gathered a 29-yard Lafferty punt at the North Carolina 44 and darted untouched into the end zone to become the first Longhorn to score on a nonblocked punt return in ninety-eight games. Mangum's point after made it 38-14.

"He was spectacular," North Carolina head coach John Bunting said of Vasher. "He was the back-breaker for us. There is no doubt about it. He was the difference in the ballgame."

North Carolina's last chance to put points on the board was thwarted when linebacker Reed Boyd intercepted a Durant pass at the Tar Heel 14. From there, backup running back Brett Robin scored on successive running plays. Surprisingly, Texas called for time just before the point-after attempt with 36 seconds remaining. Sideline reporters questioned why QB Major Applewhite lined up behind center in an apparent 2-point conversion with his team boasting a 30-point lead. Instead, Applewhite quickly took a knee after the ball was snapped. He pointed to the heavens as he walked to the emotional Texas sideline, preserving the 44th point to honor No. 44.

The Game of My Life

By Nathan Vasher

It was my sophomore year and it was my first year being a full-time starter and returning punts. I had a chance to get Hodges Mitchell's number. He was No. 3 also. The North Carolina game was definitely a great game. It ended up being one of my best ever.

It seemed like everyone was hitting their blocks on my returns, so usually I would just have to make one person miss. When they announced on the loudspeaker that I had broken some of the school's punt return records, I had to ask someone to make sure they were talking about me. I couldn't believe that I did that.

It was the first time I ever had a touchdown on a punt return but, in the same game, I had a muffed punt. I didn't make some good decisions during the game. When I was younger, the whole time I was back there I was thinking about if I would drop the football. I was down on myself after I had that drop against North Carolina. But the team said, "Don't worry about it. Get the next one." And that's what I did.

College was definitely a rollercoaster, but I've definitely become a better person because of it. I was very competitive. That's something you can't measure: the competitive nature of your heart. You always hear that DBs have to have a short-term memory, but it has to be a discipline. It has to be a conscious effort to put something negative that happens to you in the past. If you're playing cornerback, you have to have the same kind of mentality whether you have a good play or a bad play. It's something I learned from [defensive backs] coach Duane Akina, just being mentally strong, becoming a real man and just stepping up and doing what you're supposed to do. You learn to be accountable. That's something I learned at the University of Texas, and it's something I took with me into my NFL career.

I think what I remember most is just being able to persevere through both the bad and the good things you do during the course of a game. That's the game when I felt that I definitely belonged as a player. I had eight punt returns that day for a school record, but it was also a game where you learn that not everything is going to go your way. You have to be headstrong to persevere through some of those things that might happen to you, not only during the course of a game but through the course of a season. When I think about my college career, I think about that [North Carolina] game as one of the stepping stones that got me to where I am now.

It was the Cole Pittman game. It was tough when we lost Cole. Real tough. I remember the meeting when Coach Brown came in and told us that Cole was no longer with us. Cole was in an accident trying to make it back to the team meeting at the start of spring football. We couldn't believe it. We canceled the first part of spring football so we could begin to deal with losing Cole. We had a memorial service, but we also recognized Cole just before kickoff [against North Carolina]. His family was there and we presented them Cole's jersey. It was very emotional, but then you have to go out and play a football game. He wore number 44, and we didn't kick the extra point at the end of the game to keep the score at 44. Losing Cole really put things into perspective. It makes you think about what's important, about how close-knit of a family that we were as a team and not to ever take life for granted.

Upon Further Review

Vasher was named Big 12 Special Teams Player of the Week for his outing against North Carolina, but he was just getting warmed up. His 173 punt return yards against Baylor later that season set a school record as did his 554 yards for the 2001 season. His 15.0-yard punt return average ranked No. 6 nationally. Vasher's seven interceptions in 2001 tied a Longhorn single-season record. He had a career-best 12 tackles in the 2001 Big 12 Conference Championship game while playing for college football's top defense (236.2 ypg).

"We were a man-to-man team under [Defensive Coordinator Carl] 'Bull' Reese," Vasher noted. "Playing man was something I had a passion for but, when I got to the League, I had to learn how to play zone."

Vasher transitioned to cornerback his junior season, starting ten games while missing two due to an ankle injury. He earned second-team All-Big 12 honors as a cornerback after posting 33 tackles, 15 pass break-ups and 4 interceptions. He also nabbed third-team all-conference accolades at punt returner with 370 yards on 26 returns.

Vasher's senior season was one for the record books. That's when he set a new Longhorn standard for pass break-ups in a single-season (26) and in a career (64). His 1,314 career return yards also tops the Texas charts. Most impressive of all, Vasher tied the longest-standing mark in Texas football history with 17 career interceptions, matching Noble Doss's feat set in 1941. All told, Vasher completed his collegiate campaign as a First-Team All-Big 12 performer, a Third-Team All-American and as a Thorpe Award semifinalist.

"When Nate first got here, I thought he was sorry," Williams said, "but look how far he came. He was our first Thorpe Award semifinalist."

The Chicago Bears made Vasher their fourth-round pick of the 2004 NFL Draft and became the starting cornerback by the fourth game of the season. He was second in the National Football Conference with 8 interceptions in 2005 and was a Pro Bowl selection. Yet, NFL fans are more likely to recall Vasher's highlight reel return of a missed 52-yard field goal that he took 108 yards to the house (an NFL record that teammate Devin Hester tied the following season).

Vasher battled injuries in 2006 and 2007 but came up big in Chicago's NFC Championship Game win against New Orleans on January 21, 2007, with a fumble recovery and a later interception. It helped seal the deal, sending Chicago to its first Super Bowl in nearly twenty years.

Vasher battled injuries before signing a one-year contract with San Diego in March 2010 but was released in September. He signed with Detroit that same month before the Lions released him in September 2011.

Chapter Nineteen

DERRICK JOHNSON

Linebacker (2001-04)

Derrick Johnson just did not want to play football. In fact, the very thought of it left him tearfully clinging to his mother.

Say what? This from a two-time All-American? This from Texas's most celebrated linebacker since legendary Tommy Nobis set the program's standard in the mid-1960s?

Truth be told, Johnson did not want to play football that day—a Pop Warner practice, no less. It had nothing to do with the caliber of pee-wee competition ("I knew I was good," Johnson recalled) but rather the demeanor of Johnson's coach.

"He wasn't mean," Johnson laughed, "but he was one of those 'yelling' types. I was a little kid, so I wasn't used to that. I didn't want to get out of the car, but my mother made me. She said if I didn't get out, everybody would think I was a sissy. She said everybody was watching me."

That was all it took. Johnson stepped out of the vehicle and, to some extent, took one small step toward his future.

Years later, Johnson understands that his mother wasn't making him play football as much as forcing him to face his fears. Besides, linebackers are typically the most feared of all who grace the gridiron. It's just that the list of Longhorn linebackers striking fear into the hearts of opponents had been a relatively short one since Nobis won the Outland Trophy and was a Heisman finalist in 1965.

Johnson would change all that when he accepted Mack Brown's offer to play for the Longhorns starting with the 2001 campaign. By then, Johnson was a Parade All-American at Waco High and was heavily recruited by all the usual suspects.

"Everybody dreams of coming to Texas and being outstanding here," was the way Johnson saw it.

Johnson lost his redshirt during the Horns' home opener against New Mexico State. It was then that he realized he could succeed at a traditional football power when he "blew up a screen pass" midway through a 41-7 shellacking. Johnson earned his first collegiate start three weeks later in the Big 12 Conference opener against Texas Tech, registering what would be his freshman season personal-best 13 tackles during UT's 42-7 thumping of the Red Raiders.

Johnson logged his second-straight start against No. 3 Oklahoma the following Saturday as No. 5 Texas entered the Red River rivalry undefeated for the first time since 1985. He notched a team-best eight stops in what would be Texas's only loss of the regular season, a 14-3 defensive tilt unsettled until the final minutes when Sooner strong safety Roy Williams's high-flying disruption of a Chris Simms pass resulted in a pick-six.

Texas reeled off six straight wins, including a 41-7 cakewalk against No. 14/17 Colorado and a 21-7 decision at Texas A&M on the day after Thanksgiving.

The Sooners' shocking loss to unranked Oklahoma State the next day thrust Texas into the Big 12 title game against the same Colorado team it had beat by 34 points five weeks earlier. Irving's Texas Stadium provided a de facto home crowd for the Horns, who also had a legitimate shot at parlaying a win into a BCS National Championship Game appearance.

Instead, the wheels came off. Four Texas turnovers (three INTs, one fumble) resulted in 29-10 first-half deficit. Coaches remained with Simms until he injured his finger just before halftime. Backup Major Applewhite, the starting QB in 1998 and 1999, engineered a near comeback. The Horns trailed 36-30 when the defense forced a Colorado punt with 3 minutes left. But a roughing penalty gave the Buffaloes new life; the result was a clock-draining, sixteen-play field goal drive in a 39-37 decision.

Texas accepted an invitation to a second-straight Holiday Bowl. The team would not only have to overcome the crushing loss in the conference title game, but also the absence of starting RB Cedric Benson and top offensive lineman Mike Williams. The two suffered season-ending injuries in a collision trying to make a tackle on Simms's last interception in Irving.

Two-time All American Derrick Johnson won both the Butkus Award and the Nagurski Trophy as a senior at Texas (Photo courtesy of Will Gallagher)

No. 9 TEXAS vs. No. 20/21 WASHINGTON

December 28, 2001

Holiday Bowl—San Diego, California

The first 15 minutes of the 2001 Holiday Bowl ended in a scoreless tie after Dusty Mangum's 35-yard field goal attempt hit the left upright. The Huskies responded with a nine-play drive resulting in a 43-yard John Anderson field goal. Texas's next snap saw QB Major Applewhite toss the first of three second-quarter interceptions. Husky QB Cody Pickett threw three straight incompletions as his team settled for its second-straight field goal. Both defenses would force punts but, on first-and-10 from the 45, Terry Johnson stepped in front an Applewhite attempt and returned it 38 yards for the pick-six. Washington assumed a 13-0 lead with 6:54 remaining until halftime.

Applewhite shrugged off his second interception with a pair of big plays, starting with his 30-yard completion to TE Bo Scaife that took Texas to midfield. The four-play drive culminated with Texas's first TD of the evening, a 43-yard scoring toss to flanker B. J. Johnson.

Cornerback Nathan Vasher got his hands on Pickett's next attempt, intercepting at the Longhorn 46. Applewhite went to the air seven times—six aimed at split end Roy Williams—on an eight-play drive in which the only run was Ivan Williams's three-yard plunge on fourth-and-1 from the Washington 45. The Horns twice moved the chains on third down, including Applewhite's 17-yard completion to Roy Williams to the Washington 25. From there, Applewhite again connected with Roy Williams for the score as Texas took its first lead of the game, 14-13.

The Huskies immediately responded with a seven-play scoring drive, all passes, to regain the upper hand at 20-14 with 47 ticks until intermission. The Horns went to their one-minute offense but, on first-and-10, Marquis Cooper intercepted Applewhite at the Longhorn 41. The half ended with Anderson's 40-yard field goal to give his team a 23-14 advantage.

Washington added to the lead on its opening series of the second half. Pickett completed three to All-American TE Jerramy Stevens, including a 17-yard TD, to put the finishing touch on a 91-yard, twelve-play drive. Texas answered with a 26-yard Mangum field goal following a 66-yard drive but trailed 30-17 with 5:37 remaining in the third.

Pickett moved the sticks on third-and-10 from the 35 with a 16-yard completion to Stevens. That's when RB William Hurst took over, rushing for 3 yards and then for 42 before Quentin Jammer and Rod Babers lassoed him at the four. Hurst cashed in from there and, now, Texas stared at a 36-17 deficit with just 3:51 remaining until the final frame.

Texas's largest comeback had previously been a 17-point rally to upend Oklahoma in 1999. Applewhite was under center that day, and his attempt to again make Longhorn football history began when he passed his team to the Washington 5. But Ivan Williams's 2-yard loss, followed by a pair of incompletions, forced Texas to be content with a 24-yard Mangum field goal. The quarter ended with Texas trailing 36-20.

The Burnt Orange forced a 31-yard punt that Vasher returned 7 yards to the Washington 48. Applewhite converted a key third-and-10 with a 12-yarder to Scaife. A pass interference penalty put Texas in prime real estate at the 2, setting up Applewhite's first down scoring toss to Matt Trissel. The 2-point conversion failed, but Texas had narrowed the deficit to 10 points with 11:54 remaining.

The Horns desperately needed a defensive stop and Derrick Johnson produced. The freshman weakside linebacker leveled Pickett for an 8-yard loss on third-and-long, forcing a 42-yard punt from inside the Husky 20. Now, Texas was 54 yards from being back in this one. Roy Williams quickly collected 38 of those yards on first down and Ivan Williams negotiated the final 9 on 3 carries. Mangum's point after brought Texas within 36-33 at the 8:01 mark.

Once again, the Huskies faced third-and-long. And once again, Johnson came up big. This time, Johnson intercepted a Pickett pass at the Husky 25 and returned it 16 yards. It took Texas three plays to reach the promised land, but Scaife's 4-yard TD reception erased the deficit while the PAT gave Texas an improbable 40-36 lead with exactly 6 minutes remaining.

But this one wasn't over. Washington negotiated 80 yards in seven snaps, punctuated by Hurst's 34-yard TD run to regain the Husky lead at 43-40. There was just 1:49 remaining when Applewhite was forced to attempt Texas's second go-ahead drive in as many possessions. Scaife collected 12 yards on first down while, two plays later, Applewhite went up top to B. J. Johnson for 25. Applewhite found Scaife again, this time for 6, before Texas called timeout with 1:14 remaining to discuss the most critical pass attempt of the ballgame.

It would be a second-and-4 attempt from the Husky 37 and Applewhite dialed B. J. Johnson's number again. His reception quickly covered 32 yards to the

Husky five. From there, Williams carried twice to complete what was, then, the biggest comeback in program history.

The Game of My Life

By Derrick Johnson

If I had to pick one game, I'd go back to my freshman year and winning the Holiday Bowl against Washington. That was a breakout moment for me because, almost single-handedly, I probably got us back into the game to win that game. At the time, I was just a freshman running around and making plays.

We were down by 16 points at the end of third quarter. I had a big interception but, before that, I had a big play—it was a sack on third down—to knock the quarterback out of the game. We had cut their lead to 6 but they, obviously, wanted to burn some clock because there was about 12 minutes still to play. It was weird the way [the sack] happened. In that scheme, I was supposed to go the right side of [linebacker] Tyrone Jones, but Tyrone told me, "Stay to the left. We're both going to blitz." I was a young guy so I said, "All right. I'll go to the left." I got past [TE] Jerramy Stevens, who is now in the NFL. I made a little move. I made an inside move and I came scot-free at the quarterback. That sack helped us get the momentum. He [Pickens] was able to come back but I thought he was a little woozy.

Obviously, Major Applewhite had a big, big part in that momentum shift and our comeback. But that quarterback sack was on third down and it was definitely a big play. We were already in the fourth quarter and we needed something good to happen. Then I came up with an interception on the next series. I returned it about 15 yards. I don't remember how long the return was but it was near the goal line. I've seen the replay on ESPN Classic. If you watch it, you'll see our sideline is going crazy. That interception was one of my best college memories. It sticks with me all the time. It led to our go-ahead touchdown, or, to our *first* go-ahead touchdown in the fourth quarter. Washington scored again, but [RB] Ivan Williams had a real good night.

The two No. 11s [Applewhite's and Johnson's jersey numbers] were definitely on par that game. That was Major's first start of the season and it was his senior year. Of course, there had been a lot of talk from the fans and media all season long about who the quarterback should be. The guys who played on [Texas's] defense didn't care who the starting quarterback was. We just didn't want the quarterback to turn the ball over. We don't really care who the coaches put in but, as it turned out, it was the perfect time for Major. It was a perfect way to finish off his career and, I guess, the perfect way to start mine.

The Holiday Bowl definitely gave me a lot of momentum for the rest of my career because that was a big game. We finished in the top five for the first time in nearly twenty years. For me to help us win that game gave me confidence and it gave my teammates confidence in me. At that moment [against Washington], everybody knew that Derrick Johnson was going to be a great player at the University of Texas.

Upon Further Review

Johnson's fourth-quarter sack was part of a team-high 7 tackles leading to Holiday Bowl Defensive MVP honors. Offensively, Applewhite set UT bowl game records in completing 37 of 55 passes for 473 yards and 4 touchdowns while sophomore split end Roy Williams set a Longhorn bowl game record with 11 catches (for 134 yards). As a result, Texas would register its first eleven-win season and top-five finish since 1983.

Johnson's performance was a harbinger of things to come. He registered a team-high 73 solo tackles (120 total) as a sophomore en route to First-Team All-Big 12 honors. The tally included a personal-best 14 tackles during a blue-collar 17-14 October road win against a Kansas State team that would finish at No. 5 on the AP poll. His four single-season INTs tied for all-time best among Longhorn linebackers.

As a junior, Johnson emerged as Texas's first consensus All-American linebacker in twenty years. Then, he led Texas with 130 tackles during his senior campaign, capping his collegiate career as the Big 12's Defensive Player of the Year and a two-time All-American. Johnson became the first Longhorn to win the Butkus Award (honoring college football's top linebacker) as well as the Nagurski Trophy winner (recognizing college football's top defensive player). Johnson's forced fumble in the third quarter of the 2005 Rose Bowl against Michigan was his ninth of the season, setting a new NCAA record for most fumbles caused in a single season.

"It was a dream to end my career by winning the Rose Bowl," Johnson said. "I couldn't have wished for anything better."

Three months later, the Kansas City Chiefs would make Johnson their top pick of the 2005 NFL Draft. He became the franchise's first linebacker to start every game of his rookie season. In 2009, Johnson ties an NFL record with two pick-sixes in a single game. Two years later, Johnson was a First-Team All-Pro Bowl selection.

Chapter Twenty

DUSTY MANGUM

Kicker (2001-04)

Dusty Mangum was nervous before the kick.

After all, he had never been in this stadium, much less in this pressure-packed situation. But, as with many place-kickers, Mangum had long since established a pattern of self-soothing. For Mangum, it was a type of self-talk that settles the butterflies by tempering the effect of nearly 90,000 screaming fans, not to mention the heavy responsibility toward teammates as well as the lofty standards that those wearing the Burnt Orange have set for themselves. Signaled by the referee's whistle, Mangum completes the internal monologue, lowers his head, begins his approach, hoping to nail the "sweet spot" and earmark the football toward the end zone against . . . New Mexico State.

As for that last-play, 37-yard field goal attempt against Michigan in the 2005 Rose Bowl? No sweat! Piece of cake. Nothin' to it.

Never mind that Mangum's final collegiate kick would determine the outcome of Texas's first-ever BCS Bowl appearance. Never mind that this was Texas's first-ever matchup against Michigan. Never mind that Mangum had never attempted a game winner. Mangum was as cool as a California cucumber on New Year's Day, 2005, a stark contrast to his Labor Day weekend debut four years earlier.

Just four months removed from high school, Mangum was handling placekicking duties for the nationally ranked Longhorns in the 2001 home opener against the *other* Aggies.

"The only time I was nervous in my career was against New Mexico State," said Mangum. "It was actually the first time I had ever been to a University of Texas football game. There were 86,000 people there. As soon as I kicked the ball, I heard [Smokey] the Cannon go off. That's when the nerves just went away. I had butterflies up to that point."

Until then, Mangum wasn't exactly steeped in Longhorn lore.

"I even have a picture of me as a kid wearing a Texas A&M hat," he admits. "I just wanted an opportunity to play college football at the Division I level."

The opportunity would be a long time coming, given that Texas coach Mack Brown secures most of his recruiting commitments nearly one year before national signing day. What's more, few collegiate programs extend full rides to special teams players. In 2001, Texas already had one scholarship player—and three walk-ons—competing for the placekicking job. Mangum had no particular preferences in universities.

"I wanted to play for a top-ten team or not at all," he said. "Otherwise, it wouldn't be worth it. I wanted to go all the way or not at all."

It's just that few Division-I schools went out of their way to recruit Mangum. Most days during the latter part of his senior season at Dallas's Mesquite High, the kicker in-search-of-a-job dropped by his head coach Steve Halpin's office, asking, "Did anybody come by? Did anybody call? Does anybody need a kicker?"

No. No. And no.

But the day would come when Texas assistant coach Hardee McCrary attended a Mesquite game to scout defensive tackle Marco Martin. Fortunately for Mangum, McCrary arrived in time for the opening kickoff. In December, 2000, Halpin informed Mangum that a Texas coach wanted to see him after school. Texas gave Martin a scholarship, but McCrary gave Mangum a chance.

"You will be an invited walk-on," McCrary informed Mangum. "There are three other walk-ons coming on with you. Whoever wins the battle during August camp will be our kicker."

Mangum received his letter of acceptance in February and graduated in the top 7 percent of his class. His work ethic heading into two-a-days included a "let the chips fall where they may" mindset.

"It was trying, but it was a lot of fun at the same time," Mangum said.

Dusty Mangum's last-second field goal gives Texas its first BCS victory, a win over Michigan in the 2005 Rose Bowl

Just three days before the home opener, Mangum was told the starting job was his.

"I had a pretty good idea that I'd start," Mangum recalled, "but I didn't know for sure until the depth chart came out. I was so excited."

Mangum's 11 points against New Mexico State set a Texas freshman kicking debut record en route to freshman All-American honors by the Football Writers Association of America. Texas capped the 2001 season with a riveting 19-point comeback against Washington in the Holiday Bowl and then concluded Mangum's sophomore year with a Cotton Bowl win against LSU. A Longhorn program with consecutive top-five finishes was still searching for its first BCS bowl bid. Then, toward the end Mangum's senior campaign, it was apparent that the final at-large bid for a BCS bowl would come down to Texas or California.

By late November, the Longhorns and Golden Bears were a pair of one-loss teams and separated by thousandths of a point in the BCS ratings. When Texas ended the regular season with a 26-13 thumping of No. 22 Texas A&M, Brown asked voters to "take a look" at his team as worthy of BCS bowl consideration. Voters would also have a final—and originally unscheduled—opportunity to evaluate California on December 4. The Golden Bears' September contest at Southern Mississippi was delayed three months as a result of Hurricane Ivan. California was No. 4 in the BCS rankings, just ahead of No. 5 Texas, but the final result from Hattiesburg was a closer-than-expected, 26-16 Bear win.

Now, the final at-large BCS bid was in the hands of subjective pollsters and computer formulas. Partisan fans in Austin and Berkeley wrung their collective hands until late Sunday afternoon, awaiting the final tabulation. Five minutes before the BCS Selection Show aired nationally, Longhorn special teams/DE coach Dick Tomey called Mangum's cell phone.

"Congratulations, Dusty," Tomey said. "We're going to the Rose Bowl."

No. 6 TEXAS vs. No. 12 MICHIGAN

January 1, 2005

Rose Bowl—Pasadena, California

The Wolverines worked with half a field throughout the overcast afternoon as Steve Breaston's school-record 223 return yards was largely responsible for Michigan's average starting field position at its own 45. Breaston returned the opening kickoff 44 yards, but three Wolverine penalties stalled their initial series. Texas RB Cedric Benson suffered a hyperextended knee on his first carry, contributing to a season-low 70 rushing yards on 23 attempts. The Horns got things started with QB Vince Young's 20-yard scoring run, capping a twelve-play, 85-yard drive with 1:41 remaining in the opening frame.

Michigan responded on its first possession of the second quarter with a WR Braylon Edward's 39-yard TD reception. Ramonce Taylor swung the momentum back to the Texas sideline with his 40-yard kickoff return. It set up a twelve-play, 58-yard march culminating in TE David Thomas's 11-yard TD reception. Michigan, however, would capitalize on Taylor's fumbled punt at the Longhorn 34. The Wolverines knotted the affair just before halftime with Edwards's second TD reception, this time from 8 yards out.

Vince Young would convert a key third-and-10 on Texas's first possession of the second half, finding TE Bo Scaife for 11 yards at the Texas 28. Young would follow with a 60-yard scamper down the right sideline to spot Texas a 21-14 advantage. But Breaston would return Mangum's kickoff 43 yards to midfield, setting up a 50-yard TD reception. Michigan took its first lead of the seesaw contest with QB Chad Henne's fourth TD toss of the day, his third to Edwards. Young would suffer his only INT of the afternoon when linebacker Prescott Burgess stepped in front of his attempt over the middle, returning it 23 yards to the Texas 45. The Longhorn defense stiffened, holding the Wolverines to a 44-yard field goal. Now, Michigan took a 31-21 lead into the final 15 minutes of play.

Young leaned heavily on his tight ends throughout the ballgame: Thomas and Scaife teamed for nine receptions, two more than all other Longhorn pass catchers combined. The duo's contribution was never more evident than on Texas's first series of the fourth quarter. Young connected with Scaife for 18 yards on first down and then followed with a 6-yard toss to Thomas. Young's 10-yard TD run narrowed the Wolverine lead, 31-28. Michigan responded with a 32-yard field goal to extend its lead to 34-28 with 6:09 remaining.

The Horns were looking for a clock-chewing final drive but scored too soon. Texas covered 69 yards in three plays and just 73 seconds. Young's 23-yard scoring run gave Texas its first lead since the early third quarter, but the dangerous Breaston awaited Richmond McGee's kickoff. This time, Breaston's return covered 53 yards, setting a new Rose Bowl record for return yardage. What followed was a five-play, 18-yard drive culminating in a 42-yard Garrett Rivas field goal. The Horns trailed, 37-35, with 3:04 remaining.

Taylor's 32-yard kickoff return positioned Texas at its own 34. Young kept the ball on five of the drive's ten plays, picking up 32 yards with his feet before Benson rushed twice to put Mangum in position for the game-winning attempt. Mangum's 37-yard field goal as time expired marked just the third time in Texas football history that the Longhorns had won on the game's final play. While college football was abuzz with Young's MVP performance (192 rushing yards and 4 rushing TDs, 180 yards passing and 1 passing TD), it was Mangum who enjoyed the victory ride atop his teammates shoulders. The win ensured an 11-1 season for Texas, resulting in a No. 4/5 final ranking.

The Game of My Life

By Dusty Mangum

I called my parents right after I found out we were going to the Rose Bowl, and they immediately made plane reservations to Los Angeles. I had never been to LA. I had no idea what it was about. As one of the senior leaders, we let the guys know that we were there to practice and to win. We'd go have fun later.

We had some time Sunday night [of bowl week] to go out. We went to Hollywood because one of the guys I was with wanted to look for Paul Newman's footprint. For me, one of the coolest parts of bowl week was meeting [broadcaster] Keith Jackson. He came out to practice one day. You hear Keith Jackson all the time broadcasting games. More than anything, it was important for me to be with my teammates, knowing it was my last game.

On the bus ride from the team hotel, I listened to some songs my on my iPod. One of them was "Just One" by Hoobastank. I had never heard the song before, but I thought the lyrics were very cool.

Vince Young, of course, played one heck of a game. We had [RB] Cedric Benson and [linebacker] Derrick Johnson. Michigan had All-Americans like [WR] Braylon Edwards and [SS] Ernest Shazor. It was a back-and-forth ballgame.

It was clear to me after Michigan kicked their last field goal that this was the final shot. We would have just one possession left. That was it. As soon as Michigan hit that field goal, I said to myself, "It's going to come down to me. Let's go. Let's get ready."

To me, it's what every kicker dreams of. You can't play at a high level if you don't dream of being that guy. When Michigan went up [2 points] on us with 3:04 left, I knew it was on me. There's nothing you can do about it. You can't tell people to hold on and wait a couple of minutes and then I'll be all right. I'd been preparing myself in practice for years, going through situations and learning from my mistakes. All that prepared me for that one moment.

My buddy Greg Johnson, our kickoff guy, came over and stood between me and the television cameras. If you watch the game again, you'll see Greg shield them off so they couldn't come closer. He was kind of helping me out with the cameras so they couldn't get too close to my [kicking] net. [DT Larry] Dibbles tried to tell me a joke. I waved him off said, "I'm fine. I'm fine." All the guys were real supportive. There were a lot of guys that I had played with for four years: Derrick Johnson, Cedric Benson, Bo Scaife, I can't name them all.

I told myself, "You've kicked game winners before in your mind. You've always practiced your kick like it's a game winner. Why shouldn't it be this way?"

Coach Brown came up to me and said, "Dusty, you're the luckiest guy in the world. You'll get to be the hero in the Rose Bowl." That's the kind of man Coach Brown is. Most coaches would say, "Do as you're told. You know how to do it." He was confident. He wasn't worried about it. There was a calm that came over me when he told me that. The coaches were confident in me. They knew I could do it. He trusted me. That's just cool. You usually wouldn't expect that from your head coach.

I told myself, "They [Wolverines] are going to call time-out. Don't worry about it. Relax a little bit."

During the first time-out, I was singing that song from my iPod because it was in my head. It was "Just One" by Hoobastank. I didn't know most of the lyrics until after the game. I was singing it because I was trying to relax myself. I later thought about how it kind of fit my situation. It had to do with needing just one chance, just one opportunity.

During the second time-out, I was thinking about my teammates. I was thinking, "We've gotten this far. Let's close it out. Then, let's go have a good time." We always had this Longhorn party in the locker room, this chant and cheer. I was thinking that's what we need to do. We came all the way out here. We needed to finish the season right. I thought about all my teammates and all my coaches and what they meant to me. I thought about my four years at Texas. I was thinking that the type of season we had was coming down to a last-second kick in the Rose Bowl, in Hollywood.

It probably seemed like hours on TV but, honestly, it felt like seconds in real life. When you ice the kicker, it usually means the kicker thinks about the kick too much. When kickers have too much time to think, they over-analyze everything. For me, singing that song, thinking about other things, the kick wasn't that big of a deal. When we practiced field goals at Texas, you'd wait for the right people to get on the field. I was used to waiting around and getting ready. It just comes down to the kicker being prepared for that situation, knowing they're going to call time outs and relaxing.

After the final time-out, I said, "That's it. I'm going to kick this." We'd worked too hard during two-a-days, too hard at 6:00 AM, to let it come down to this and not take advantage of this opportunity.

I went up to kick. I approached it. I kept my head down. I hit it sweet. Michigan got a good push. Man, they had a heavy rush. As soon as I kicked it, I looked up and there was a Michigan guy right in my face. [SS Ernest Shazor] came through unblocked. The ball went right through his hands. If he had crossed his hands like he was supposed to, Michigan wins. Game over. Then the linebacker [Prescott] Burgess jumped up and got his fingers on the ball. I looked at the ball. That got the rotation changed on it but it kept going straight. It was angling to the right but I knew it was going through. I'd seen too many of those. Before the ball went through, I turned and started running off the field. All I can remember was the sea of orange, the light bulbs, the confetti, and the excitement. It was surreal.

Upon Further Review

Mangum and several of his teammates spent one more day in Los Angeles to celebrate Texas's first BCS bowl win.

"I went to breakfast the next morning at a little diner," Mangum recalled. "Someone said, 'Do you know who this guy is? He just won the Rose Bowl.' They sat us immediately at the table. To me, it wasn't like, 'Wow, I did it,' because I didn't do it by myself. I had a snapper, a holder, and teammates who believed in me. I was just doing my job. My job is to make field goals. I don't need praise. I went out there, did my job, and we had fun."

The win propelled Texas to a final No. 4/5 national ranking, its best finish in twenty-one years. More important, members of the 2005 Longhorn team would view the Rose Bowl win as a precursor to the national championship the following season. When Texas returned to the Granddaddy of Them All one year later, this time facing top-ranked USC, the experience of having already won a Rose Bowl game was deemed invaluable. The win over the Wolverines, however, was the centerpiece of a twenty-one-game winning streak culminating in Texas's first national championship in thirty-five years. For Mangum, it was clearly the climax of a career that began with the happenstance attention of a Longhorn assistant.

"One of the things that I loved is that I played in both the Cotton Bowl and the Rose Bowl, two historic bowls, in my career," Mangum concluded. "I feel fortunate that I was able to play in two historic bowls. You feel like you're part of history. It's hard for me to imagine, though, that when I'm forty or fifty years old, people might ask me if I remember that Rose Bowl game. It's hard to imagine that right now, but it's going to be really cool to have been part of the history of Texas football."

Chapter Twenty-One

LIMAS SWEED

Wide Receiver (2004-07)

There it was, scrawled on a chalkboard, for all to see:

Whoever wants to beat Ohio State, meet me at the field tonight at 8.

Texas's voluntary summer workouts had yet to reach the midway point. The September 10 tilt at Ohio Stadium, the first meeting between the Longhorns and Buckeyes in 136 years of college football, was still months away. But there was no questioning the urgency of the statement, much less its author.

Quarterback Vince Young already had his game face on.

Whoever wants to beat Ohio State . . .

It wasn't so much an inquiry as it was an imperative. Just like it was imperative that Texas come away with its most significant road win since traveling to Arkansas on December 6, 1969. The consensus was that the victor in what promised to be 2005's marquee intersectional matchup, slated for a prime time national telecast, would have the inside track to face top-ranked and defending national champ USC for the BCS title.

Moments after Texas upended Michigan in the Rose Bowl on January 1, 2005, Young vowed that his team would return in one year's time to the Pasadena venue and play for the national championship. Now, No. 4 Ohio State represented the biggest hurdle in the '05 season to that promise. The only chink in the Buckeye armor was that QB Troy Smith had been suspended for the last game of 2004 and the 2005 opener against Miami [Ohio]. Head coach Jim Tressel planned to start Justin Zwick behind center, but Smith would play. Otherwise, the Scarlet and Gray returned nine defensive starters, including All-American linebacker A. J. Hawk. The Buckeyes had also won thirty-six straight nonconference home games; they had never lost a night game at the fabled Horseshoe.

It was Vince Young's midsummer night's dream that his squad would shape the national championship race by the second Saturday in September. In the eyes of Texas, Columbus Day would come early this year.

Among those who heeded Young's summons to practice that evening was sophomore split end Limas Sweed, arguably the offensive jewel of Mack Brown's 2003 recruiting class. The Brenham product was a second-team Texas 4A all-state selection as a senior after nearly half of his 72 career catches [31] went for touchdowns. The fact that Sweed not only wore Roy Williams's jersey number but also looked conspicuously like Williams in height and stature raised expectations among Texas fans to stratospheric levels. He *looked like* Roy, but could he *catch and run like* Roy?

There was also a gaping void in Texas's receiving corps after Williams, B. J. Johnson, and Sloan Thomas completed their eligibility in 2003. The Horns relied heavily on high-percentage tosses to tight ends Bo Scaife and David Thomas in 2004 as Sweed slowly matured as a redshirt freshman. He started the last seven games of the season, posting 23 catches for 263 yards on the year. Those were modest numbers, given that fans had grown accustomed to record-setting stats back when *the other No. 4* terrorized Big 12 defenders. Texas's inexperienced receivers had drawn heat during an otherwise splendid 11-1 campaign. There had been dropped balls, missed blocks, and busted assignments. The receivers simply had to upgrade their overall productivity, especially since RB Cedric Benson [Texas's third all-time leading rusher] had taken his game to the NFL.

Sweed was a late bloomer; more than half of his totals came during the final three games of the 2004 season. But fans and players were still anticipating his breakout game. Texas's 60-3 home opener against overmatched Louisiana-Lafayette didn't count. Besides, Sweed was still looking for his first collegiate touchdown when the underdog Horns boarded their charter plane to Ohio.

No. 2 TEXAS vs. No. 4 OHIO STATE

September 10, 2005

Columbus, Ohio

For the second time in three games, Texas faced one of the Big Ten's premiere programs. The Horns had parlayed the dramatic Rose Bowl win against Michigan into a preseason No. 2 ranking, but a bigger stage waited in Columbus. The crowd

Limas Sweed breaks the Buckeyes' backs with this fourth-quarter touchdown grab in Columbus, 2005

of 105,565 crammed into the 'Shoe set a new stadium record, and represented the largest crowd ever to attend a Texas game. Tailgates were at full-throttle nearly twelve hours before kickoff, while Ohio State coaches had long since added a wrinkle to the game plan. The Buckeyes spun an outside linebacker closer to the line of scrimmage, hoping to contain Vince Young's Zone Read threat. Texas offensive coordinator Greg Davis opted to dictate the tempo by opening with a no-huddle offense. Davis also countered with a play-action package out of the shotgun intended to draw in linebackers and open up passing lanes.

Young converted a key third-and-7 on Texas's opening series when he ran for 10 yards from his own 15. The eleven-play, 64-yard drive set up David Pino's 42-yard field goal. Three of Young's first six completions went to Billy Pittman, including a 33-yarder to over the middle on a slant to open the Horns' second drive of the game. Pittman would tally 130 yards on five catches, including a five-yard TD reception to put the finishing touches on that ten-play drive. Pittman's first career touchdown, in front of a stunned Ohio Stadium, saw Texas take a 10-0 lead with 1:37 remaining in the opening frame.

Smith entered the game on Ohio State's third series, but not until a 15-yard personal foul penalty was tacked on to Antonio Holmes's 47-yard kickoff return. That put the Buckeyes in prime real estate at the Texas 36 but the home team settled for a 45-yard Josh Huston field goal. Texas had a chance to regain the momentum when safety Drew Kelson stepped in front of a Smith pass inside the Buckeye 40, but Ohio State would dodge a bullet when the ball glanced off Kelson's jersey. Smith would then hook up with Anthony Gonzalez for 12 yards to move the chains on third down. It set up Holmes's 36-yard reception to cap a nine-play, 80-yard march. This one was tied at 10 apiece with 8:11 remaining until halftime.

Texas's attempt to answer was short-lived when Hawk returned a Vince Young interception 24 yards to the Texas 18. But defensive end Tim Crowder's 8-yard sack on third down forced a 36-yard Huston field goal. The Buckeyes led for the first time with 4:33 remaining before the break. Things continued to unravel for Texas when Hawk recovered RB Selvin Young's fumble at the Longhorn 30. Smith overcame a third-and-19 when he found Gonzalez for 21 yards. A 12-yard toss to Holmes made it first-and-goal from the 6. Ohio State would score on all four of its possessions in the second quarter, but the Texas defense forced field goals on three of those drives, including Huston's 25-yarder with 35 ticks left until intermission.

Texas took over at its own 46 following Tarell Brown's 12-yard kickoff return and a personal foul against the home team. Freshman RB Jamaal Charles replaced an injured Selvin Young and, on first down, turned on the jets following a short reception, racing 36 yards to the OSU 18. It set up Pino's 37-yard field goal cutting Ohio State's advantage to 16-13 heading into the locker room.

Vince Young's first attempt of the second half saw him suffer his second interception when safety Nate Salley came away with the steal. The Buckeyes operated from the Texas 37 and, again, the Horns forced a Huston field goal. Texas answered with a 72-yard drive, 63 of them courtesy of Pittman's catch-and-run. Young was thrown for a 4-yard loss on 3rd-and-goal from the four. Pino's field goal narrowed the deficit, 19-16.

For the sixth time (of eight on the night), Ohio State would begin a possession outside its 40 following Ted Ginn Jr.'s 46-yard kickoff return. From the Texas eight, Zwick fired a third-down bullet to tight end Ryan Hamby, alone in the middle of the end zone. Hamby bobbled the ball and, for a moment, looked poised to give his squad a 10-point lead. But cornerback Cedric Griffin, as if shot out of a cannon, leveled Hamby from the left. The wicked hit forced an incompletion and then a chip-shot 26-yard field goal, Huston's fifth of the night. Ohio State nursed a 22-16 advantage late in the third.

Early in the fourth, Vince Young took Texas from its own 12 to midfield on three straight completions, including a 27-yarder to Pittman. But Charles's 11-yard loss on a reverse—he would recover his own fumble at the end of the play—was a dagger in the seven-play drive.

The Buckeyes took over on their own 30 with 10:07 remaining. Mixing pass and run, Zwick efficiently moved the offense to the Longhorn 29 with a fresh set of downs. Here, another field goal would have forced Texas to score twice during the final 5 minutes. On first down, strong safety Michael Huff and middle linebacker Rashad Bobino stopped running back Antonio Pittman for no gain. Then, defensive end Brian Robison swatted a Zwick pass back into Antonio Pittman's hands, a reception that lost 4 yards. At that moment, Vince Young was on the sideline rallying his offense.

"I was telling the guys that we've been through this before," Young said, "and that the defense was going to get us the ball."

Indeed. A third-down incompletion led to Huston's only missed field goal of the night, a wide-left attempt from 50 yards out after Robison's play pushed Huston outside of his comfort zone. Texas took over at its own 33. A defensive pass interference penalty resulted in 15 yards of real estate, but then Young faced a critical third-and-6 conversion attempt. After a time-out, Young's 9-yard completion to Charles gave Texas new life at the Buckeye 39. Young went to Charles two plays later, this time for 8 yards. An offsides penalty moved the ball to the 25. Charles managed a yard on first down, but Texas had already burned two time-outs on the drive. There were less than 3 minutes remaining.

When Young broke huddle on second-and-9, he noticed Ohio State had dropped into a Cover Two zone for the first time. He faked the handoff to Charles and went through his progressions. There! Streaking toward the left pylon was a young receiver who had never caught a collegiate touchdown. Sweed had a step on Salley as Young lofted the ball. The arching lob reached Sweed's fingertips just before an outstretched Salley knocked them both into the end zone. Officials quickly surveyed the tangled bodies before making the call.

Touchdown! Texas 23, Ohio State 22 with 2:37 remaining.

As if to atone for a dropped interception, Kelson stripped Zwick as the Buckeyes attempted a game-winning drive. Robison returned the fumble 9 yards to the Ohio State 21. Running back Henry Melton was stopped at the one-inch line on fourth down, but linebacker Aaron Harris would sack Smith in the end zone for a safety, completing the scoring with 19 seconds left.

The Game of My Life

By Limas Sweed

The first touchdown pass I ever caught in college was at Ohio State. It jump-started my career and it definitely was a big confidence builder. I had always been a confident person, but maybe I was a little too quiet or didn't show enough emotion during games. Or, at least, that's what some people probably thought about me. That catch at Ohio State definitely helped me out as far as making plays. I had a good high school career but that catch proved I could make big plays in big games. I was a sophomore and that jump-started my collegiate career.

We were a great road team. We had won something like 21 of 22 road games, but this was Ohio State. There was a lot of hype.

We had a fast start, but then we had some turnovers. Our defense kept us in the game. Vince had led us on so many comebacks already that I think we were confident we would win [trailing late in the game]. I remember there were less than 3 minutes to play and we were driving into the loud end of the Horseshoe. What's interesting is that Ohio State went into a Cover-Two defense when I made my catch. That was the first time they went with that coverage all night.

All the routes on that play were streak routes. I think David Thomas was the first read, but the ball could have gone anywhere. I just ran by my guy and kept running. Vince threw the pass and I caught it. I think I caught the pass over Nate Salley. It was a falling down catch at the left pylon. Brian Carter ran over to me and asked, "Did you catch it? Did you catch it?" I said, "Yeah, I caught it! It's good." But they did an instant replay and we took the lead with the touchdown. The defense forced a fumble on Ohio State's next series and then came away with a safety.

Vince had a great game. The defense had a great game. Billy Pittman had a great game. Jamaal Charles didn't play like a freshman. He came up big with some catches out of the backfield. But without that [game-winning] catch, I don't think we would have played in the [2005] national championship game. That's why it meant so much to me. It wasn't just me catching a pass; it was me catching a pass that helped my team go to the national championship.

Upon Further Review

Sweed would earn Honorable Mention All-Big 12 honors as a sophomore after he finished second on the team with 36 receptions for 545 yards and 5 TDs. He would set a career high with 8 catches for 65 yards in Texas's 41-38 thriller against USC for the National Championship.

Sweed would earn first-team All-Big 12 accolades as a junior. He led the team that season with 46 catches for 801 yards. His 12 TDs that season tied Roy Williams's school record, but Sweed would break Williams's mark for touchdown catches in consecutive games with 7.

Sweed was a 2007 Preseason All-American, but his collegiate career was cut short by a wrist injury suffered during August camp. He accounted for 19 receptions for 306 yards and 3 TDs through six games before aggravating the wrist against Oklahoma. He opted for season-ending surgery and began to prepare for the 2008 NFL Draft. Sweed finished among Texas's Top 10 all-time leaders with 124 career receptions.

Sweed became the second-round pick of the Pittsburg Steelers. He remained with the franchise until he was waived in September 2011.

Chapter Twenty-Two

VINCE YOUNG

Quarterback (2003-05)

Even Superman gets the blues.

It had been a tough two weeks for Texas football and an even tougher fortnight for one Vincent Young. It began when the Horns not only lost to Oklahoma for the fifth straight year, but also saw their NCAA-leading scoring streak (spanning a quarter-century) snapped with the 12-0 setback to the Sooners. Texas would eke out a listless 28-20 win against Missouri the following Saturday, but it was backup Chance Mock sealing the deal after Young exited early with a bruised sternum with all of 19 yards passing on just 3 completions plus 2 interceptions in 9 attempts. Now, some odds makers listed No. 8 Texas as a slight underdog heading into an October 23, 2004, road test against dangerous No. 24 Texas Tech.

Young's sternum would be fine; it was his morale that needed a lift. His record as the Longhorn starter stood at an impressive 11-2, but it was the third time in nine games that the strong-armed Mock was summoned to relieve him of his duties. All Texas quarterbacks, to some extent, carry the weight of extraordinarily high expectations on their shoulder pads. For Young, those expectations were stratospheric. He was, quite simply, the prized recruit of Mack Brown's Texas tenure and the most coveted Texas schoolboy athlete since the days of Earl Campbell.

To be sure, Young enjoyed flashes of brilliance as a redshirt-sophomore in 2003. He rallied Texas to a 24-20 comeback against eventual Big 12 champ Kansas State. He made good on his first start with a 40-19 thumping of Iowa State. The Zone Read offense, with Young at the helm, was gobbling up real estate the way the Wishbone used to when Texas won thirty straight and pair of national championships. Texas steamrolled No. 12 Nebraska 31-7 before reeling off 41 unanswered points to dispatch of No. 21 Oklahoma State, 55-16. The '03 regular season ended with a 46-15 thumping of Texas A&M at Kyle Field.

Texas had never possessed a running quarterback quite like Young, prompting Brown to observe that it "was like having an extra running back on the field." Still, critics fixated on Young's half-cocked throwing motion that made him look like he was releasing darts rather than lofting passes. When Mock replaced Young in the third quarter of the 2003 Holiday Bowl loss to Washington State, there was a groundswell of opinion that the only thing keeping Vince Young from becoming, well, *Vince Young* was his suspect passing game. When the topic of his throwing motion surfaced *again* following the 2004 spring scrimmage, it was clear that Young was more than ready to put the matter to rest.

"I know what I want to play," Young said, "and I want to play quarterback. I mean, just *deal with it.* Vince is going to play quarterback."

Still, Texas was lucky to be 5-1 midway through the 2004 regular season. A late fumble recovery secured a 22-20 nail-biter at Arkansas while blowouts against North Texas, Rice, and Baylor did little to deter Young's naysayers. Oklahoma was the only *real* team Texas had faced in 2004, some argued, and the Sooners had pitched a shutout. Superman was not allowed to fumble or throw interceptions. He certainly could not be turned away from the Sooner end zone as if it were loaded with kryptonite. Something had to change, and some suggested that the most sensible thing would be a position change for Young. Move him to wide receiver, many suggested, and let Mock throw to him.

Young actually considered the switch, according to reputable insiders, the day he arrived at offensive coordinator Greg Davis's office for a little heart-to-heart heading into the Texas Tech game. Instead, Davis asked Young to consider all he had done to lead Houston Madison to a 14-1 record as a high school senior. Davis surprised his quarterback that day with a highlight reel of Young's jaw-dropping plays that resulted in 2001 national high school Player of the Year honors. The contrast was evident: Young was clearly more relaxed, fluid, and confident as a prepster. But the biggest difference was not so much the quarterback, Young suggested, but rather the game plan.

Typically, Davis prefers a drop-back passing attack because a rollout game can eliminate nearly half the field. However, the highlight reel indicated Young excelled while on the move. Davis agreed. He added rollout passes, lead options, and sprint-

Vince Young scores the game-winning touchdown against USC in the 2006 National Championship game

pass options to the game plan for Texas Tech. There would be bootlegs, draws, and keepers. There would be counters, stretch plays, and end-arounds. In short, it would be a creative and aggressive game plan to offset Texas Tech's point-a-minute attack that was averaging 70 points per game at home.

A school-record 55,413 crammed into Jones Stadium on Saturday night and saw the Red Raiders draw first blood with an 86-yard first quarter march that required all of five plays. But that only meant Vince Young would get the football, and Texas outscored the home team 51-14 during the next three-and-a-half quarters. Young coolly and efficiently threw for 142 yards and 1 touchdown on 10-of-15 passing. Just as impressive, he added 158 yards and 4 touchdowns on 25 carries.

All in all, it was the turning point in Young's college career. During the first six games of 2004, Young completed 62 of 113 passes (54.8 percent) for 758 yards; during the final six games, Young went 86 of 137 (62.7 percent) for 1,091 yards. Beginning with the win in Lubbock, Texas would not lose another game with Young behind center.

Sure, there would be moments that would test the mettle of any Man of Steel. But fans hardly seemed worried two weeks later, when No. 19 Oklahoma State jumped to a 35-7 lead with 1:21 left in the first half. It would only be a matter of time before Young donned his red cape and rallied his team with 49 unanswered points for the biggest comeback in school history.

The Horns would dodge a speeding bullet the following Saturday at Kansas. The Jayhawks were on brink of one of the most improbable upsets of 2004 with a 23-20 lead against No. 6 Texas late in the fourth quarter. Young faced fourth-and-18 at the Longhorn 45 with little more than a minute remaining. He dropped back to pass, quickly went through his progressions before darting around right end. Then, stepping out of the grasp of a crashing Jawhawk linebacker, he glided out of bounds 22 yards down field. The play gave Texas new life and then, with 11 seconds remaining, Young connected with Tony Jeffery in the left side of the end zone with a season-saving 21-yard touchdown completion.

Texas's 26-13 win against No. 22 Texas A&M represented the third straight game where Young rallied his team after trailing at halftime. Texas parlayed its strong finish into not only the program's first BCS bowl appearance, but also its first meeting against Michigan.

The Rose Bowl showdown against college football's winningest program represented Young's biggest stage to date and he was, quite simply, a human highlight reel. His 5 touchdowns (4 rushing, 1 passing) tied a Rose Bowl record that had stood for 102 years. His 24 points scored also tied a Rose Bowl record while his 372 yards (192 rushing, 180 passing) ranked No. 4 all-time in the Pasadena venue. Most important, when Texas trailed 37-35 at its own 34 with just 3:04 remaining, Young rushed on five of Texas's next seven plays to set up Dusty Mangum's game-winning 37-yard field goal as time expired. The obvious choice for the game's Most Valuable Player, Young was already thinking ahead to the 2006 Rose Bowl —the site of the BCS National Championship game—when he vowed, "We'll be baaaack!"

He was right. But, first, there would be the thrilling 25-22 comeback at No. 4 Ohio State with Young's 24-yard touchdown toss to split end Limas Sweed giving Texas the lead for good with 2:37 remaining. There would be Texas's 45-12 thumping of Oklahoma followed by the 52-17 shellacking of No. 10 Texas Tech. There would be another incredible comeback against Oklahoma State, this time from 19 down. By November, Young was directing a monster offense that was shattering school records (508.9 yards per game) that had stood for thirty-five years. The Horns outscored Baylor and Kansas, 128-14, on successive weekends before getting past Texas A&M, 40-29, for its third straight win at Kyle Field. UT's 70-3 annihilation of Colorado in the Big 12 Championship game sent No. 2 Texas to the BCS National Championship game against top-ranked and two-time (*Associated Press*) defending national champ USC.

One week after the resounding conference title game victory, Superman had the blues—again. December 10 was a frigid night in Manhattan, and Young finished a distant second to USC running back Reggie Bush in the 2005 Heisman Trophy balloting. It marked the highest finish by a Longhorn underclassman in the history of the award. Even so, Young thought that his also-ran status had disappointed, well, nearly everybody.

"I feel like I let the guys [teammates] down," Young said. "I feel like I let down my family and I feel like I let down our fans. I feel like I let down the city of Austin and the city of Houston."

If there was a silver lining for "disappointed" fans, it was that Young's second-place finish served as an incentive toward a larger goal: the national championship tilt against Bush's Trojans.

"This gives me a little bit of an edge," Young concluded. "I'm going to go on, work hard, and get prepared for January 4."

No. 2 TEXAS vs. No. 1 USC

January 4, 2006
Rose Bowl—Pasadena, California

No college football dynasty had ever put two Heisman Trophy winners on the field at the same time until USC lined up against Texas with running back Reggie Bush and quarterback Matt Leinart.

The Horns opened the showdown guilty of the one cardinal sin that could not be committed against what had been called the best offense in college football history: giving the Trojans not one, but two, shortened fields. Aaron Ross's fumbled punt after Texas forced a three-and-out on the opening drive kept the Trojan offense on the field. The result was a five-play, 46-yard scoring drive culminating with running back LenDale White's 4-yard scoring run. The Men of Troy had jumped to a 7-0 lead just 2:33 into the contest. Then, Texas coach Mack Brown's fourth-and-one gamble saw RB Selvin Young thrown for a loss at the Trojan 49.

Yet, Texas returned volley when it stopped Leinart for no gain on fourth-and-1 from the Longhorn 17. Linebacker Drew Kelson was credited with the tackle and, in all likelihood, kept USC from jumping to an early double-digit lead. The Horns quickly negotiated 36 yards to the Trojan 47, the big play courtesy of Vince Young's 15-yard run. The drive stalled when Texas lost 5 yards on running back Jamaal Charles's fumble, recovered by wide receiver Billy Pittman at the Longhorn 48.

The Trojan offense was back in business following a 39-yard Richmond McGee punt to the 17. A 9-yard Bush run and a 4-yard Leinart completion collected a pair of first downs. Yet, the tide turned for the rest of the opening half following Leinart's first completion of the second period. The two Heisman winners connected on an inside screen, and Bush was off to the races. Yet, 30 yards later, Bush attempted a lateral to unsuspecting wide receiver Brad Walker. Kelson was credited with a forced fumble while 2005 Thorpe Award-winning strong safety Michael Huff pounced on the precious pigskin at the Longhorn 18. Texas parlayed the gift into its first points of the game with David Pino's career-best 46-yard field goal.

Mixing pass and run, USC efficiently moved to the Texas 25 in seven plays. Then, on second-and-9, free safety Michael Griffin's leaping goal line interception staved off what momentarily appeared to be USC's second TD of the evening. The touchback put Texas 80 yards away from pay dirt, but now the Texas offense was humming. Young followed a 10-yard completion to Limas Sweed with a 9-yard toss to tight end David Thomas. He came back to Thomas for 9 more yards after Selvin Young carried for 8. Charles's 15-yard dash set up shop at the Trojan 22, but it also set the stage for some razzle-dazzle. Bush's ill-fated attempt at a lateral was engrained in Young's mind when, after sprinting for 10 yards around left end, he pitched to Selvin Young, who darted for Texas's first touchdown. (Replays indicated that Vince Young may have had one knee on the ground when he pitched to his roommate. Consequently, Texas hurried its next snap to beat a review of the scoring play. Pino's extra point attempt failed, but Texas now held its first lead of ballgame at 9-7.)

USC could not overcome a pair of 5-yard penalties and settled for a 40-yard Tom Malone punt. Ross's 15-yard return spotted Texas at is own 49 with 3:46 remaining until intermission. Young kept the drive alive with a 13-yard completion to Thomas on third-and-2 before running back Ramonce Taylor's 30-yard scoring run on a sweep-left. The Trojans answered with an eleven-play drive, but tackle Frank Okam registered back-to-back sacks, forcing USC to be content with a 43-yard field goal and a 16-10 halftime deficit to the underdog Horns.

The Men of Troy forced a three-and-out on Texas's opening series of the second half and then deftly collected 62 yards in seven plays, the big play coming on Dwayne Jarrett's 24-yard reception. White followed his 14-yard run by careening into the end zone from three yards out to reclaim the Trojan lead, 17-16.

Young sandwiched a pair of completions to Sweed, totaling 20 yards, with an 18-yard scamper. Charles rushed for 6 to the Trojan 14 and, from there, Young extended his arm toward the pylon as he dashed unmolested into the end zone. Texas was back on top, 23-17, following the seven-play response. It didn't last long. Leinart passed his team to the Texas 21 after, again, finding Jarrett for 24 yards. A one-man battering ram, White cashed in from 12 yards as USC jumped back on top, 24-23, with 4:07 remaining in the third quarter.

This one had become a track meet. Young immediately drove his team 66 yards to the USC 14, but Pino's 31-yard field goal attempt was wide right on the first play of the fourth quarter. Leinart hooked up with Jarrett, this time for 12 yards, to move the sticks on third-and-6 from the 24. White netted 21 yards on consecutive carries, upstaging the 2005 Heisman winner for most of the night. But it was patented Bush when, on the next play, he flew down the right sideline and, 26 yards later, somersaulted into the end zone to stake USC to an 8-point advantage.

A pair of Pittman receptions were good for 35 yards but the Texas drive stalled at the USC 17. Young was visibly agitated when Texas settled for a 34-yard field goal to draw within 31-26 with 8:46 remaining in what was becoming a down-to-the-wire thriller.

"Vince didn't speak to me when we kicked the field goal," Brown laughed. "I didn't think he would ever speak to me again."

After a four-play, 80-yard drive that gave USC a 38-26 lead with 6:42 remaining, Leinart had completed 14 of 15 passes since halftime. Michael Griffin and cornerback Tarell Brown's goal line collision knocked both of them out of the game on Jarrett's touchdown reception that capped the Trojan drive, but there was no panic on the Longhorn sideline.

"Vince is the Heisman Trophy winner in our books," said Huff. "We knew that, whatever it takes, Vince is going to go out there and make a play."

Or, in this case, a succession of plays. Young came out firing, completing five of six, including a couple to Thomas. The senior tight end's 6-yard reception over the middle converted the only third down of a 69-yard scoring march. Thomas led his team with 88 yards on 10 catches and had little trouble against USC's inexperienced outside linebackers.

Young ran just twice on that eight-play drive, but the final one was a highlight reel scramble where he reversed field, swept right and ran virtually untouched into the end zone from 17 yards out. It narrowed the Trojan lead to 38-33. Both offenses lived up to their considerable hype: USC rolled to 574 yards on the night while Texas countered with 556. Now, the Longhorn defense would have to accomplish something it had not done during the entire second half: keep USC out of the end zone.

Leinart's 9-yard completion to Jarrett moved the chains on second-and-6. But three plays later cornerback Aaron Ross stopped LenDale White at the end of a 5-yard run to force a fourth-and-2 decision at the Texas 45. A first down, here, would be a dagger to the Longhorns' national title hopes. Texas called time-out with 2:13 left. Brown quickly huddled his defense.

"I told them if we stopped this fourth-down play," Brown said, "we'd win the national championship. That's what it was down to."

The call from the Trojan sideline was almost obvious to the 93,986 packed into the stately stadium: White would surely get the football. After all, he'd been virtually unstoppable all evening, averaging 6.2 yards per carry. Besides, Bush wasn't even on the field when Leinart broke huddle. Texas's defensive front, anticipating an off-tackle play, stayed low and clogged their gaps as Leinart took the snap. The linebackers crashed the middle of the scrum with Texas's defensive backs on their heels. After all, White only needed two yards.

He got one.

Huff was officially credited with the stop but at least four Longhorns had a hand, or a helmet, or a shoulder pad in on the play, including defensive end Brian Robison, who split a double-team to disrupt White's effort. Robison signaled 'Texas ball' as White stood with his hands planted on his hips. By then, Vince Young's chinstrap was already fastened.

Texas's drive for the ages would start at its own 44 with 2:09 remaining, yet things started poorly. A 2-yard loss and an incompletion meant Texas needed 12 yards on third down; it got just 7 of them on Quan Cosby's reception. But a Darnell Bing face-mask infraction gave Texas new life at the Trojan 46. Wide receiver Brian Carter had battled injuries throughout his senior year, but came up big with a pair of catches totaling 26 yards. It put Texas in prime real estate with a fresh set of downs at the Trojan 13. Young collected 5 yards on second-and-10, and Texas called time-out with 30 seconds remaining. Young would look to Sweed for the third time during the era-defining series; the result was a third-straight incompletion.

In the end, the single, perfect Rose would stem from this: fourth-and-5 from the 8, down by 5, and just seconds separating the 2005 Texas Longhorns from college football immortality. Young first looked for Thomas before going through his progressions. Trojan defensive tackle LaJuan Ramsey pushes between a pair of blockers but Young has already run to his right, again looking for Sweed, who has just broken past cornerback Justin Wyatt. But, now, Young has made his decision. He runs. He bolts around right end, where defensive end Frostee Rucker has a shot at him just outside the 5 before the Texas quarterback scampers to the right pylon and into Longhorn legend.

Touchdown!

The celebration from the Longhorn sideline spilled onto the field while the offense calmly lined up in an empty backfield for the 2-point attempt. Young kept for two, giving Texas a 41-38 lead with 19 seconds remaining. From his 31, Leinart found Bush down the right sideline for 27 but USC was out of time-outs. Leinart needed another 20 yards to set up a game-typing field goal, but on the final play, Leinart scrambled and scrambled before firing incomplete for Jarrett as time expired.

On cue, fireworks exploded as a blizzard of confetti tumbled from the starry California night. Look! Up in the sky! No need that night—Superman was on the ground, wearing No. 10, and kissing the crystal of the BCS National Championship trophy.

The Game Of My Life

By Vince Young

[The week of the game], my teammates and I walked around Los Angeles, and everybody had their opinion about how we were going to get beat bad. I never feed into that. We knew who was going to win. . . . We didn't get respect from the media all year, and we just worked hard to prove we deserved to be there.

USC was 34-0 [dating back to the 2003 season] and a great football team, but we were a great football team as well. Nobody just gave us our 12-0 [record]. We worked hard for it. We were used to being the underdog. It doesn't matter what other people think. There were a lot of things said about the University of Texas [during the 2005 Rose Bowl game against Michigan]. They said Texas can't win the big game, or Texas was not physical enough, Texas this or Texas that. We wanted to show the world what it was all about. To go out and get it like we did answered the critics. It was nice . . . From the [2005] Rose Bowl, [the team's success] just took off and carried over.

I said all week it would come down to the last play of the game, and it did.

We'd been down at the end of the game before, and it's all about focus and poise and to not worry because, in the end, it's all about heart. We just went out there and performed. On the [game-winning] fourth-down play, you're thinking about what you're going to do. I went through all my progressions, but no one was open. Their defensive line went inside and that gave me a little edge. I went through my third progression and took off.

I was actually hoping those guys [USC] would score a field goal and send the game into overtime so we could keep playing. But I was so happy with the results and seeing my coaches, teammates, and the fans so happy.

It was all about heart, poise, and nobody getting frustrated with each other. Everybody showed so much heart on both sides of the ball.

After the game, there was a lot of prayer [with family members and teammates] because it was such a blessed moment to be in that position, not just for me but for my teammates, the coaches, the coaches' wives, and the fans. It had been a long time since the University of Texas did the thing we did.

Upon Further Review

Young was named Rose Bowl "Most Valuable Player" for the second straight year after he rushed for 200 yards and 3 touchdowns while adding 267 yards through the air on 30-of-40 passing with no interceptions. Young became the first player in NCAA history to rush for 1,000 yards and pass for 2,500 in the same season.

Earlier in the week, however, Brown was asked what he would do if Young became his first Texas player to forego his final year of eligibility and declare for the NFL draft.

"I'd kiss him," Brown said.

It was another way of asking what more the fourth-year junior could do after posting a 30-2 record while handing Texas its fourth national title. Four days later, Young arrived at a news conference in a limo.

"That's when I knew he was leaving," Brown smiled.

The Tennessee Titans made Young their first-round pick, the first quarterback selected and third player overall in the 2006 NFL draft. He agreed to a six-year contract worth $58 million and started his professional career in a preseason matchup against Reggie Bush and the New Orleans Saints. He led the Titans to an 8-5 record as a rookie starter, doubling the franchise's total wins from the previous season, en route to NFL Offensive Rookie of the Year honors and a Pro Bowl invitation. Young played with an injured quadricep during most of the 2007 campaign but guided Tennessee to a wildcard spot in the AFC playoffs.

He re-enrolled at Texas in the spring of 2008 to finish his degree requirements, yet the upcoming season would be a difficult one for Young. He injured his knee in the season opener, and Titans coach Jeff Fisher named Kerry Collins the starting QB for the remainder of the season. Fisher announced during the 2009 preseason that Collins would remain the starter, but Young was handed the reins after Tennessee opened 0-6. The Titans won five straight as Young went 8-2 as starter that year.

The Titans struggled to a 5-5 mark with Young as the starter to open the 2010 campaign. By then, there had been several reports of the tumultuous relationship between Young and Fisher. It all came to a head during a loss at Washington. Young injured his right thumb and Fisher would not allow him to re-enter the game. Following the loss, Young threw his shoulder pads into the stands and had an altercation with Fisher in the locker room. Days later, Fisher named Rusty Smith as the starting quarterback.

In July, 2011 Young was released from the Titans after compiling a 30-17 record. Earlier that year, Fisher and the Titans also agreed to part ways. Young signed a one-year contract with Philadelphia. He served as Michael Vick's backup but started three games, including a 17-10 win over eventual the Super Bowl champ New York Giants.

Young signed a one-year contract with Buffalo in May 2012.

Chapter Twenty-Three

JORDAN SHIPLEY

Wide Receiver (2006-09)

The bitter irony is that it happened during a preseason, noncontact drill. And to a former prep-All American with little to prove.

The 2004 season opener was weeks away but, already, veteran Longhorn players gushed that true freshman WR Jordan Shipley had established himself in the starting lineup. Didn't matter that Shipley had yet to take a collegiate snap: QB Vince Young had nicknamed him "ESPN" for his highlight reel receptions.

Everything changed on a muggy, overcast August morning.

The toss from Young was behind Shipley's back but not beyond his reach. It would have been a routine incompletion, a nondescript play, as forgettable as a bad summer movie. But Shipley *wanted* that ball. Instinctively, he twisted his upper body to reach for the pigskin. It's just that his right knee twisted in another direction.

Moments later, Shipley lay crumpled on the turf as the mood of the practice session became understandably somber.

"I knew right away," Shipley said. "I felt my knee pop. I heard it pop. At first, I was real upset. Then I started thinking about it. I understood that I had this put before me, and I had to deal with it and make the best of it. I tried to get past that initial shock."

No small part of the shock was Shipley had never before suffered an injury. The initial diagnosis was a torn ACL; the final prognosis was nine months of intensive rehab before he could play again. Understandably, Shipley found a second opinion. His own.

Six months max, he vowed. Shipley was determined to run routes on that same field with the start of spring drills. True to his word, Shipley was cleared to practice when the 2005 Longhorns began spring workouts in late-February. He took solace in that the injury had occurred during the preseason, and that he had not lost a year of eligibility.

"If it was going to happen, it happened when it needed to, right at the beginning," Shipley said during 2005 spring drills. "It's one of those deals that you didn't want something to happen but, if it was going to happen, it happened at a good time."

OK, so that was the first season-ending injury.

When Shipley suffered a summer hamstring injury that sidelined him for the entire 2005 national championship season, coach Mack Brown wondered if Shipley would ever return. It took another year of rehab but, three years into his career, Shipley notched his first collegiate reception in the 2006 home opener against North Texas.

He started seven games as a sophomore, highlighted by his 60-yard reception in the final 5 minutes at Oklahoma State. The deep completion from Colt McCoy was critical to Texas' biggest fourth-quarter comeback in school history, erasing a 21-point deficit in the final frame. Texas took its first lead, as time expired, with Ryan Bailey's game-winning 40-yard field goal.

Shipley's 43 total receptions heading into his junior season were by no means disappointing, but there was a pervasive sentiment among Texas fans that his potential remained untapped. Relatively speaking, there was little preseason buzz surrounding the 2008 Longhorn campaign. Texas had gone a respectable 20-6 in 2006 and 2007, although one national sports publication stated that the program had grown stale in the three years since its national championship.

Texas probably would have opened 2008 with a ranking loftier than the No. 11assigned by the *Associated Press* were it not missing key players at critical positions. Jamaal Charles' decision to forego his senior season for the NFL left Texas without a breakaway running back. The Horns also took a double hit at tight end: Jermichael Finley declared early for the draft while Blaine Irby's gruesome knee injury, suffered against Rice just three games into the season, would sideline him for the better part of three years. Defensively, Texas boasted a solid line but was

Jordan Shipley turns the tide against Oklahoma in 2008 with a 96-yard kickoff return for a touchdown

fielding a pair of inexperienced safeties in redshirt freshman Earl Thomas and true freshman Blake Gideon.

Texas steadily climbed in the rankings by opening with five convincing wins, including three by the score of 52-10. The Horns were No. 5 in both major polls when rankings were released on October 5, but there was some question if Texas' mettle had been tested. The verdict would come on national television the following Saturday with its annual litmus test against No. 1 Oklahoma.

The last time Texas had faced a top-ranked Sooner squad, the 2003 Longhorns suffered a historic 65-13 beat down, the most lopsided margin in series history.

No. 5 TEXAS vs. No. 1 OKLAHOMA

October 11, 2008
Cotton Bowl—Dallas, Texas

Oklahoma entered the game having outscored opponents, 103-3, in the first quarter. The up-tempo Sooners twice jumped to early 11-point leads against Texas, and drew first blood on their opening possession with QB Sam Bradford's 5-yard touchdown pass to Manuel Johnson.

When Texas touched the ball for the first time, offensive coordinator Greg Davis unveiled a formation he had not used in eight years. The Horns went with a no-tight end, four-wide set that placed Shipley as an inside receiver.

The Sooners took a 7-3 lead, and little bit of luck, into the second quarter. OU was in prime real estate at the Texas eight just 1:46 into the period. Bradford fired a pass at Jermaine Gresham, but safety Earl Thomas nailed the big TE as the ball arrived. The pigskin ricocheted into the arms of WR Ryan Broyles, who was standing inside the end zone, for Oklahoma's second score and a 14-3 lead.

All the momentum was squarely on the Sooner sideline, but the nation's No. 1 team had one discernible Achilles' heel entering the fray: kickoff coverage.

Shipley gathered Matt Moreland's kick just inside the four and looked upfield. He cut to his right, found a crease and, behind the clearing blocks of Eddie Jones and Lamarr Houston, blazed a trail along the Texas sideline for a 96-yard return. It was the first kickoff return for a touchdown by a Longhorn in five seasons and the longest in the history of the Red River Rivalry.

Bradford and company quickly answered. Gresham was standing all by his lonesome on the drive's sixth play and galloped 52 yards into the end zone on Bradford's third touchdown pass of the first half. Meanwhile, Texas had yet to mount a touchdown drive and, once again, was staring at an 11-point deficit.

The McCoy-Shipley combination got untracked when Texas took over at its own 20. The two hooked up three times for 28 yards on a twelve-play march, but the big play was McCoy's 19-yard toss to Quan Cosby to move the chains on third-and-2. It set-up first-and-goal from the 8. The Horns hit pay dirt with redshirt freshman Cody Johnson's 1-yard plunge to narrow the Sooner lead, 21-17, with 3:41 left until the break.

Bradford had plenty of time to maneuver his squad for a momentum-shifting score just before the half, but the pendulum swung back to the Texas sideline 49 seconds later. Thomas' diving interception gave Texas the ball at its own 33. McCoy quickly found Cosby for 36 yards on the first snap. The Horns would have faced third-and-long, but Travis Lewis was flagged for pushing McCoy when he was out of bounds. It was the first of two such calls against the redshirt freshman, who later insisted he was trying to stop McCoy's momentum. The first infraction spotted Texas at the Sooner 20. It led to hunter Lawrence's field goal as time expired. This one was a 21-20 instant classic at intermission.

The Bradford-Johnson combo was just as effective on OU's first series of the second half as it was on the game's first drive. Johnson's 31-yard catch-and-run over the middle set up his 14-yard TD toss. It took OU all of 90 seconds to rebuild its lead, 28-20.

The intended mismatch of aligning Shipley in the middle was further exploited when OU lost middle linebacker Ryan Reynolds to a third-quarter, season-ending knee injury. The big play in Texas' 89-yard response was Chris Ogbonnaya's 30-yard run, but McCoy was six-of-six passing on the touchdown drive. Four of those completions went to Shipley, including his 2-yard reception in the back of the end zone. The Horns were back in it, 28-27.

Bradford directed his offense to near midfield before DE Brian Orakpo threw him for a 6-yard sack. The Sooners faced fourth-and-6 at their 48, but coach Bob Stoops was willing to roll the dice. Mike Knall lined up for what appeared to be OU's fourth punt of the game. Instead, he took off running. Cornerback Curtis Brown stopped him just one foot shy of the first down marker. Texas took over at its own 47.

The Horns benefitted from two questionable calls on their next possession, including Lewis' second late-hit infraction against McCoy following an 18-yard scramble. Officials spotted the ball at the Sooner 20. Then, on third-and-one from the 11, linebacker Lamont Robinson appeared to have intercepted McCoy. Officials ruled it an incomplete pass, allowing Lawrence to boot a 28-yard field goal. Texas had its first lead, 30-28, with 64 seconds left in the third quarter.

A questionable roughing-the-kicker penalty sustained Oklahoma's next series. The Sooners faced third-and-14 at the Longhorn 40, but Bradford found Juaquin Iglesias for 26 yards over the middle. Next play, Johnson registered his third receiving touchdown of the day on the 14-yard toss from Bradford. Oklahoma regained the lead, 35-30, with 3:18 eclipsed from the final frame.

McCoy recovered his own fumble at the Longhorn 38 on Texas's next series. A 10-yard completion to Shipley had Texas at midfield. Then, on third-and 8, McCoy found Shipley alone in the middle of the field. Shipley was brought down at the goal line, and scoreboard officials put 6 points on the board. Moments later, the points were removed after game officials spotted the ball at the one. Next snap, Cody Johnson burrowed for his second score of the afternoon. It was a 38-35 Texas lead with 7:37 remaining.

Will Muschamp's defense forced a three-and-out. Texas scrimmaged from its own 20, needing to milk the clock for the final 6:32. Ogbonnaya's 10-yard reception moved the chains on third-and-4. Then came the backbreaker. Ogbonnaya was a senior but making just his second career start. He took the handoff off right tackle and patiently waited for the downfield blocking to develop. He then switched into a higher gear and careened 62 yards down the Sooner sideline. Two plays later, Johnson carried across from the one. By now, nearly everything was going Texas's way. McCoy's pass to Cosby on the 2-point conversion bounced off his chest and went straight in the air. But Cosby was so wide open that he held his ground and waited for the ball to land in his arms. When it did, the scoreboard read 45-35, Texas, and that's how it ended. The 2008 game set a new series record for most total points.

Shipley finished with 225 yards (112 receiving, 113 returns) and two TDs on the day.

The Game of My Life

By Jordan Shipley

We were ranked No. 5, but Oklahoma was No. 1. There was a general feeling on the team that, no matter what situation we were in, we were going to find a way to come back and win. Everybody on the sideline knew Oklahoma was No. 1 in the country, but I think everybody on the sideline went in believing that we were going to win that game.

Coach [Greg] Davis put in a package for that game that our team never used before. We basically put in an extra slot guy, so I moved inside for that game. We did some stuff that they hadn't seen before, and it worked pretty well. I don't know that [the package] was because of anything Coach Davis had seen in Oklahoma. It was just something he had been working on prior to the game. That's always such a huge game, and so we put it in the game plan. It was pretty productive from the very beginning.

They were beating us 14-3, and I had a kickoff return for touchdown that helped spark the come-from-behind victory. Sometimes when you're returning kicks, you just have a feeling that it's going to be a special play. I kind of had that feeling as the ball left the tee. They kicked it right to me. It was a middle-return. I remember running toward the middle of the field and then hesitating for just a second. I looked at where our guys were blocking. There wasn't a big crease, but it was a perfect, little crease. I squeezed through there and, after that, all I saw was the kicker. All I had to do was make a move toward the sideline. It was off to the races from there.

It was a breakout game for (safety) Earl Thomas. He was a redshirt freshman that year. He had a huge interception just before halftime. It led to a field goal, and we were within a point at halftime. That was a big momentum shift for us. We had just come off a road win at Colorado, and were undefeated, but I guess some people questioned if we could hang with the No. 1 team in the country. I think everybody knew at halftime that we were as good as college football's top team.

Quan Cosby had one of the best blocks I've ever seen in that game. I saw it out of the corner of my eye. I had caught a ball over the middle during the fourth quarter, and I thought I had scored. To this day, I still think that maybe it was a touchdown. One of the officials signaled that it was a touchdown, but another guy came up and overruled it. It was from that inside-slot package. I caught a post route over the middle and turned it upfield. Quan came from the sideline, and I believe it was Lendy Holmes that he blocked. Quan came across the field and just took him out. It was like slow motion. It seemed like that the first thing that hit the ground was his helmet. It was an unbelievable hit.

Chris Ogbonnaya had a great second half. He was a senior, but this was his first start against OU. He wore the defense down. We were just trying to run some clock at the end of the game and then he had that long [62-yard] run down the sideline during the closing minutes. That was huge for us. He established himself during that game.

We came together more as a team after that game. We figured that if we could beat No. 1 Oklahoma, then we could beat anybody. We were No. 1 in the polls the week after we beat them. That win gave us a lot of confidence going forward.

Upon Further Review

Texas took over the nation's No. 1 ranking, but the OU game was just the start of a murderer's row in which the Horns faced four straight top-eleven teams. Texas made short work of No. 11 Missouri, 56-31, before fending off No. 7 Oklahoma State, 28-24. But the last-minute loss at No. 6 Texas Tech ranks among Texas' all-time heartbreaks.

The Longhorns would run the table, but the final 90 seconds in Lubbock (in all probability) cost Texas a shot at the national championship. Texas, OU, and Texas Tech each finished tied atop the Big 12 South standings with 7-1 marks. But Oklahoma leaped over Texas to take the No. 2 spot in the last Bowl Championship Series ratings of the regular season. The Big 12 used the final BCS standings to determine which teams represented each division in the league's championship game. It meant Texas was shut out of the Big 12 title game despite the fact that it beat both participants (OU, Missouri) by double-digits.

Texas's consolation prize was a 24-21 Fiesta Bowl comeback in the final 2 minutes against No. 10 Ohio State. Shipley registered 10 catches for 78 yards that night in Tempe. The result was that Shipley and Cosby became just the eleventh duo in college football history to each have more than 85 receptions and 1,000 yards in a single season.

Texas would go undefeated and win the 2009 Big 12 championship before facing No. 1 Alabama for the BCS national championship. Colt McCoy's iconic career came to a shockingly abrupt conclusion when he was lost to injury in the first quarter. Texas trailed 24-6 at halftime but, thanks primarily to Shipley's 122 yards and 2 touchdowns on 10 receptions, trimmed the deficit to 3 points with 6:15 remaining in the game. A forced fumble on a sack of backup QB Garrett Gilbert resulted in the first of two Alabama touchdowns in the final 2:01 that sealed the deal for the Tide.

Shipley would be named consensus All-American that season. He concluded his collegiate career by owning every major Texas receiving record, including single-game receptions (15), single-season receptions (116), career receptions (248), single-game yards (273), single-season yards (1,485), and touchdowns in a single season (13).

Shipley was the 2010 third-round Draft pick of the Cincinnati Bengals. He suffered a concussion in week four of the NFL season following an illegal helmet-to-helmet hit from Cleveland safety T. J. Ward. He returned two weeks later and finished his rookie campaign with 600 yards and 3 touchdowns on 52 catches.

Shipley missed virtually all of the 2011 season after tearing his ACL and MCL against Denver in week two. It meant another eight or nine months to rehab torn ligaments in a knee. Shipley was cleared on May 7 to play in the 2012 NFL season.

Acknowledgments

I first want to thank Robert Heard, founder of *Inside Texas*, for giving me a chance years ago to work with him on his newsletter. Without that chance, I would have never been involved with this book. I also want to thank my partner and co-owner of Inside Texas, Inc., Clendon Ross, for his help not only in editing the chapters of this book, but for being there to discuss ideas and to help shepherd the project to completion. I am particularly grateful to the folks at Sports Publishing and Skyhorse Publishing for giving us the opportunity to tackle this project, and to our editors Meg Distinti and Niels Aaboe. Thanks for all your help in getting the book to the finish line. The former players whose stories appear in this book, as well as Coach Royal, deserve a special thanks. I personally want to thank Robert Brewer, Steve Worster, Pat Culpepper, Johnny "Lam" Jones, Brian Jones, Dan Neil, and Jerry Gray for taking the time to talk with me. You guys were open and willing to talk for as long as I had questions. It was a privilege and a pleasure to meet all of you. I hope you all enjoy the book. Also a special thanks to Lee Corso for agreeing to write the foreward. I look forward to seeing you on Game Day, Coach! Thanks also to my co-author Bill Frisbie. I appreciate all of your efforts to make this book great, and for all the work you've done at *Inside Texas*. And thanks to photographer Will Gallagher for being a part of this project, and for providing *IT* with so many great photos over the years.

Finally, I want to thank my wife, Mari, for bearing with me through this process. It's been a long road, but we made it through. Eu te amo.

—Michael Pearle

There is a bumper sticker in my office that states: 'I love my job so much, I'd do it for free. (Unfortunately, they know that).' It's intended as tongue-in-cheek, but it speaks well of the vocational choices I have made. Among those decisions was to cover Longhorn football for *Inside Texas* and that, of course, led to my affiliation with *Game of My Life* co-author Michael Pearle.

The book's most intriguing element is its basic premise: a Texas great reflects on a game that was particularly meaningful and perhaps career-defining. In some cases, a contest was described as life-changing, but we never knew in advance which game a player would pick. Longhorn fans might assume, for example, that Roosevelt Leaks would have picked his record-breaking game against SMU in 1973. Or that quarterback Duke Carlisle might have selected the 1964 Cotton Bowl showdown against Navy's Heisman Trophy winner Roger Staubach as the capstone to Texas' first national title. Or that James Brown would have chosen the 1996 Big 12 Conference Championship game against Nebraska. They did not. Quite often, the deeply personal reasons for their selections superseded outstanding performances in games we would ordinarily associate with these former lettermen. I very much appreciate their time and candor in this project.

Michael Pearle, it was terrific sharing this experience with you. As you well know, the hours spent conducting interviews, transcribing notes, collecting background information, and putting words to the page would not have been possible without the patience and understanding of *Inside Texas* co-publisher Clendon Ross and InsideTexas.com editor Ross Luckinger. I am thankful that Dr. John Butler, Pat Culpepper, Bob Shipley and Sammy Gilbert were instrumental in securing interviews for this publication.

Much love to my daughters, parents, family members and friends.

—Bill Frisbie